SOCIAL ISSUES, JUSTICE AND STATUS

EMOTIONS, TEMPORALITIES AND WORKING-CLASS IDENTITIES IN THE 21ST CENTURY

SOCIAL ISSUES, JUSTICE AND STATUS

SOCIAL ISSUES, JUSTICE AND STATUS

EMOTIONS, TEMPORALITIES AND WORKING-CLASS IDENTITIES IN THE 21ST CENTURY

MICHALIS CHRISTODOULOU
AND
MANOS SPYRIDAKIS
EDITORS

nova science publishers
New York

Library of Congress Cataloging-in-Publication Data

Names: Christodoulou, Michalēs, editor. | Spyridakēs, Manos, editor.
Title: Emotions, temporalities and working-class identities in the 21st century / edited by Michalis Christodoulou, Manos Spyridakis.
Description: Hauppauge : Nova Science Publishers, 2019. | Series: Social issues, justice and status | Includes bibliographical references and index. |
Identifiers: LCCN 2019037573 (print) | LCCN 2019037574 (ebook) | ISBN 9781536162035 (hardcover) | ISBN 9781536162042 (adobe pdf)
Subjects: LCSH: Working class--History--21st century. | Working class--Greece--History--21st century. | Group identity--Greece. | Industrial relations--Greece. | Labor unions--Greece. | Global Financial Crisis, 2008-2009.
Classification: LCC HD4855 .E56 2019 (print) | LCC HD4855 (ebook) | DDC 305.5/62--dc23
LC record available at https://lccn.loc.gov/2019037573
LC ebook record available at https://lccn.loc.gov/2019037574

Published by Nova Science Publishers, Inc. † New York

"Class issues are back forcefully : This is an excellent and insightful collection of empirical and theoretical essays on the making of working-class identities today. Very timely and well-researched, it draws not only on the global state-of-the-art debates but most importantly, grounded in Greece, the book contains brilliant macro-sociological extrapolations, drawn from the most violent austerity 'laboratories' of the European Union."

Nicos Trimikliniotis, Professor of Sociology, Social Sciences and Law, at the School of Humanities and Social Sciences, University of Nicosia

Our efforts to explain and confront the growing inequalities in western societies have to include discussions about the ways that individuals experience and make sense of their positions and of the precariousness of modern living as well as explorations of societies' tendency to sleepwalk into crises. This volume contributes to these discussions by turning the attention of the reader to two significant dimensions of human relevant experiences: the temporal and affective. The result is an original, systematic and insightful exploration of modern life which does not shy away from the complexity of the task to describe the ways that social phenomena are rooted in the human condition.

Dr Michalis Kakos, Carnegie School of Education, Leeds Beckett University

CONTENTS

FOREWORD A

Paul Durrenberger
Emeritus Professor of Anthropology, University of Iowa and Penn State

Part of the neoliberal turn is that every person can, must and cannot avoid living by individual decisions. Government agencies create training programs for unemployed individuals to provide them with marketable skills. When they turn to the market to sell their skilled labor, these individuals frequently find that nobody is buying. They've done what they were told. They lost their jobs. They did what they were advised and endured the training programs. Now they are unemployable again.

One of the fundamental assumptions of the theology of the discipline of economics, the bed rock of neoliberalism, is called methodological individualism. This is the assumption that institutions and larger social forms emerge from the acts of separate persons acting in their own best interests. This is no more a fact than the virgin birth of the Catholics. But it fuels a powerful religious force backed by global corporations and governments just as Catholicism once did.

Anthropologists, on the other hand, have observed that whatever people do is rooted in larger social structures that transcend them. Consider language. All people learn the languages of the people they grow up with.

They aren't free to invent their own language, or even grammatical forms. They are constrained by the language they found at birth. They may elect what they say, but not how they say it. If we tried to understand language as economists describe economic systems, we could never arrive at the concept of a language. There would be only so many individual choices of utterances, each motivated by personal benefit. The original tower of Babel.

For all of their talk of cultures and institutions and other abstractions, anthropologists like to keep their feet on the ground and move with the people they are trying to understand. So we do ethnography and no theoretical musings can transcend what we see and hear on the ground. Spyridakis and his colleagues here show us how the individual choices of those caught up in the recent economic turmoil of Greece are coping with the uncertainties of their lives. It is just as absurd to suggest that they have chosen that uncertainty or that historic moment or that language or that place on the planet as that they have chosen their responses. People make choices from among those available to them.

Does an insurance man elect to be dishonest? No, it is a precondition of his work. Does that make it acceptable? Perhaps not, but then we must question the institution of insurance and not the person destroyed by his dishonesty determined by his position in it. So these colleagues have done what anthropologists do—they have moved with the people, spoken with them, and endeavored to understand them. Sometimes they take flight into the abstracted theoretical language of the academy, but like dishonesty in the insurance industry, this is a hazard of their trade, determined not so much by their individual choices as by their structural positions. Those thoughts are worth sustained attention in an era that is so divorced from realities and one in which so many lives are determined by the workings of so many mythologies, many of them centered on the pure magic of money. But even more valuable is the experiences and thoughts of the people they represent in this volume.

Those thoughts and experience are largely determined by their positions in a global economic system whose masters are far above and far away, that 1% of the people on the planet who manipulate the global economy for their own benefit in a global class system whose concentration of wealth is unprecedented. We hear *their* perspectives in the media, in schools, in any example of that ideology of choice with which I began. So we don't need to hear it again. We need to hear the perspective of those whose labor has created the wealth of the planet and who deserve their share of their creation.

For anthropologists and for everyone else this poses the question of whether we want to serve solidarity in a war between classes or perpetuate illusions to serve the capitalist class. The sooner those perspectives are realized as political action, the better for us all and for our planet.

5/19/2019 EPD

FOREWORD B

Thomas Hylland Eriksen

Sitting in Oslo, Norway, I am writing these lines from one European periphery to another. Yet, however much Greece and Norway may have in common, what separates them is more striking these days, not least concerning work and time. Norway, outside the EU and the Eurozone (but part of Schengen and the European Economic Area), is obscenely rich, largely due to the considerable deposits of fossil fuels in the North Sea. Unemployment is low and the standard of living high. The temporalities struggled with by Norwegian wage-workers typically concern the life-work balance, stress and overwork, disruptions and distractions, and the relentless feeling of lagging behind with important tasks.

The Greek situation could hardly have been more different. A member of the EU and part of the Eurozone, Greece was hit hard by the financial crisis of 2007–08, and the economy remains precarious with high unemployment numbers, not least among youth, and with austerity policies resonating through Greek society. To many Greeks stricken by the crisis, the problem is not too much to do, but too little. The unemployed Greeks features in this book spend much of their time waiting.

The present contribution, edited by Michalis Christodoulou and Manos Spyridakis, represents a fresh and original perspective on the economic crisis and its long-term effects. By studying the temporalities that shape and are shaped by unemployed people's lives, the authors connect their situation to fundamental features of contemporary societies, ranging from forms of historical consciousness and their relationship to ideas of progress and development, to the phenomenology of everyday life, where the loss of the routines and temporal structures of the working life seem to lead to an eternal present where the past becomes distant and the future dim. In fact, research on life satisfaction suggests that being unemployed in a capitalist society reduces the quality of life more than most other dramatic life events, including serious accidents and divorces.

The editors use the term 'future bracketing' to describe an important dimension of the uncertain situation of their informants. Getting by from day to day becomes a matter of priority in the absence of realistic, cumulative, future-directed projects, where the flow of the life-story grinds to a halt when one is laid off. Interestingly, this kind of life may entail a form of presentism which is quite different from that described e.g., by François Hartog and other critics of information society: this is an enforced presentism where the past vanishes into an idealised mist and the future loses its relevance because formerly held narratives about a meaningful life trajectory can no longer be sustained.

Seen in a generational perspective, the continued precarity, not least among young people, in several European countries represents a serious threat at the systemic level, seriously questioning the hegemonic narratives of growth and development. In several European countries, including Greece, it is no longer widely assumed that young people will achieve a higher standard of living than their parents. When unemployment is presented as an individual problem rather than a structural issue, which is a characteristic expression of neoliberal ideology, the credibility of standard narratives about development is seriously impaired.

This book, importantly, also addresses the systemic issues connecting, or perhaps disconnecting, the expanding present of financial capitalism and the enforced presentism of the new precariat. Whereas cumulative linearity is the temporal backbone of a working-class life, underpinned by the predictability of a stable job, the demands for flexibility entailed by the new economy, often in the guise of a 'gig economy', is incompatible with a cumulative life where the aging of the body is intertwined with a work career. I have formerly spoken of a temporality where life stands still at enormous speed; in the case of those left out of the labour market owing to the repercussions of financialised fast-capitalism, life has instead ground to a halt.

This book is a highly readable and significant contribution to the research literature on work and precarity in contemporary Europe, especially through its emphasis on temporalities. It would be very interesting to see a companion volume, or parallel research, from a society which is otherwise quite different. Such as Norway. The differences may be less pronounced than they may seem at a first glance.

Oslo, 15 June 2019
Thomas Hylland Eriksen

In: Emotions, Temporalities …
Editors: M. Christodoulou et al.
ISBN: 978-1-53616-203-5

Chapter 1

INTRODUCTION: EMOTIONS AND TEMPORALITY AS INSTANTIATIONS OF CLASS IDENTITY

Michalis Christodoulou* and Manos Spyridakis†
[1]Department of Philosophy, University of Patras, Patras, Greece
[2]Department of Social and Educational Policy, University of the Peloponnese, Corinth, Greece

INTRODUCTION

Class identity is the main ground upon which this book is based. It aims at exploring the embodied, relational and processual dynamic of social class. According to an old but well grounded conception of class identity:

* Corresponding Author's Email: hristodoulou@upatras.gr, mikechristod7@gmail.com.
† Corresponding Author's Email: maspyridakis@gmail.com.

> "Class has both objective and subjective components. That is, it is not simply a position, but a complex lived cultural and bodily reality. It is a process, not merely a 'thing.' Thus, it should always be seen not as a static entity, but as a set of processes that are both creative and destructive and in constant motion. Furthermore, it is a relational concept in that it is defined in opposition to other classes. Finally, it is historically contingent." (McNall et al. 1991, 141, as cited in Apple 2007, viii)

Our aim is not to repeat known analyses on social class identity but to bring to the foreground two aspects of this processual, embodied and relational dynamic of class identity, which have not yet been researched by means of an integrative social-class theoretical lens, namely temporality and emotions. Although there is a lot of literature highlighting the relevance of class for explaining all kinds of inequalities (educational, health, income, lifestyle etc.), what has not yet been paid full attention to is the conceptualization of the intersection of class identity, emotion and temporalities. There is no doubt that in one of his most-cited books expanding on this issue, Sayer (2011) has stated some leading ideas regarding the existential and relational nature of class identity. We believe that these ideas could be summarized as follows:

1. Humans are evaluative beings in the sense that they evaluate themselves and others in order to asses how much respected they are.
2. These evaluations are shaped by class forces in the sense that it is class hierarchy which gives rise to such emotions as deference, shame, guilt, envy, resentment, arrogance, contempt, fear and mistrust.
3. Class hierarchy is not only an external force which affects the unequal distribution of resource-related life chances but an emergent reality which is reproduced or transformed by the way this emotional dynamic frames life projects as well.
4. Emotions should not be seen as counter-posed to reason but they carry a peculiar rationality which is fallible and guides deliberation and decision making.

5. "Lay normativity" is a term Sayer introduces for describing the usually inconsistent and disparate ethical rationales regarding "what is of value, how to live, what is worth striving for and what is not" (Sayer 2011, ch 2).

It is by means of these moral and ethical rationales that one can detect (upwardly and downwardly) life course trajectories as well as the reproductive or transformative effect of both agency and structure. The reason for this lies in that these "lay conceptions of good" constitute the core of class identity through which people make sense of themselves. In this light, what is the point in studying lay normativity as the par excellence expression of class identity? Surely it is not to prioritize either voluntaristic conceptions about social class or about its socially constructed nature. On the contrary, lay normativity is a useful path for the social researcher in order to tap what Critical Realists call causal mechanisms. Taking the risk of being accused for oversimplification, we could say that causal mechanisms are what make things what they are or else, make things in one way and not another, and are to be found in the emergent level of social relationships in the form of a social group, of a social institution, of a discursive formation or of a social class (Collier 1994).

In other words, we believe that lay normativity is the main field of exploring first-person experiences of class identity that social researchers draw upon in order to identify third-person causal mechanisms which explain why these experiences are specifically these ones and not others. In that sense, one of the main thrusts permeating the chapters of this volume is that class identity is a powerful means for explaining the logic of various kinds of inequalities such as those related to the topics contributors deal with. As a consequence, it is obvious that we are in line with those who see social class not as an obsolete explanatory category of social science but as a scientific concept capable for producing understandings of how society works.

However, we do not approach class identity as equivalent to collective action or as something which enlightens class consciousness and motivates class struggle but as a way of studying the way agents experience their existence in the world. This does not happen as Rational Actions Theorists have suggested, that is in a computer-like way, but in a practical, embodied and mostly in non thematized terms. It is through this embodied, practical and non intended way of reproducing and transforming boundaries that class identity works. In her famous analysis on the interconnection of drawing boundaries and social class, Michelle Lamont (1992) has stated that people obtain the sense of who they are (and who they are not) by drawing upon biographically sedimented stock of knowledge through which they classify themselves regarding what kind of person they would like to be (or deserve to be) and what they want to become or are afraid of becoming. Lamont has identified three historically and class-based resources people use for drawing boundaries. First, through economic resources agents draw boundaries related to wealth, occupational success or social status, second, cultural boundaries are formed according to how cultural-capital preferences make people construe "high" and "low" culture or "refined and "brutal" manners and, third, moral boundaries are formed in conjunction with how agents use such moral terms as honesty, integrity, compliance, prudence etc in order to separate those whom they would like to be close with from those whom they want to be distanced from.

Two important ideas stemming from Lamont's approach are of much relevance for empirical research. The first is that in researching the kind of boundaries groups of agents draw, one is able to detect the identity claims they forge. Put it in inverse terms, by focusing on how the members of a social group collectively form significant symbols and vocabularies of motives in order to frame life plans or emotional states, one can tap the class-formed ground of subjectivities. Second, in so far as the boundary drawing process Lamont talks about is inscribed within power relations and structures of inequalities which sustain various social fields, it follows that the nature of this process is formed independently of whether agents are aware of the emergent causal dynamic which gives shape to it.

Three Traditions of Class Identity

Lamont's and Sayer's approaches on the class nature of emotions, who develop and dig into Bourdieu's theory of habitus in order to qualify it and to empirically test its strength, constitute two of the main elaborations through which our book conceives of the "feeling structure" of class identity. Regarding social time, we believe that although all of the scholars who have grappled with time theorizing stress its absence from its connection with class identity and try to explain it, a comprehensive framework conceptualizing temporality and class identity has yet to be stated. A notable exception is Atkinson's work on integrating Bourdieu's theory with temporality experiences. In particular, the core idea of Atkinson's reading of Bourdieu's theory about time (2018) is that the two dimensions of the temporal structuring of consciousness, i.e., the Husserlian "retention" and "protention", are tied up with the various social fields agents live in, that is "multidimensional structures of domination and struggle defined by possession of one or more form of capital, or property securing legitimacy and authority (i.e., misrecognition) in the eyes of those struggling for that capital" (Atkinson 2018, 3). Agents' temporal orientations and experiences are formed according to the position they occupy within these fields of power relations, positions which are distributed in accordance with the volume and the composition of capitals that correspond to them. It is for this reason why agents' conceive of some of their actions and life plans as likely or unlikely, possible or impossible or as within their reach or beyond it. In other words, the extent to which one possesses the resources to deal with present uncertainties shapes his/her future orientation, or to put in Bourdieu's terms, time consciousness is conditioned by the fields' doxa.

Notwithstanding its deterministic overtones, this way of conceptualizing temporality has two merits, first it acknowledges that each field is structured according to its own patterns regarding timing, sequentiality or temporal locations and, second, it underlines the role of generational battles and of the struggles between the "newcomers" and the "old school persons" on the transformation of the field which enables/restrains/alters agents' trajectories within the field or across the fields. Atkinson notes two additional factors affecting the peculiarity and the transformation of the social time of the field, the "increasing pressure to be more productive, to work quicker, with more and tighter deadlines" (Atkinson 2018, 8) and the transport and communication technologies. What these factors underline is the openness of agents' temporal orientations stemming from the fact that they have 'extra-field' experiences issuing from their location in a multitude of fields and that they move across them throughout their life course.

However, the problems which this openness face are the following: 1) what is the class-formed temporality of those who are simultaneously located both into an advantaged position in one field and into an disadvantaged one in an other field and 2) what about the interconnection of class identity and temporal experiences of those whose social trajectories are upward or downward during the life course? Atkinson's answer is twofold. He says, first, that one should research into how the different fields are interrelated with each other, how one field affects the other and how these inter-field dynamic create a dialectical relationship which impacts upon individuals' temporal orientations (a process termed by Bourdieu as "legitimation circuits"). Second, he maintains that, regarding the experience of competing schedules and demands related to the different fields agents are in, researchers should pay attention to the specifics of the multiple positions agents hold and in relation to which they set in motion "temporality strategies", like those Hochschild identified (2005).

Atkinson's attempt to develop Bourdieu's theory of fields for exploring issues related to our society is remarkable. However, given that a lot of things have altered since Bourdieu's time, it follows that the explanatory power of these attempts seems unable to deal with a) how the interdependency of the fields affects temporal experiences and b) the unequal life-course effects on people's trajectories in the contemporary globalized world. We believe that Atkinson's explanatory limitations stem from the fact that Bourdieu himself privileged space in his theorizing and that Atkinson subsumed Husserl's protention/retention distinction to the field's distribution of recognition and to agents' misrecognized interiorization of its *illusio,* as Bourdieu did.

As a proof of this, we think that Carrier's remarks show why the subsumption characterizing Atkinson's analysis needs refreshment. According to Carrier, (2015, 32), one of the main process through which contemporary capitalism affects people's life plans and trajectories concerns how the growing importance of financial capital changes both their place and their sense of it. Given capitalism's rapid changes, the specific forms that classes take in capitalist societies will vary across the course of both time and space.

We believe that Scott's conception of social class (2001) is more appropriate for researching how these developments influence the way class situations affect agents' experience of time. In elaborating Weber's three-dimensional class/status/party conception of stratification, Scott viewed class and status as two different ways through which the unequal distribution of power shapes people's life chances. As to the "party", Scott approaches it as a kind of authority or command which structures stratification, as well. The crucial detail Scott recontextualizes from Weber's theory is that people's life chances are formed according to the peculiar characteristics of their circulation through various class situations. Association and mobility are the two main features affected by the unequal distribution of power and which are expressed in these class situations. Within this scheme, class relations can be researched both as "class situations" (comprising the property and market situations through which economic resources are distributed), as "status situations" (comprising the specific lifestyles and identities through which 'social honour' or prestige is attributed to individuals) and as "command or authority situations" comprising various social élites which are formed in organizations and in institutions. All these three dimensions of power circulation through which class relations are formed affect interdependently, causally and unequally people's life chances.

It seems that "class as (mis)recogntition" (in Atkinson's elaboration of Bourdieu) and "class as life chances" (in Scott's elaboration of Weber) (Atkinson 2015), despite their differences, are more close in considering class as that which affects causally people's destinies and through which one could explain social inequalities. Both of them share what philosophers would call "instrumentalism" in the sense that they view social classes not as real entities "out there" ready to be researched and discovered in the process of capital accumulation but either as "class on paper", clustered around similar capital volume/composition or as social groups having unequal power within similar situations. The danger one faces in case he/she sees class in instrumental terms is that he/she tends to implement nominalist data-gathering strategies to the extent that classes are researched as occupational categories or as measurable entities. Be that as it may, we believe that this danger concerns more the Nuffield School and not so much Bourdieu's cluster analysis. In addition, both of them privilege how the field of power affects the structuring the heterogeneity of class fractions and the inequalities ensuing from it. Finally both of these approaches to class point to the fact that the causal factor for explaining late modernity's inequalities is always emergent and dependent on the specifics, the peculiarities and the details of time and space.

However, what both of these approaches miss is a real life situation which takes place in how people develop relations to their means of production and this is exploitation. In this "class as exploitation" tradition, what matters is how ownership of the means of production enables researchers to explain the creation of new class fractions in late modernity. Wright's famous and Marxist-inspired notion of "contradictory class locations" (1997) taps the ways through which relations of ownership and control, decision-making powers and authority define capitalist societies. In this scheme, exploitation refers to the fact that those who dominate the labour process have the power to control the extraction of its surplus value. In that sense, exploitation in contemporary capitalism is a matter of degree related to where the various social classes are located in the continuum from being fully in control of the production means to being fully dispossessed of any skill or loyalty to rent.

Now, what this tripartite approach of class has to offer us regarding the study of temporality and emotions seen from a class-identity point of view? We believe that the above mentioned theories of class entail a different conception of temporality and of emotions upon which they frame class identity. In particular, the "class as exploitation" tradition, in prioritizing commodity production and the labour theory of value as the primary explanatory factor of experiencing class, tends to reduce the multiple ways of experiencing temporality and emotions to the social time of commodity production. Within this tradition, dominant role is attributed to how those who control the labour process set the stage for experiencing temporality and emotions in dominated ways. Or to put it in inverse terms, the way one experiences temporality and emotions depends on where he/she is located in the continuum of the ownership of the production means: in case he/she is located in a contradictory class position, he/she tends to experience temporality and emotions in contradictory ways. We believe, in other words, that this tradition is not so much suited for answering questions related to the subjectivity of class identity as for critiquing capitalism.

Things are somehow different for the other two traditions which we consider to have affinities between them. We believe that one defining feature of class uniting the "class as life chances" and the "class as (mis)recognition" tradition is that they see class as an emergent entity of which the form varies according to time and place and which has causal power to produce various and severe inequalities. In other words, temporality and emotion, as cardinal expressions of class identity, are better approached in relation to group dynamics of which the causal power is independent of agents' reasons and courses of actions. We believe that the key for explaining how temporality and emotions as instantiations of class identity are shaped in relation to such emergent entities as group power, class structure, political discourses, status situations etc, is to explore how values and rationality are enmeshed in practical reason. Andrew Sayer (2005) has made a relevant contribution which might give us a clue as to how one could conceptualize emotions in relation to class identity.

The Emotional Dispositions of Practical Reason

The core idea Sayer proposes is that often agents act not according to a means/ends scheme but in an embodied, non discursive, implicit, responsive to context and value/emotion-laden way. Values and emotions should not be treated as irrational parts of humans' souls but as fallible and corrigible guidelines for navigating in the world through which they take decisions. By means if this practical reason humans navigate into their everyday lives according to criteria of effectiveness which concern the particular and not the universal, as a scholarly conception of rationality would have us think. Within this line of argument, emotions offer crucial "discerning commentary on situations" (Sayer 2005, 65) though which humans display their sensitiveness and are seen as reasonable persons. In acting wisely, humans do not follow formal procedures but take into account (consciously or unconsciously) their strong evaluations by means of which they form criteria for making ethical judgements when they face dilemmatic situations. Sayer considers three distinguishing features of practical reason.

First, it is embodied in so far as agents know much more than they can tell and it is through the body's skilful way of dealing with the world that they obtain the sense that they know this world. While Bourdieu's theory of practice is the main source of inspiration of Sayer's approach to practical reason, Sayer provides some crucial qualifications in relation to habitus' shortcomings. While for Bourdieu habitus acquisition is in its most part unconscious, Sayer thinks that people acquire the "feel for the game" by using, more or less, a conscious monitoring of their actions. In the meantime, habitus' dispositions "once learned they change from something we struggle to grasp to something we can think *with*, without thinking *about* them" (Sayer 2005, 23). The point that Sayer is trying to make is that emotional dispositions should be seen neither as rational nor as irrational but as constitutive of agents' being in the world. What researchers need to take into account is not whether embodiment runs counter to rationality but the extent to which agents develop internal conversations when they face situations they are not familiar with. It is the interplay between internal conversation and embodied knowledge which makes habitus conditioned not by external stimuli but in conjunction with agents' social trajectory. There is ample of research evidence regarding how the production of cleft habitus is intimately connected with such emotions as confusion, shame, fear and resentment and is more or less independent of its corresponding habitat. For example, Thacher and Halvorsrud (2016) highlight the moral grounding of class identity by showing how Polish migrated from Poland to England try to deal with the resentment of the people in the host country by invoking that they are "hard workers". A similar finding regarding the habitus dislocation of upwardly mobile working-class adolescents has been found by Christodoulou and Spyridakis (2016). No matter how dislocated or ambivalent, emotional dispositions enable people to navigate into the world because they are part of agents' package providing them with the means of dealing with present life demands or future life plans. As Sayer puts it: "To understand how inequalities are lived we have to come to terms with actors' ambivalent responses of compliance, resignation, rationalisation, resistance and longing" (Sayer 2005, 39).

Second, practical reason concerns how agents make judgements for concrete situations they live in, which means that its effectiveness should not been assessed according to Logician's philosophical logic but in relation to how agents immediately come to grasp gestalts. Finally, in addition to being embodied and concerned with the particulars, practical reason entails ethical dispositions in so far as agents are engaged with the world by means of ethical judgements. Conceptions of good and bad, of the desirable and not despicable and of the valuable or invaluable constitute the heart of agents' grasping of situations they live and of how they relate with others. Ethical dispositions, of course, are not tied to one's character but are formed in conjunction with his/her cultural, economic and social determinants of their lifeworlds and with the biographical details of their social trajectories. This means that the crucial thing about agents' ethical and emotional dispositions is not whether they are in harmony with their habitat or not but that, as part of the class identity, they are the most sensitive part of how they relate with status and power hierarchies. It is not only through emotions that agents come to feel that some situations are seen as taken for granted or as being their place but also it is through emotions that they shape their criteria for taking decisions in unfamiliar and uncanny situations. Recall here the classic Sennett and Cobbs' argument (1973) that manual workers suffering from 'injured dignity' turn to their families as a way of recovering lost pride and Crompton's (2001) point that middle class men who feel unsuccessful in their careers may also seek solace in their family lives.

Another field of class identity research in which one can see how emotions work as class identifier is the literature on "emotion capital" in which what is underlined is that working-class mothers come to adopt parenting styles promoted from professional discourse that individualize marginalization and depict working classes as too ignorant and as having low moral standing. In that way, working-class mothers in order to deal with this disrespectful image they develop a kind of emotional labour regarding parenting which tries to imitate middle-class worldviews by creating in them criteria of guilt in case they are not aligned with this emotional labour (Gillies 2006). Historians have made excellent contributions on how working-class emotional dispositions are shaped through political regimes and through the historically contingent class structure. Buchanan (2014) shows that nineteenth-century Northern elites promulgated the emotional rules of the powerful Christian middle-class by valuing sympathy, grief, and exemplary suffering as appropriate emotional states. In a similar vein, Peter Stearns (1994) analyzes how anger was applauded only in case that it promoted young middle-class adolescents' competitiveness in the world of work, an emotional style which became more "cooled" in the twentieth century while the work environments became more post -industrial.

The Temporality of Class Identity

It is not an exaggeration to say that the sociological and anthropological literature on the temporal grounding of class identity is rapidly growing. One of its main theoretical origin draws from what we previously analyzed as the "political economy side" of class culture. By refreshing E. P. Thomson's classic, these approaches hold that the whole spectrum of social time is structured according to the workings of industrial or commodity time. The structuring of industrial labor makes social time experienced by people as a quantifying and measurable entity not only regarding work life but regarding the rest of their lifeworlds such as school and family life. People's allocation of activities in a timetable is directed according to the time of capital accumulation and their duration, sequence, synchronization and rate takes a predictable, invariable and standardized form. This kind of time patterning through which people experience temporality as it is seen in the case of punctuation is controlled by employers. Labour is exchanged for money and time is the medium by means of which labour obtains its abstract exchange value. Repetitiveness of work rhythms, the separation of work time and free time, time divisibility in small units and time as abstracted exchange value, are all expressions of a commodified time as it has been nested within the industrial wage labour. Hohn (1984 as cited in Adams 1990, 112), in reversing the moto "time is money" to "money is time", argues that the more time one has, the lower its value is as the cases of prisoners, of unemployed and of all those having "plenty of time" show because the value of time fluctuates in accordance with the supply and demand. In these cases, time is accorded a low social value and the less time one has the more precious it becomes. In other words, time is conceived of as resource only within societies for which clock time has been reified through labour commodification and those who dominate capital accumulation have the power to dominate the time of others.

Bob Jessop (2009) applies this line of reasoning to the world scale of the globalized society by considering as its most defining feature the time-space distanciation and the time-space compression: the former concerns the fact that social relations are stretched over time and space so that they are controlled or coordinated for long periods of time and for long distances or great areas, while the latter has to do with the intensification of "discrete" events in real time and the increased velocity of the material or immaterial flows over a given distance (Jessop 2009, 137). Modern societies are extremely disrupted and disoriented by these two features which in turn affect people's lives in the following regions. First, there is a growing sense of stress due to time-space compression as it is expressed in the tension between the biological and sentient temporality of human existence and the abstracted time of labour commodification. Second, contemporary capitalism promotes the interdependence between the economic and extra-economic factors as it is reflected in the passage from Fordist productivity to post-Fordist precariousness and in the hegemony of social capital, trust and learning. A deep-seated contradiction permeates the time structure of post-Fordist finance capitalism: according to Hope (2011) the fast short-term profit making of finance undermines the long-term strategies of capital accumulation while at the same time supra-national and state-executive elites make fast decisions which marginalize the national-political rhythms of public law, representative assembly, the election cycle, policy formation and mediated public debate. The 2008 financial crisis brings to the fore a corresponding crisis in humans' temporalities in the sense that the priority given to the financialized acceleration of profit making is at odds with the temporalities of duration, sequence, planning and chronological ordering demanded by the longer-term requirements of capital accumulation. This in turn creates huge contradictions in people's temporal experiences since they are pressed to obtain such resources as skills, trust, reflexivity and transnational forms of capital that take years to stabilize and reproduce in order to exchange them into a rapidly changing and short-term finance-based economy.

In this constellation of "new economy", in which information and communication technologies play a crucial role, the temporal and spatial boundaries of paid work are extended and make people work more flexibly, for longer working hours and in accordance with precarious, fragmented and unsecure working patterns.

A "new temporality" emerges out of this "new economy" of which the mark is that firms are employer-led in the sense that it is employers who rule employee's working time and not the Fordist "9 to 5" pattern, with the effect that employees work harder and longer in order to the labour cost be minimized. Entrapped in this work environment, people instead of colonizing the future, they give prominent role on inventing time management policies for dealing with the pressures stemming from work intensifications. Within this "extended present" of experiencing temporality what matters is the day-to-day overcoming of precariousness in individualized and non collective terms (Perrons et al. 2005; Shirani 2011).

A SOCIAL PROFILE OF GREECE AFTER 2010 FINANCIAL CRISIS

One of the measures taken by the nation states for dealing with the banking crisis of 2010 was the supplying of banks with huge sums of money in order for the finance system to be saved. Greece, the frontline country of this crisis, received 214.9 billion Euros so as to be saved, money that Greece has the obligation to return on the basis of Memorandum obligations. Spyridakis (2018, 140-144) provides six reasons why the Memorandum solution imposed on Greek society is insufficient for explaining the Greek fiscal derailment and for justifying it: (1) the very low real taxation of capital achieved mainly by tax exemptions. In 2009, business taxes were equal to 16.5% of GDP when the EU average was 28.8%. Greek political elites chose to borrow from the rich instead of taxing them; (2) the addiction of Greek business to state subsidies, which culminated in the 2004 Olympic Games. Their final cost is very close to the deficit of 2010, 24.11 billion euro. (3) The provocative record, in European terms, of military spending (as percentage of GDP), which is due only partially to the Turkish aggressiveness. In 2009, Greek military spending was equal to 3.2% of GDP, when Germany's was 1.4%, and both the UK's and France's spending were 2.5% (4) The vicious circle of servicing the public debt reveals the trap where any indebted country is caught. From 1992 to 2016 the servicing of sovereign debt or, in other words, the fee of keeping it viable, cost Greek taxpayers 640.157 billion euro on December 31, 2016; (5) The participation of Greece in 1981 in the (then) European Economic Community and in 2002 in the Eurozone. The economic integration of Europe helped German manufacturers and others from northern countries with productivity benefits. These benefits helped to transform the whole continent to an internal market through the intensification of the competition and the assistance of visible hand of the European Commission, which led to the bankruptcy of industries who historically lagged in productivity. The result wasn't so apparent in the 1980s and 1990s because of the influx of subsidies from EU funds, basically in primary sector. However, it became thoroughly apparent recently due to diminishing tax revenues and a huge deficit on the foreign account balance; (6) and, finally, and more important, is the underlying crisis of Greek capitalism. This crisis was evident in the falling rates of increase of the GDP, which in 2008 turned to a reduction in the third quarter of 2008 (for first time since 1993), ending a long period of increases, that were higher than European ones. In contrast to the press stereotyping of Greeks as South lazy people who do not work, Greece got the third position on the average ranking of actual annual hours worked per worker, with 2032 hours. What one learns from the above picture is that the measures demanded by Troika's Memorandum like spending cuts, reductions in wages, sell-off of public enterprises, and massive redundancies of public servants were a failure for the simple reason that Greece's problem wasn't excessive expenses but the deficient revenues. This is why all of the Troika's predictions regarding the GDP and unemployment reduction rates have been disproved. Despite the fact that Greece's sovereign debt increased during the years from 2010 to 2014, European elites knew very well that the price of the fiscal consolidation would be the recession, given that GDP six years after the collapse of Lehman Brothers hasn't came back to its pre-crisis levels.

In practice, Troika tried to implement in the case of Greece what has been termed as ordoliberalism, the German version of imposing neo-liberalism on the South-European countries. According to Hadjimichalis (1987), its main features are: a) a powerful central intervention for safeguarding market competition, b) an independent central bank dedicated to promoting monetary stability and low inflation, c) privatization of public services and of its property and d) deregulation of job market. Hadjimichalis has powerfully argued (2011, 2018) that it was ordoliberalism that destroyed the second-sector model of economic development in South Europe during mid-90's. One of the main effects of this violent implementation was the transformation of family structure and culture because a) family could no longer be the core of small entrepreneurship or of small-medium sized business and b) younger generations (mostly women) lost interest in continuing the economic plans of these business and started searching for educational credentials in order to survive in the new and precarious job landscape.

Papadakis et al's empirical research on NEET (2015) corroborate the above-mentioned findings as far as Greece's work situation is concerned since they contend that the gap of unemployment rates between Greece and EU has been extremely widened during the years 2009-2015 and that the long-term unemployment rate has been dramatically increased from 47,1 to 73,5%, as well. Youth unemployment was (and is) the par excellence negative consequence created in Greece by the Memorandum measures. Even though in August 2016 youth unemployment has fallen from 49,1% (September 2015) to 46,5%, the fact remains that Greece's unemployment rate is twice that of European median and that 1 out of 2 youth is unemployed (Eurostat 2016). As far as the NEET's rates in Greece are concerned, one can note that Greek NEETs' rate (17,2% in 2016) is higher than that of EU (12% in 2016), that ¼ of them holds a university diploma and 59,1% comes from low income families (Papadakis, Kyridis, Papargyris 2015). Regarding the job market, males' rate employment has been decreased during the years 2010 – 2016 (from 74,4% to 58%) while women's employment rate increased and the reason is that finance crisis affected mostly "manly" jobs such as those related to the secondary sector (for example building constructions). These developments had severe consequences on marginalization and poverty increase, on physical and psychical health and on brain drain (Zacharopoulos et al. 2014; Aleksiou 2016; Charakioulafi et al. 2014),

CHAPTERS OUTLINE

The unifying core of the chapters of the volume revolves around three interrelated issues: first, they touch upon the themes we analyzed in the previous sections, which means that some of them grapple with the temporal or the emotional dimension of the working-class class identity and some with its socio-political expression. Second, all of them use qualitative research methodologies which are connected with most of the philosophical traditions of the qualitative paradigm and, third, almost all the samples upon which all the chapters are based have a temporal and contextual mark: they concern informants who, firstly, belong to the working classes (in the broad sense of the term) and, secondly, have experienced the vicissitudes of 2010 Greek crisis. Hence, we believe that the volume's chapters are indicative of a case which is typical of a contemporary socio-economic and political phenomenon, which is how working class as a group deals with a disruptive situation tending to shake the foundations of its existence.

Given the priority we give to the temporal grounding of class identity, *Michalis Christodoulou* in *chapter 2* tries to articulate the theoretical dimensions of a research agenda focused on temporality-related research questions. Michalis shows how Gurvitch's, Rosa's and the micro-sociological conceptions of time and temporality could be implemented in the research fields of mobility studies, youth studies, anthropology of work and sociology of education. By using examples from these fields, he highlights the details of forging theoretical propositions regarding how phenomena of synchronization and of de-synchronization impinge upon the subjective experience of temporality.

Chapters 2, 3 and 4 are all based on field research and try to connect the above-mentioned theoretical issues with first-hand research evidence. In particular, *Michalis Christodoulou and Manos Spyridakis* in *chapter 3* present the research findings of a narrative-ethnography research related to the impact the Greek crisis had on working-class people aged between 50 and 65. Michalis and Manos describe the temporal nature of living in precarious situations and try to explain its life-course determinants by exploring the causal mechanisms which give shape to a peculiar kind of temporal dislocation. *Giorgos Bithymitris* in *chapter 4* presents interview-based research findings from his five-year fieldwork experience with workers from the Ship repair Zone of Perama, the largest ship repair and shipbuilding industrial site in Greece. Giorgos brings to the fore how the restructuring processes in global shipbuilding industry affects the interplay of their political//cultural identity with their working-class location. He argues that it is not only class-as-relationship that forms the thoughts, affects and acts of the workers, but also it is class-as-trauma that frames their narrativized identities by means of which they negate their structural location. Finally, in *chapter 5 Eleni Giannakopoulou*, in her PhD research, explores in what ways emotional temporalities, class identification and future life plans are embedded in the biographical identities of second generation Albanian immigrants in Greece. Eleni argues that to the extent that crisis disrupted most of their life experiences and made them rearrange their decisions and life plans, emotions affect mostly how they will orient themselves towards both past and future. Fear, shame and resentment are some of the driving forces through which they are trying to change their precarious present conditions and to be protected from future vulnerabilities.

The next two chapters have a theoretical and a macro-sociological interest on the shaping of working-class identities as far as trade unionism and immigration is concerned. In particular, *Christina Karakioulafi* in *chapter 6* examines working-class labour solidarity and union inclusiveness in light of the declining rates of unionization, diminishing political power and distrust as to their public legitimacy, of the rise of precarious employment and of an insider-outsider division within labour force and inside unions. Christina holds that class-oriented identities are not inexistent in the Greek unionism but remain active both within precarious workers unions, marked by a left-wing political orientation and the presence of rank-and-fil activists, as well as within unions close to PAME (Communist-party organized unions). *Spyros Sakellaropoulos* in *Chapter 7*, by setting in motion a Marxist methodology, is researching the social stratification of foreign workers in Greece before (2001) and during (2017) the crisis. In using quantitative data and macro-structural evidence, Spyros compares the social stratification of the country's total workforce with that of the foreign workers (2017). Spyros maintains that within a very brief period of time Greek workers would have to become accustomed to living with a significant number of their foreign fellow citizens and the foreign citizens to become accustomed to a quite different, and to a significant extent hostile, social environment.

The final section of the book offers anthropological and psychoanalytic insights into the interplay of emotions, temporalities and working class identities. In *chapter 8 Ioannis Kyriakakis* provides a global perspective on class and examines in what ways the transformation of global capitalism affects working-class identity formation. Ioannis argues that the strengthening of the global class-systems, although it does not change the nature of capitalist exploitation, has the effect that class-consciousness and class-struggle become extremely difficult for workers because, first, workers have their patrons thousands of miles away, and second, because they live side by side to an extremely numerous underclass, ready to replace them at any moment at work. Psychoanalyst *Nikos Papachristopoulos* in *chapter 9* explores how working-class families deal with the internet use of their children. Nikos tries to connect the precarious job histories of these parents with their inability to comprehend and evaluate their children's use of the Internet. In *chapter 10 Kalliopi Orfanaki* provides participant-observation research evidence which bring to light how the emotional experiences of prisoners interact with their temporal orientation. Kalliopi's long-term engagement with the prisoners as part of her PhD research gave her the opportunity to conduct 235 narrative inteviews through which she shows how the prison time affects subjectivity. She concludes that prison overturns time correlations, bringing the past to the present, catalysing reality whereby prisoners start to confuse their lies with the truth, and simulating myths with reality. Finally, *Konstantina Bada (chapter 11)* explores the role of emotions in the everyday life of Ukrainian and Bulgarian women, who work as domestic workers in Greece. Konstantina draws upon her rich ethnographic material which has been collected through intensive narrative interviews carried out with twenty five immigrant women. She analyzes the ways though which emotions redefine a) one's identity as a migrant domestic worker, b) the forms of sociality—developed in conditions of precariousness, non-formal and low-profile work and social inequality—and c) their relationship with their place of origin and family. The constant care they invest in improving the lives of their underage or adult children and the parental relationship that they often develop with the children of the employers' family gives meaning to their everyday lives as immigrant domestic workers and helps them to establish an identity as mothers and good women. Konstantina maintains that their identity is preserved primarily through their role as mothers and not as salaried workers, as workers especially in work with a low-ranking social recognition.

References

Adam, Barbara. 1990. *Time and social theory*, Cambridge: Polity Press.

Aleksiou, Thanasis. 2016. *Social class, social inequalities and life conditions*, Athens: Papazisis (Greek book).

Apple, Michael. 2007. Foreword to *social class and schooling in the new economy,* edited by Jane A. Van Galen and George W. Noblit, vii-xi, NY: State University of New York Press.

Atkinson, Will. 2015. *Class*, Cambridge: Polity.

Atkinson, Will. 2018. Time for Bourdieu: Insights and oversights, *Time & Society*, DOI: 10.1177/0961463X17752280,.

Buchanan, C Thomas. 2014. Class Sentiments: Putting the Emotion Back in Working-Class History, *Journal of Social History,* pp. 1–16 doi:10.1093/jsh/shu044.

Carrier, James. 2015. Anthropologies of Class. Power, Practice and Inequality, *in Anthropologies of Class. Power, Practice and Inequality,* Edited by James G. Carrier and Don Kalb, 28-41, Cambridge: Cambridge University Press.

Charakioulafi Christina, Manos Spyridakis, Eleni Giannakopoulou, Dimitris Karalis and Giorgos Soros. 2014. *Unemployment and work insecurity in a time of crisis.* Study 31 of the Economic and Social Observatory of the Greek Syndicate Work Institute, Athens: Kampili (Greek book).

Christodoulou, Michalis and Manos Spyridakis. 2016. Upwardly mobile working-class adolescents: A biographical approach on habitus dislocation, *Cambridge Journal of Education,* 47(3): 315-335.

Collier, Andrew. 1994. *Critical Realism: An Introduction to Roy Bhaskar's Philosophy*, London: Verso.

Crompton. Rosemary. 2001. *Employment and the Family* Cambridge: Cambridge University Press,.

Eurostat. 2016. *Eurostat, news release - Euroindicators*. Available online at: http://ec.europa.eu/eurostat/documents/2995521/7720354/3-0311 2016-AP-EN.pdf/bf3d493b-9596-4ac9-b5ff-4e078523622a.

Gillies, Val. 2006. Working class mothers and school life: exploring the role of emotional capital, *Gender and Education*, 18(3): 281-293.

Hadjimichalis, C. 1987. *Uneven development and regionalism. State, territory and class in Southern Europe*. London: Croom Helm.

Hadjimichalis, C. 2011. Uneven geographical development and socio-spatial justice and solidarity: European regions after the 2009 financial crisis, *European Urban and Regional Studies*, 48(3), 254-274.

Hadjimichalis, C. 2018. *Landscapes of crisis in southern Europe. Pathways of uneven geographical development*. Athens: Aleksandria (Greek book).

Hochschild, Arlie. 2005. On the edge of the time bind. *Social Research* 72(2): 339–354.

Hope, Wayne. 2011. Crisis of temporalities: Global capitalism after the 2007–08 financial collapse, *Time and Society*, 20(1): 94–118.

Jessop, Bob. 2009. The Spatiotemporal Dynamics of Globalizing Capital and Their Impact on State Power and Democracy in *High-speed society: social acceleration, power, and modernity*, edited by Hartmut Rosa and William E. Scheuerman, 135-159, USA: The Pennsylvania State University Press.

Lamont, Michelle. 1992. *Money, Morals, Meanings*, Chicago: Chicago University Press.

Perrons Diane, Colette Fagan, Linda McDowell, Kath Ray and Kevin Ward. 2005. Work, Life and Time in the New Economy. An introduction, *Time & Society* 14(1): 51–64.

Papadakis Nikos, Argiris Kyridis and Andreas Papargyris. 2015. Searching for absents: The State of things for the Neets (young people Not in Education, Employment or Training) in Greece. An overview, *Journal of Sociological Research,* 6 (1): 44-75.

Sayer, Andrew. 2005. *The Moral Significance of Class*, Cambridge: Cambridge University Press.

Sayer, Andrew. 2011. *Why Things Matter to People. Social Science, Values and Ethical Life,* Cambridge: Cambridge University Press..

Sennett, Richard and Cobb Jonathan. 1973. *The Hidden Injuries of Class* New York: Vintage Books.

Scott, John. 2001. If class is dead, why won't it lie down?, in *Inclusions and Exclusions in European Societies*, edited by Alison Woodward and Martin Kohli, 127-147, London and New York: Routledge.

Shirani, Fiona and Karen Henwood. 2011.Taking one day at a time: Temporal experiences in the context of unexpected life course transitions, *Time and Society*. 20 (1) 49–68.

Spyridakis, Manos. 2018. "We are all socialists". Greek crisis and precarization, in *Market vs Society*, edited by Manos Spyridakis, 133-153, Amsterdam: Palgrave McMillan.

Stearns, N Peter. 1994. *American Cool: Constructing a Twentieth Century Emotional Style,* New York: New York University Press.

Thacher, Jenny and Kristoffer Halvorsrud. 2016. Migrating habitus: a comparative case study of Polish and South African migrants in the UK, in *Bourdieu: The Next Generation. The development of Bourdieu's intellectual heritage in contemporary UK sociology*, Edited by Jenny Thatcher, Nicola Ingram, Ciaran Burke and Jessie Abrahams, 88-107, London and New York: Routledge.

Wright, Erik Olin. 1997. *Class counts,* Cambridge: Cambridge University Press.

Zacharopoulos Thanasis, Stavros Gavroglou, Olympia Kaminioti and Chrysa Paidousi. 2014. *Work and Employment in Greece. Annual Report of the National Institute of Work and Human Resources*, Athens: Ministry of Work, Social Security and Social Solidarity (Greek book).

In: Emotions, Temporalities …
Editors: M. Christodoulou et al.
ISBN: 978-1-53616-203-5

Chapter 2

ON THE TEMPORAL NATURE OF SOCIALITY: A GUIDE FOR RESEARCHING SOCIAL TIME

Michalis Christodoulou*
Department of Philosophy, University of Patras, Patras, Greece

ABSTRACT

The aim of the chapter is to present an argument as to how one could translate philosophical and social-theoretical approaches to social time into research tools. My intention is to identify how the sub-fields of sociology/anthropology of work, of transition studies and of sociology of education could be benefited by using these tools for handling research material. I have structured my argument as follows. First, I provide a sketch of two ideas from Heidegger's and Ricoeur's theories of temporality which are relevant for temporality-related social research. In order to overcome the impasses stemming from the first-person perspective-ness of these philosophies, I present, second, three sociological theories of temporality of which the focus is on the emergent nature of sociality. Finally, I explain in what ways the synchronization/de-synchronization phenomena and the temporality of occupations constitute two main research domains for

* Corresponding Author's E-mail: hristodoulou@upatras.gr, mikechristod7@gmail.com.

producing substantive theorizing on the temporal nature of decision making, of mobility experiences and of habitus dislocation.

Keywords: temporality research, social time, synchronization/de-synchronization phenomena, occupational temporality

INTRODUCTION

When a philosopher studies the phenomenon of time he will find himself engrossed in grappling with the essence of time or with how human consciousness makes sense of temporality. When sociologists and anthropologists study the same phenomenon, their exclusive focus is on how society's institutions produce various symbolic and material means for creating conventional time structures. Undoubtedly, both of these approaches do not move in opposite directions since what unites them is the aporia they feel when they try to explain in what way(s) time can be at once both objective and subjective. In this chapter my aim is not to rehearse famous sociological and philosophical analysis of time and temporality but to propose a sociological idea for carrying out social research on social time. In my view, up until now there have been excellent theorizations on time and temporality from philosophers and sociologists alike but what is missing is how one could "translate" them into research tools. I am not intending to provide a theoretical framework because I do not think that it is what social research needs but a conceptual grid for implementing social research in the various fields of sociology and anthropology. I have structured the chapter as follows: first, I present the ways through which some of Heidegger's and Ricoeur's ideas on temporality could be of use for social research. At the same time, I bring to the fore the limitations of these approaches and show why a conceptualization of sociality's temporality is needed. Second, I elaborate on three sociological approaches to time which could overcome traditional dualisms and, third, I provide an argument of how the above elaborations could be merged in a conceptual map for posing temporality-related research questions. In particular I will bring to the fore how the sub-fields of youth studies, migration studies and social anthropology of work could be renewed by implementing as sensitizing concepts these theoretical approaches.

The Temporality of Care and Narrative Identity

When Heidegger says that the Being of Dasein is to care for, he means that humans care for things (including themselves) in a temporal manner. In experiencing my lifeworld in a temporal way, I experience past, present and future states not sequentially but in a unified manner. This means that when humans think of the present, they think of it as something between the former and the later, the formerly and the then. Heidegger defines this unifying feature of experiencing temporality as "world – time" which has four characteristics. First, datability, which means that experiencing "Now", concerns things that humans have to complete. For example, "now that I am doing this" or "before when I was doing that" means that humans make sense of the "Now" through their practical dealings. Second, spanned-ness or during-ness, which means that "now" has duration. Third, world time is structured by the web of significance. This means that events accrue meaning in relation to conceptions of appropriateness which frame them, for instance when one says that "it is (not) the right time to do this or that", he has in mind an "in order to" motivational structure which construes this sentence. This means that appropriateness is tied up with the structure of the "in order to" motives. One can not make sense of him/herself but only through the framework of "in order to" motives which form the "first things first" structure. If my salient identity is that of the father, this means that the significance of the entities making up my lifeworld is structured according to what things have to be done first and what things have to be done later. Fourth, in so far as the temporality of care is the Being of Dasein which is amidst others, it follows that world time is collective and public. In other words, when Heidegger says that "now" is public he means that its essence is tied up with the being-amidst of Dasein's Being (Heidegger 1978, 350-420; Blatner 1999, 127-164).

To sum up, when Heidegger says that temporality is unified, he refers to the three facets of the identical "now" which lies between the "no longer now" and the "not yet now". In that sense, the retaining of the past and the waiting of the future coexist in the temporal nature of "that-for-the-sake-of-which" way of experiencing the world. Sociologically speaking, it is through practice that humans experience the world in a tensed way and eventful way, for the simple reason that events accrue meaning as temporal "until", "then", "after", etc. The kind of temporality Heidegger describes is practical and embodied, not cognitive, which means that humans' capacity of experiencing things as temporally embedded is pre-reflective and emerged through their being-with-others engagements.

Ricoeur follows Heideggerian theorizing by adopting Bergson's critique on Newtonian time and by rejecting the commonsensical idea of time which conceives of it in terms of extension and of counting, that is in terms of space. According to this idea, time presupposes isolated parts connected by means of intervals which are positioned in space. In that sense, space crates time. However, duration can not be understood in spatial terms but it is an effect of consciousness. Present takes shape according to the attention humans dedicate to it and this is the reason why present's duration varies. Ricoeur's argument on time has been influenced by this solipsistic-Bergsonian style of thought but he adds the famous idea that temporality is premised upon humans' story-telling capacity. It is through the emplotement of life events that humans are experiencing time. This narrative grounding of temporality means that time horizons are understood by humans as meaningful wholes within which duration and change are taking shape. In other words, Ricoeur draws a connection line between narrative activity and our ability to give time meaning. In that way, narrative identity is created through temporality (Ricoeur 1980; Muldoon 2006, 179-225).

We belong to groups (familial, generational, cultural, sport, or other) by means of the stories we tell during our lifetime which make us recognizable as group members. It is only to the extent that we are embedded in a web of prior stories that we understand ourselves as members of a group. Narrative time is meaningful only as a response to the question "who am I?" and in that sense temporality concerns what Ricoeur defines as the *ipse* identity, that is the self-interpretation of change and mutability over one's life course. In order to respond to the "who am I" question, humans narrate life experiences by emploting past events, present situations and future expectations. For those unfamiliar with philosophical theorizing, let me underline the sociological/anthropological connotations of Ricoeur's line of reasoning.

Despite the fact that temporality is forged through narratives, they are not individual inventions but socio-historical creations. This means that meaning is never given directly to consciousness but it is rooted in social interaction. In other words, meaning, as emplotted in stories, is to be found in the conversation with institutions, roles and social groups. Narrative resources humans draw upon for emploting life events are not idiosyncratic in nature but are parts of the stock of knowledge of the life-worlds they live in. In the same way, knowledge and self-knowledge are neither immediate to us nor issuing from consciousness. Rather, we are faced with a pre-given world of things and meanings which pre-exists and is outside of us. We come to know this world by orienting our actions through narratives. While we organize our actions to the world, we give a temporal shape to our experience because actions take place in time (Ricoeur 1979).

It is needless to say how much innovative Heidegger's and Ricoeur's approaches are for seeing time in conjunction with how humans conceive of it. Their contribution lies at highlighting that it is pointless to study time without researching the temporal nature of human consciousness and action. However, they are formulated in a way which taps temporality only as a first-person phenomenon and not as an emergent feature of humans' relations. By viewing temporality exclusively from the first person perspective, one is unable to theorize how sociality has a temporal nature different from that of the persons which compose it. This is exactly what a sociological and anthropological theory of temporality has to offer. While being-with-others is one of the cornerstones of Dasein's temporality and ipse-identity sets the stage for narrative time, what is missed is how social formations' temporality is an emergent feature of social interaction. Obviously, such a statement presupposes a social ontology quite distant from reductionist or individualistic meta-theories for which explanation is to be reduced to humans' rationality. On the contrary, in stating that social groups present an emergent temporality different from its members, I am committed to a holistic social ontology (or at least stratified). I believe that there are three sociological theories of temporality which highlight in what ways institutions', relations', roles' and groups' temporality, while emergent from humans' actions, gives shape to their experience of time. These are Gurvitch, Rosa and Zerubavel whose main theoretical ideas I present in the next sections.

Gurvitch's Theory of Social Time

Gurvitch starts his theorizing about time by turning his attention to what Mauss has termed total social facts. By keeping from Mauss' conceptualization of total social facts that humans' actions express both subjective (cognitive, emotional and volitional) and cultural/economic/family or other external dimensions, Gurvitch conceives of social phenomena as layered realities, as structured in levels of which the relations are best depicted in a depth/surface manner. Social time is understood in conjunction with how, whether and to what extent these layered realities are connected through relations of divergence or convergence. As himself puts it, "social time is the time of divergencies and convergencies of total social facts". In that way Gurvitch is trying to elaborate a conception of time that will tap the temporal nature of social relationships' totality and not to divide their components into subjective temporality and Newtonian time. Since human beings are not isolated atoms but they are embedded in relations with others, Gurvitch theorizes the relational nature of social action and he does not prioritizes neither humans' interior duree nor clock time per se. Studying social time is to study the pulsations of continuity/discontinuity or divergence/convergence which are developed among these total social facts' depth levels (Gurvitch 1965, 39-44)

Then, Gurvitch describes in detail the peculiar characteristics of eight kinds of social times that are met, invade and permeate these different depth levels. First of all, there is the *enduring time* (the time of slowed down long duration), in which the past prevails over the present and the future. Despite its remoteness, the past dominates by means of its projection to the present and to the future. For Gurvitch, kinship groupings of rural areas tend to move according to this time. Second, it is the *deceptive time* which means that behind a guise of long duration, unexpected crises are to evolve and discontinuities between past and present are possible to emerge. Large cities, organizations and political "publics" are characterized by this time. Third, *erratic time* (time of irregular pulsations between the appearance and disappearance of rhythms) is "the time of uncertainty par excellence" where contingency prevails. In that way, what matters is only the present and not the past or the future. Four, *cyclical time* is the time in which past, present and future are blended together into a kind of continuity. Five, *retarded time* concerns a delayed time awaiting to unfold and it is expressed in the lives of symbols. Social groups that move in this time are closed circles or for which admission is difficult to obtain. Six, *time alternating between delay and advance* is when discontinuity is stronger than continuity and contingency prevails. Seven, when discontinuity and contingency triumph and the future becomes present, then *time is in advance of itself*, or pushing forward. For Gurvitch, this is the time of aspiration and of collective acts of decision and is indicative of competitive individualism. Finally, eight, whenever past and present fall back in favor of a transcendent future, *time is explosive*. Discontinuity and contingency are maximized due to acts of collective creation that intervene social reality. The explosive time puts in danger durable features of social reality (Gurvitch 1965, 45-52).

Regarding the social fact's depth levels, one can pass from the exterior crust of its ecological level (demographic, spatial or geographic elements) to its organizational or patterned level, then passing to its roles/attitudes level and finally to its symbols/values level. Each of these layers of social facts is crossed with the abovementioned varieties of social time. In particular, distribution and density population and migration are some of the dimensions of ecological social time which moves through the logic of enduring time. Deceptive time, the time of surprise, permeates organizational patterns due to the fact that organizations, even though role behaviors are constrained through rigid schemes, have to display a readiness both to innovation and to the unexpected. As to the behavioral patterns which prevail in social life, their time is stamped by an endless struggle between delay and advance, between immobility and flexibility, between future and present. As to the social roles and attitudes, Gurvitch makes two points. First that there are foreseen or foreseeable roles and unpredictable roles and second that their enactment is open to multiple interpretations because of collective attitudes. As a consequence, discontinuity predominates over continuity and ruptures characterize the enactment of roles and role transition, which means that the time of roles and attitudes is the erratic time of uncertainty in which contingency prevails. Finally, symbols, ideas and collective values, due to their fluctuating character and their dependence upon the contents of various religious, political or other worldviews, unfold in a time in which delay and advance struggle but never achieve alternation nor compromise (Gurvitch 1965, 53-59.

For Gurvitch, humans are being bound to others through the various forms of sociability, of we-ness as he terms it, which constitute the micro level of total social facts. Most of the social times belonging to the various depth levels are actualized in the manifestations of sociability which are classified according to three degrees of intensity (Mass, Community and Communion) and to three degrees of relations with others (relations of approach, the mixed relations, and the relations of withdrawal). As he himself underlines, Mass, Community and Communion are not groups but *degrees* of partial fusion in the we-ness. In analyzing the roles of the degrees of intensities, Gurvitch says that Mass sociability moves in erratic and deceptive time because of the peculiarities of its bonds. In a different orientation moves the time of Community in which time alternates between delay and advance because the dominating depth level is that of signs, signals, patterns, rules, and sometimes also of symbols. Finally, the time of Communion differs from both the previous forms of we-ness since it moves in a time ahead of itself in a way that sometimes becomes explosive and never is in equilibrium. Regarding the time related to the degrees of relations with others, erratic and alternating time permeates "separation of partners, temporary isolation, struggles, rejections, antagonisms, and systematic hatreds, passing through jealousies, competition and rivalry", that is relations of withdrawal. In contrast, relations of attractions, affinities, like interests, passing through gifts, mutual or unilateral concessions, that is relations of approach, move in a time of delay combined with a time of long duration and slow motion. Finally relations found between approach and withdrawal, mixed relations, (for example barter, contracts, property returns, credit, mortgages and different kinds of promises) are characterized by combinations of deceptive, delayed and advancing time (Gurvitch 1965, 61-62).

THE INSTITUTIONALIZATION OF SOCIAL ACCELERATION

The main thesis of Rosa is that only on condition that one takes into account the nature and character of temporality is he/she able to make sense of modernity's essential features. Rosa thinks that social acceleration (SA) pervades all of these defining features of contemporary society in ways that it was not happening before (in the first modernity, in Beck's terms). In particular, SA does not refer only to the technological advancements which have radically transform transportations, communications and production of goods. SA refers mostly to the acceleration of social change and of the pace of life. The defining feature of the acceleration of social change concerns the "contraction of the present" (Rosa 2013, 15-30, 63-71). In order to make it clear, Rosa sets in motion this term to note that present is a period of stability in which the space of experience and the horizon of expectations are unchanged. In this period one can learn from the past in a way that he/she can orient him/herself to the future. What happens today is that the increasing rate of obsolescence leads to a situation called the non-contemporaneity of the contemporaneous (what is still valid within one geographical or social realm has already lost its validity in another) and social de-synchronization (job market changes faster than its members). Within this remark in mind, Rosa states that

> The acceleration of social change can thus be defined as an increase of the rate of decay of action-orienting experiences and expectations and

> as a contraction of the time periods that determine the present of respective functional, value, and action spheres (Rosa 2013, 77).

As an example of the acceleration of social change, Rosa makes use of life course sociology in which there is a plethora of studies highlighting the passage from an *inter-generational* pace (dominant in early-modern society), to a *generational* pace (dominant in 'classical modernity) and today to an *intra-generational* pace abound. As far as the acceleration of the pace of life, Rosa notes a paradox. While technological innovations give us the opportunity to save time and to slow down the pace of life, what is dominant is that we experience time as a scarcity, that people feel that time is going by too fast and worry that they might not be able to keep up with the pace of social life. Rosa tries to explain this paradox by saying that while technology increase free time, the quantity of activity itself has risen faster than the corresponding technological rate of acceleration. As himself says,

> when the speed of transport doubles, half of the time previously used for transport is available as 'free time.' However, if speed doubles while the distance we need to cross quadruples, we need twice as much time as we did before: time becomes scarce.

In other words, while technology provides us with the opportunity of doing more things by increasing our free time, the social world presents us with a range of possibilities which run faster than what humans can pursue. Human beings today feel that have access to whatever society offers but they have not the temporal means for obtaining them. There is a temporal gap between the opportunities the social world offers and what humans are accessed to realize within a finite time span (the truth is that it sounds like a Mertonian argument). While one could see social acceleration as a *promesse de bonheure*, what lies beneath is a vicious circle of social inequalities because the more the gratification means are augmented, the more exhausted are those who have not the means to remain close to the possibilities capitalist order offers. As Rosa puts it: "the rate of growth of options exceeds the rate of acceleration" (Rosa 2017, 38).

Rosa draws specific conclusions from how SA affects personal identity. First, he concedes that personal identity becomes a temporal project of which the main task is to foresee future. Life plans are identity projects with temporal grounding which are tied up with the above-mentioned SA dynamics. Second, SA heightens the consciousness of contingency in the sense that individuals are called to find their own place in the world through narratives which are in continuous remaking in so far class, political, religious or other memberships have become obsolete. In that way, since identity becomes transitory, it is temporalized given that people in our days are on the move for various reasons (for example migration for education or for work). However similar this argument may seem with Beck's individualization of risk, Rosa adds that the substitution of polygamy of place for the monogamy of jobs for life has the effect that people lose control over their life plans because of the unpredictability of the future (Rosa 2013, 224-231).

Social Layers of Temporal Patterns

The exposition of these analyses show us that for sociologists time is neither Newtonian nor mind dependent (only), but its meaning and nature is to be found on the institutional structure of society. As already as 1937 the then leading sociologists Sorokin and Merton had pointed out how groups' social life forms temporal patterns. Forty four years later Zerubavel (1981) systematized this reasoning by recontextualizing Durkheim's conception of temporal regularities. In particular, Zerubavel states that social events and situations present 1) a sequential structure (in what order they will take place), 2) duration (how long they will last), 3) temporal location (when they will take place) and 4) rate of recurrence (how often they will happen) (Zerubavel 1981, 12-14). These four features provide social events with normativity by enabling people orient themselves motivationally and practically. Such expressions as "too often", "hardly ever", "too late", "too long", "too early", "when" and others, delineate durational expectancies and the temporal spacing of social events. Schedules (for example dieting) and life plans (for example post graduate transitions) are empirical realities in which one can see how this kind of temporal structuring forms individual time horizons and people's reasons for taking actions.

Within this line of reasoning, Lewis and Weigert (1981) reflect on what it means to experience the passage of time as a social process by developing a three-level typology which is comprised of biographical time, interactional time and institutional time. In order to expand upon biographical time, Lewis and Weigert refer to Heidegger's concept of "nearing nearness of nearhood". In simple terms this means that the experiences of events in the past and future are ordered with respect to their nearness or remoteness to what is taken as present. Interactional time refers to the temporal flow of social interactions and to the rules that define appropriate "turns" in interaction. Lewis and Weigert (1981, 448) note that this feature is imbued of power relations like those which frame who has the power to set barriers on waiting and delay. Finally, their conception of institutional time draws upon Chicago School theorizing on how careers shape identities. Career, in this perspective, is the meeting point of biographical and social time. Social institutions, in laying out the time track for each one of us, delineate the temporal frame of the statuses and positions we have to pass. They set out temporal expectations about when and for how long we have to stay in each status. Career, in other words, refers to the number of statuses which are meaningfully related to each other in a recognized sequence. Through the concept of career one can tap both the values and meaning people invest to their status passages and the socio-temporal structuring in which it is developed. People who pass too slow or too fast from the temporal structures society defines are considered either age deviants (for example, giving birth "too late") or age exceptionals (for example, charismatic children), depending on the temporal expectations each institution imposes. In that sense, temporal structures, albeit conventional, obtain a binding and external forming force as any other "social fact".

A Sociological and Anthropological Temporality-Related Research Agenda

The socio-theoretical conceptions of time I presented should not be taken as recipe for use without taking into account geographical and social contexts of which the details do not fit to each of the above-mentioned approaches. In addition, one has to be attentive as to the peculiarities of the sample by means of which he/she tries to respond to specific research questions. In that sense, one should not impose them indiscreetly to the research material he/she gathers. On the contrary, my aim is to see how these theories can be implemented as sensitizing concepts to specific temporality related research questions.

Two main groups of research areas can be detected through the socio-anthropological analyses of temporality I sketched. First, there are issues related to phenomena of synchronization and of de-synchronization issuing from how modern society forges its temporal structures. Second, there are issues related to how organizational and occupational time structures impinge upon the subjective experiencing of temporality. Let me expand on them respectively.

Regarding synchronization and de-synchronization phenomena, in the field of lifelong learning one could explore how the varieties of Gurvitch's social time interact with the temporalities of the narrative identities of its members. In particular, one research orientation could be the investigation of the ways through which these varieties (for example the enduring, erratic, deceptive, retarded or cyclical time) affect the organizational structure of lifelong learning. For example, what about the narrative temporalities of large group of people who left school early in their teen years and decided to return to attend Second Chance Schools? In what ways these temporalities have been shaped by the lifelong-learning's social time varieties? What about the biographical time of postgraduate students who decided to start postgraduate studies "too early" or "too late"? Given that tertiary education constitutes a global market and that the percentage of tertiary-educated students has been increased, it follows that such questions could refresh the field of sociology of education.

It seems to me that a very interesting substantive field of research concerns how one could conceptualize decision making as a temporal matter. I believe that it is the temporal structure of motives which drives people's actions. Since decision making is motivated action, it follows that researchers should explore the interplay of because-of motives with in-order-to motives within actors' narrative identities. By researching the temporality of decision making one could find the key for conceptualizing motives not through psychoanalytic or old-fashioned ego-psychological theories of motives seen as internal/external but as biographically formed.

Two other research fields which could be benefited from the social time theorizing we developed are youth studies and anthropology of work. In particular, one could detect in what sense social inequalities are in essence temporal inequalities through two interrelated theoretical ideas. The first concerns the mobility paradigm of Elliot & Urry (2010) who, in stating that the major and most dominant feature of contemporary life is movement (of bodies, objects, ideas), they believe that this movement entails power relations in the sense that those who are able to move (or to be able voluntarily to stay still) are in advantageous position in comparison to those who are not. Elliot & Urry point out that movement takes place within networks of which, however, the power varies and are unequally distributed. In that way networks are a form of power or influence that can operate to benefit some social groups at the expense of others (2010, 45). Thus, how their network-laden conception of temporality is combined with synchronization and de-synchronization phenomena? I think that youths' international mobility could be approached as a practice related to unequal temporality resources groups of students draw upon for realizing transition decisions. For example, how the prospect of going to study abroad affects students' habitual paces of life? In what ways their narrative temporality is re-shaped by means of their prospect of studying in a foreign country? In other words, how synchronized/de-synchronized are youths' biographical time regarding the temporal structure of living within different paces of life? I believe that within this temporality-related frame of posing research questions one could investigate phenomena of brain drain (or circulation) across the globe.

The second theoretical development relating social inequalities with temporal inequalities concerns the domain of work. The Bourdieusian toolbox is very useful here in so far as it enable us to conceptualize the subjective perception of upward and downward mobility. In particular, when habitus and field are synchronized agents tend to find as taken for granted the temporal structures of the field and to adjust their subjective expectations to objective possibilities (for example the scholars' scholastic preference for reflexivity). Given that for Bourdieu each field has its own temporal structure (pace, sequentiality and rhythm), actors experience their lifeworld in terms of these structures (the "feel for the game" tries to capture this experience). On the contrary, in cases that agents change field because of upward/downward mobility, of migration, of political upheavals or of field transformation, they experience habitus dislocation of which the major determinant is temporal dislocation. In such cases the mismatch between habitus and field undermines the sense agents have of the likely and unlikely, possible and impossible (Atkinson, 2013). Regarding the case of work/unemployment, Rosa thinks that it is the technology-provoked intensification of work that marginalizes those who are in a disadvantaged position as far as the volume and the structure of capital is concerned. Either because agents can not tolerate the speed by means of which they should deal with work demands (e.g., burnout) or because they do not have the resources to overcome the speed through which the necessary job skills are transformed, unemployment affects in various ways and disproportionately those who are on the margin or are becoming marginalized. Will Atkinson (2013) has shown how the temporal sense of presentism is formed by those who are amongst the least resourced and Rosa (2013) has highlighted the vicissitudes that will face those who lack the means and the opportunities to form concrete and realizable expectations and are excluded from the hamster wheels of work by unemployment.

Besides the research of how synchronization/de-synchronization phenomena impinge upon socio-temporal inequalities, life-course decisions and upward/downward mobility, one other unexplored terrain of investigating social time concerns research on the temporalities of occupations. The working hypothesis is that the nature of labor produces peculiar temporalities. Individuals working on specific jobs set in motion specific technologies of self through which the try to synchronize with the time of other people or to make others synchronize to them. For example, one could investigate in what ways the temporal structures of administration-related jobs shape the conceptions of past, present and future of its members and how this shaping affects in turn their interaction with other social groups. In one of the best ethnographies on the temporality of taxi drivers, Sharma (2014, 55-81) describes how they are trying to adjust their pacing to the temporal demands of their clients. As she underlines, there are different struggles over time that occur when one's labor entails directly synchronizing to the time demands of other populations' temporalities.

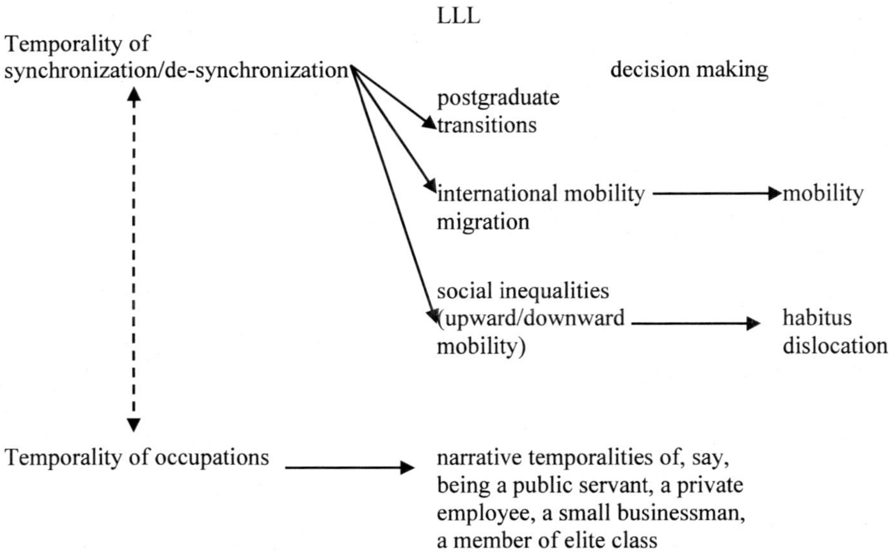

To conclude, we believe that the sub-fields of sociology/anthropology of work, of youth transitions and of education could be benefited from putting temporality-related research questions to the forefront of their priorities. Research on the generative mechanisms producing the temporality of synchronization/de-synchronization phenomena and the temporality of occupational lifeworlds can provide us with new insights on both the reproductive and transformative dynamics of late capitalism. The previous scheme tries to capture my line of reasoning. Decision making, mobility and habitus dislocation constitute the three substantive terrains in which specific explanatory propositions could be developed. For instance, research on these research domains could end up in conceptual propositions explaining the temporal peculiarities of decision making, mobility experiences and habitus dislocation.

REFERENCES

Atkinson, Will. (2013). Class habitus and perception of the future: recession, employment insecurity and temporality, *The British Journal of Sociology*, *64*(4), 643-661.

Atkinson, Will. (2018). Time for Bourdieu: Insights and oversights, *Time & Society*, DOI: 10.1177/0961463X17752280.

Blatner, William. (1999). *Heidegger' temporal idealism*, Cambridge: Cambridge University Press.

Elliott, Anthony. & Urry, John. (2010). *Mobile Lives*, London: Routledge.

Gurvitch, Georges. 1965. *The spectrum of social time*, Dordrecht: Reidel Publishing Company.

Heidegger, Martin. (1978). *Being and Time*. Trans. John Macquarrie and Edward Robinson. Oxford: Basil Blackwell.

Lewis, J. David. & Weigert, J. Andrew. (1981). The Structures and Meanings of Social Time, *Social Forces*, *60*(2), 432-462.

Muldoon, Mark. (2006). Bergson, Merleau-Ponty and Ricoeur in search of time, self and meaning, Pittsburgh: Duquesne University Press.

Ricoeur, Paul. (1979). "The Human Experience of Time and Narrative." *Research in Phenomenology*, *9*, 17–35.

Ricoeur, Paul. (1980). "Narrative Time." *Critical Inquiry*, *7*, 169–90.

Rosa, Hartmut. (2013). *Social acceleration: a new theory of modernity*, translated by Jonathan Trejo-Mathys, New York: Columbia University Press.

Rosa, Hartmut. (2017). "De-Synchronization, Dynamic Stabilization, Dispositional Squeeze: The Problem of Temporal Mismatch", in The Sociology of Speed Digital, Organizational, and Social Temporalities Edited by Judy Wajcman and Nigel Dodd.

Sharma, Sarah. (2014). *In the Meantime. Temporality and Cultural Politics*, Durham and London: Duke University Press.

Sorokin, A. Pitirim. & Merton, K. Robert. (1937). Social Time: A Methodological and Functional Analysis, *American Journal of Sociology*, *42*(5), 615-629.

Zerubavel, Eviatar. (1981). *Hidden Rhythms Schedules and Calendars in Social Life*, Berkeley, Los Angeles, London: University of California Press.

SECTION 1. RESEARCHING WORKING-CLASS TEMPORALITIES

In: Emotions, Temporalities …
Editors: M. Christodoulou et al.
ISBN: 978-1-53616-203-5

Chapter 3

The Life-Course Determinants of Falling from Grace: On the Temporality of Precariousness

Manos Spyridakis[1,*] and Michalis Christodoulou[2,†]
[1]Department of Social and Educational Policy, University of the Peloponnese, Corinth, Greece
[2]Department of Philosophy, University of Patras, Patras, Greece

Abstract

Greece was one of the most discussed countries during the 2009 world financial crisis because of the severe austerity measures the crisis provoked in various facets of the citizens' social and personal life. In this chapter we present research findings from one-year fieldwork research carried out with unemployed aged between 50 and 60 years old, who used Greek government facilities for the protection of those affected by the crisis.

* Corresponding Author's Email: maspyridakis@gmail.com.
† Author's Email: hristodoulou@upatras.gr; mikechristod7@gmail.com.

Given that most of the informants had a similar profile regarding generational and social-class background, we tried to capture the temporal nature of living in precarious situations and to explain its life-course determinants. For that reason we implemented a Critical-Realist framework for carrying out Biographical-Narrative interviews in order to tap generative mechanisms. We explain the ways in which the dual nature of standing still forms peculiar emotional dispositions by means of which the informants' temporality becomes displaced.

Keywords: precariousness, temporal dislocation, downward mobility, biographical time, standing still

INTRODUCTION

In the 90's interventionist labour market policies were demonized due to the ascendance of neo-liberal economic mindset which conceived of workers as autonomous and self-motivated economic actors who are responsible for their own fates or for their job-related search outcomes. The responses promoted by neo-liberal advocates was that workers should learn to accept the risks related to job changes and that the role of state or of various counselling regimes was to provide them with the tools to manage risks effectively. According to such individualized understandings of the labour market, career outcomes were seen as manifestations of workers' psychological or emotional functioning. Nowadays, neo-liberal capitalism presents three features which make it differ in qualitative ways from the 80's and 90's. First, today's job losses mostly affect skilled workers and middle-income households. Second, those who lose their job cannot rely on termination payments to ease unemployment and to fund job search practices. Third, given that household debt has been increased and its savings are kept to a minimum or are hard to achieve, it follows that financial and social risks are more threatening for household members who lose their jobs (Weller, 2012).

In her classic *Falling from Grace*, Newman (1988) has shown that downward mobility related to job loss, as it affects the material, the psychological and the family aspects of people's lives, has to be explained in relation to the life course formation of their class identity. In this process emotions are crucial since they bind individuals with dominant ideologies (meritocracy for example) and frame how active or inactive they will be during this downwardly mobile trajectory. Although it has not passed unnoticed, the temporality dimension of the class-formed feeling structures of those who lose their jobs has yet to be examined. In this chapter we examine this temporality dimension of emotions by presenting research findings stemming from a generation of 55-year-old working-class workers who experienced the loss of their respectable jobs in the age of financial crisis in Greece by moving from a state of prosperity to a situation of precariousness. Our aim was to explore the life course formation of the temporal nature of the emotional structure during this transition process.

Literature Review: The Ambivalence of a Research Paradigm

In social theory the above-mentioned economic and social development has been expressed in Beck's and Gidden's works as the "individualization thesis" or "risk society thesis". Although popular and much used in work and transition studies, we will try to show how this thesis underpins the fields of life course studies, youth transition studies and sociology of time. Regarding youth transition studies, Woodman (2009:249) argues that individualization is a term Beck proposes for legitimizing life decisions at critical biographical moments and that ambivalence prevails due to the diffusion of uncertainty. Furlong and Cartmel (2003) try to link Beck's individualization thesis to a view that theorizes the social reproduction process and the structural bases of action. To do this they develop a conceptual model for researching transitions which centres on how and to what extent agents mobilize capacities either of a structural variant (economic, social and cultural capital resources) or of an agency variant (motivation, drive and determination). This two-dimensional scheme is framed by the critical incidents related to biography. The concept of "situated rationalizing action" they implement seeks to underline that past experiences affect present choices. Along the same line of reasoning, Walther (2009) in explaining the de-institutionali-zation of transitions states that contemporary life courses have been "biographized" in the sense that individuals are confronted with the need to make decisions, and they are increasingly alone in making them because their trajectories differ from those of their parents as well as their peers. For him what makes a transition successful is the biographical competence to make decisions which are both meaningful and viable. To give more strength to this reasoning, Walther points out that the concept of biographical coping is the most appropriate term for tapping the interaction between subjective motivation and structurally accessible resources and opportunities.

In the field of job loss research what has been emphasized is that the responses to the experience of being laid off are hugely emotionally charged, painful and conflictual experiences. Gabriel et al. (2013) propose the concept of "narrative coping" for understanding how managerial and professional employees make sense of unemployment as lived experience. They found three patterns of such narrative coping. First, there are those who see unemployment as a "temporary derailment" from which they can recover. Second, there are those who believe that they are at the "end-of the line" in the sense that unemployment is a blow which they cannot overcome; it is the beginning of a new period of stress. Third, there are those for whom unemployment is a kind of moratorium, a period which, however permanent, temporary or unknown, they believe they will do their best to get out of. The main research finding is that workers try to resist in an individualized way. Life course research follows the same line of thought as one can see in the work of Heinz (2002). The author believes that the way persons deal with work uncertainty depends on how they connect their education, training, and employment biography with the contexts and options at work and that this process "is mediated by action orientations which relate to selected aspects of work in specific ways and are personal guidelines for job-related activities" (p. 225). In that sense, transition biographies "are determined neither by action contexts nor by social class; instead they are individually constructed in the course of the person's training and work history" (p. 229).

However, while he recognizes that within the context of "risk society" transitions in the life course initiate reciprocal socialization processes between the individual and social contexts, he accepts that "since life chances are distributed unequally according to social origin, gender and age, there is no completely individualized choice in life-course transitions" (p. 237).

Regarding time studies, Carmo et al. (2014), by examining how precarious youth construct conceptions of future, highlighted two types of "future projections", the cumulative and the non-cumulative projections which contain the "contingent", "the immobile" and the "rupture" sub-types. Those who see their future work lives as cumulative projections are more optimistic and draw upon educational resources either for job change or for improving upward mobility. In contrast, the contingent sub-type of the non-cumulative projection looks powerless and refuses to conceive of future projects, while for the immobile non-cumulative type there is no place for considering employment paths due to parental responsibilities. Finally, the non-cumulative type who opts for rupture refers to unqualified workers who migrate to foreign countries. Despite its merit regarding the aim of relating temporality with precarious conditions, it seems that the typology's failure to distinguish social class condition from precarious condition leads to an individualistic separation of those who rely on educational and training capital from those whose projections are defined through discontinuity and a series of non-cumulative ways of thinking. In the same way, the findings from research aimed at understanding how young people deal with "future crisis" are handled by means of such a first-person perspective (Leccardi, 2005). By describing a typology depicting various ways of coping with crisis, Leccardi presents two life stories the first of which has a positive and the other a negative conception of the future. What is not highlighted, however, is why this difference could not be explained though their different cultural capital or through the concept of habitus dislocation, given that those with more educational capital are more prone to see uncertainty as a resource for future planning and as a kind of "existential autonomy". In an attempt to overcome this theoretical ambiguity, Facchini and Rampazi (2009) try to reconcile the institutional with the subjective dimension of temporality. In this research, which is one of the best within the "risk individualisation thesis" paradigm and which examined the temporal orientations of educated workers/craftsmen, of white-collar workers and of teachers in their mid-50's, two temporalities were identified. First, the traditional temporal orientations corresponded to people with a working class background with a medium-low standard of culture whose temporal horizons are still pervaded by the standardized logic of linearity. Despite the fact that within such a temporality there is empty time to be filled,

> it is annulled by a prevailing sense of insecurity whenever the following conditions are met: a) the life plan has been strongly, if not exclusively, anchored to work and when this is no longer present, an acute sense of identity loss occurs; b) the death or absence of the partner creates a sense of loneliness that is so strong and pervasive as to lead to self-isolation; c) there is the risk of an incapacitating illness and/or economic precariousness (361).

Second, the innovative temporal orientation is prevalent among the culturally educated who enjoy physical health and economic stability and who see the "deinstitutionalization/de-standardization of life courses as an opportunity for experiencing uncertainty as a *chance"* (362). Would it be an exaggeration to say that the first group looks like the Willis "lads" who are close to their retirement and that the second group consists of people whose practices could easily be described through a Bourdieusian toolkit of "distance from necessity"?

In extending the critique of Bruckner and Mayer (2005), we believe that this conception of risk individualization can be critiqued on three additional points. First, in the above-mentioned five propositions that make up the "risk individualization" thesis, one cannot distinguish the premises from the conclusion. Since structural inequalities exist as much in modernity's class identifications as in late modernity's biographicity, how can one explain that the same cause (inequalities) gives shape to different outcomes in two different historical periods ("normal" biographies in the first case and "choice" biographies in the second)? Second, the weakness in theorizing the collapse of social class identifications in non-nominalist terms is expressed in the ambiguity which permeates the research findings of this literature. While acknowledging the existence of the structural dynamics of external reality, researchers in this tradition end up repeating in other words the common-sense perspectives of their informants by classifying them typologically. There are no solid grounds for why one should disregard explanations which rely upon such "modern" concepts as social class, opportunity structures or generative mechanisms and replace them with biographical types in so far as the research findings do not justify this replacement. Finally, by prioritizing narrative coping, risk individualization researchers reduce the temporality of social relations to its cognitive dimension. Should one restrict the temporal forming of identities only to its cognitive dimension he/she remains blind to the emotional dynamics of identity and to its social or life course formation. Since one sees the "not yet" conception of temporality as constitutive of all reflexive life planning, he/she fails to see other possible ways of temporality formation, especially for those who do not see their future in colonized terms (e.g., Shirani and Henwood 2011). At a methodological level, research undertaken through the "risk individualization thesis" lens ends up in a kind of fragmented descriptivism by means of which one is unable to produce a non tautological explanatory framework through which he/she can establish why some temporalities and feeling structures are formed in that way and not another. At the theoretical level, our main reservation concerns the fact that the theoretical gains of using the risk individualization reasoning in order to talk about something that is obvious (life-course fragmentation, reversibility of transitions, work flexibility and precariousness etc) seem unclear and unconvincing, or to put it in other terms, it is not clear what the sociological gains are from focusing exclusively on the prioritization of the first-person perspective and ignoring how one could forge a third-person explanation (Bruckner and Mayer 2005, 34). Finally, the "risk individualization" thesis suffers from its inadequacy to account for the temporality of being-together with others. It is one thing to theorize the temporal orientations of unique individuals ("me", "you", "him/her") and it is quite another to theorize about how sociality's temporality is instantiated in social agents' thought and action.

METHODOLOGY

One of the measures the SYRIZA Government in Greece took for coping with the financial crisis was the establishment of the Social Grocery (SG), the Social Pharmacy (SP) and the Social Solidarity Income (SSI) measures. Beneficiaries of the SG are those with a 6000 euro income limit (conditions of relative poverty) while for the SSI and the SP are those with a 2400 euro income limit per year (conditions of absolute poverty). Beneficiaries of SG are provided with a card with which they can obtain clothes or food for free. The three social services are run by local authorities and by the Municipalities in the majority of most large towns in Greece like Athens, Patra, Heraklion, Thessaloniki, Larissa etc. One of the authors (Manos Spyridakis) visited three of the most crowded SG in Athens over the course of one year in order to collect life story data from the SG's members. The sampled SGs are located in three neighbourhoods which differ regarding their socio-cultural composition and population density. The aim of this choice was to trace possible class or other differences as far as their demographic profile is concerned. In addition to the narrative interviews, Spyridakis researched the demographic profiles which were kept by the municipality staff on all the beneficiaries of the three SG. This kind of archival research showed us that those who benefit from the social services constitute a more or less homogeneous group in the sense that they share similar generational, educational and work histories. Given that most of the SG beneficiaries were reluctant to participate in the interviews for several reasons, Spyridakis managed to collect 36 life stories.

Data were collected through biographical interviewing because we think that it is the most appropriate means of studying self processes related to life disruptions and to how members of social groups develop strategies for coping with them. However, in our research we did not limit the value of biographical interviewing only for tapping lived experiences but used it mostly for tracing causal processes. In particular, through biographical interviews we can both highlight first-person perspectives and explore the generative mechanisms which form them. As Wengraf and Chamberlayne (2013, 63) put it: "to avoid being seduced by interviewees' storytelling, for a critical realist understanding it is crucial that the researcher separately gathers together as much hard biographical and contextual data as they can in order to understand the 'situated subjectivity' of the story teller".

Despite the fact that the biographical method tends to be identified with a constructivist epistemology, we adopted the Critical Realist (CR) social ontology for framing biographical interviews. What distinguishes CR from the constructivism-oriented epistemology is, mutatis mutandis, that the roots of the interviewee's meaning formation are not inscribed in the interview context but in the external social reality which is stratified in Empirical, Actual and Real layers. The Empirical layer concerns lived experiences, the Actual entails events and the Real entails generative mechanisms. This means that causality is found not only in the informants' reasons for acting but also in the emergent reality whose peculiar features are not reduced to the individual actor him/herself (Iosifides 2017).

Life story data were analyzed according to the scheme of "Sequences, Actants and Narratives" proposed by Demazier and Dubar (1997). The analysis focuses on how the horizontal axis of Sequence is articulated with the vertical axis of evaluations and narrations. This articulation is expressed in pairs of conjunctions and disjunctions in which the interviewees' meanings are formed. In other words, informants' deeper meanings are to be found in the "code of Discourse" which is constructed through relations of difference. According to Demazier and Dubar, what is analyzed is not the psychology of individuals but the embedding of their narratives in particular social situations. This is the reason why their style of analysis is compatible with a CR social ontology. Informants talk about themselves and their life course through normative judgments within which past experiences, present situations and future potentialities are emplotted.

Narrative and Social Determinants of Working-Class Cyclical Time

As far as the informants' social class background is concerned, their social origin is close to a "respectable working-class" situation in the sense that their fathers are either semi-skilled workers or self-employed owners of small businesses, their mothers are housewives and most of them are primary or vocational school graduates. However, fathers hold stable jobs which permit the informants to engage in—long-term life planning. Informants are either early school drop-outs or vocational school graduates, without on the job training. One should not forget however, that when our informants were adolescents (they were born between 1950 and 1966), that is in the seventies and in the mid-80's, mass education and educational expansion were something of a *terra incognita* in Greek society, in the sense that those who chose educational pathways as a post secondary life route were a minority. In other words, the parents of the working-class generation we examined experienced what is termed a (working-class) "institutionalized life course" and it is exactly this temporal horizon that our informants tried to act out after finishing high school. Needless to say they tried to follow their parents' life pathways not as a consciously-stated life goal or work plan but as a pre-reflexive and taken-for-granted lived experience. This is obvious in how they emplot the beginning of their biographical self-presentation.

See how John May (all the names are fictional), a 54-year-old informant who is married with two children chose to respond to the initial prompt of the interviewer (Manos Spyridakis) to narrate his life by starting from whatever event or life period he wished:

> May: I was born and raised in Brahami, my family is one of the oldest in this neighborhood, I spent my school years here, elementary and vocational school and I worked in a garage I was one of the few guys who had a job 'cause my friends left school early. Then I got married and worked for 25 years in this garage. Next I opened my own garage for 10 years, as you see I have been working in the garage for 35 years, since I was 15.

In the same tone, Haris Hatzidis, 65, divorced and remarried, recollects his adolescent school-to-work transition:

Hatzidis: I was born and raised here in Likovrisi, I have worked as a clock repairer since my teen years because of our family tradition, my uncle and my father did the same job, so I learned the job first hand and through our tradition.

Locality and family traditions are the spatial and the cultural determinants which provided them with the temporal resources for making the passage to adulthood. Informants' past experiences are organized narratively by how they make sense of their spatial movements, of their early entry into work life and of their marriage responsibilities. Local membership dominates in the generation of the working-class we examined since it is the subcultural capital (acquaintances, and embodied skills) they accumulate in manual work that secures them a safe work future. One could say that informants respond to the "who am I" question by narrating the "where I started from" question.

This is the temporal dimension of narrative identity Rickoeur talked about (Muldoon, 2006) in the sense that locality and family traditions are not just "themes" which stabilize the informants' self-understandings but meaningful wholes through which they make sense of the succession between "before" and "after", before the passage to precariousness and after it. Finding themselves as always already belonging to local communities and family traditions, informants develop temporal orientations shaped in relation to the fact that these groups promote enduring and cyclical social time by means of which they feel that their lives are predictable. However, this predictability has gendered grounding in the sense that women informants, when asked to talk about their present lives, had a "male's domination" story to tell which was tied up with their divorce. For instance, Kolona and Meropi start as follows:

Meropi: look, I have been hit by the financial crisis, a lot of people have and not only me but I have a personal story to tell, let me begin by stating that I am a single parent 'cause I have two kids, I got divorced from my husband when the financial crisis started, I receive 500 euro in alimony with the prospect that it will be increased so as to cover my child's needs. However, since my ex-husband's salary was cut, things are too hard to handle, I have nobody to share economic and emotional burdens with.

Kolona: I got married and I divorced…I was married in my teen years, I was 18 and attended an art vocational school in order to follow university studies but my husband moved to another place because he found a job, so I went to stay with him but I could not find a job there. Given that my son was 2 years old I had no one to take care of hım should I attend an art class, so I quit this project 'cause I had no options, my parents were too strict, my dad told me "forget university, I will not let you go", so I saw my husband as a route to get out of this impasse.

While both women are asked to talk about how they cope with present difficulties, they choose to put an order between past experiences and present situations by emplotting their broken marriage. For Meropi, it is the financial dependence on her husband's income that affects her here-and-now life while for Kolona the strict upbringing of her adolescence made her marry a man whose occupational demands annulled her life plans at the age of twenty. In other words, there is a gender difference as to how informants emplot their temporalities.

For men, the predictability of the future was connected with local membership and with the sub-culturally structured work life whilst for women it was connected to male domination. However, for both genders, beyond the obvious gender inequality issue, future predictability is tied up with the fact that past, present and future are blended together into a kind of continuity (cyclical social time) through which they forge a time horizon of the type "life will always be the same". One of the main working hypotheses of our research is that while the informants' lives were moving forward they encountered social and class situations whose social time was incompatible with this time horizon. It is this incompatibility that set for them the stage for entering the road to precarity, or the "road to hell".

Feeling Structures and Temporal Displacement

In an excellent approach to the strengths and weaknesses of Bourdieu's theorization of time, Atkinson (2018) notes that while each field has its own distinct temporality structured according to its internal struggles between insiders and outsiders or between newcomers and "old-school believers" who fight to retain or to transform its sequence, its pacing or its calendar, things are more complicated when one's biographical time is not aligned with the social time of the field which he/she enters. In other words, in cases of upward mobility the temporality of the habitus is displaced because its dynamic is incompatible with the social time of the field the actors encounter. As we shall see, it is this temporal displacement which acted as the generative processes for the marginalization of our informants. Let's see the biographical details of this process which, one should not forget, has intense emotional connotations. Hatzidis, the clock repairer, narrates the rise and fall of his work career as follows:

> Although I entered the job due to our family tradition, I was always searching for something new, I was not content doing such a routine job, I wanted to do something more creative. Then I realized that such demands as insurance, tax and electricity payments are difficult to satisfy, so I had to enter the trade part of the job and become a clock merchant, a part I find too fortune-seeking, most of my colleagues are such people because there is huge tax evasion, I can guarantee you that no one at the age of 69 can obtain two or three floor buildings by relying only on the clock repairer's wage.

Hatzidis, while he started as a repairer of mechanical watches and clocks, entered the trade of silversmith because his daily earnings could not satisfy the demands related to tax payment. Note that he biographically presents himself as an honest man who scorns fraudsters and fortune seekers, that is, those who do the same job but are not as honest as he is. Be that as it may, in entering the merchant life of silversmith, it is his ignorance of how things work that gradually marginalized him:

> Then I started moving to the silversmith trade and managed to have a good reputation but soon I fell from grace 'cause I was not the fraudulent type, silversmith trade demands frauds, so I was robbed, these are very valuable metals, which means a lot of money, I mean…I buy the raw material and make a necklace for example, I made a huge mistake because I did not manage to save money considering it useless, this carelessness hurt me a lot 'cause I reached 69 with no house and hunted by 3 banks to repay huge debts.

Honesty has a double meaning for the informant, on the one hand it protected him from becoming a fraud but on the other it kept him ignorant concerning how the silversmith trade worked. Honesty, however, is not an internal and ethical substance attached to an individual but it is Hatzidis's way of being in the world, of seeing how things should be done in the world in which he lived, it is an embodied understanding of how one should treat past, present and future dealings. In particular, an honest man keeps his word, he remains loyal to what he promised in the past or he promises that he will stick to the job's moral codes not only now but in the future as well. The emotion of honesty prioritizes a temporality of continuity, of the sense that things will proceed as they always have proceeded. One could say that the temporality of honesty is at odds with the temporality of fraud which prevails in the silversmith trade in which discontinuity and contingency define the erratic and deceptive time of being a silversmith trader. To recall Gurvitch, deceptive time is full of unexpected crises and of discontinuities between past and present while erratic time is structured through irregular pulsations which govern the tempo of work and in which it is only the present that matters, not the past or the future. Similar is the biographical self-presentation of Diamandis, a 65-year old insurance broker who uses the narrative pattern of honesty in order to manage the serious health problems that followed his social fall:

> *Spyridakis:* could you tell me a few things about your job history?
> *Diamandis:* I was an honest citizen until 2004, financially speaking, I took a loan in order to buy a house for my 5 kids, when my wife was

pregnant I said to her "ok, we do not kill children", but in 2004 I lost all of my assets in the stock market, about 100,000 euro.

Spyridakis: what did you do then?

Dimantis: the shock was so big that I had seven heart attacks, I have 7 stents in my heart, then my wife died and I married the wife I have now but since then I have declined rapidly due to coronary disease, I feel that I have fallen apart.

Spyridakis: what was your job?

Dimantis: I was an insurance employee but I didn't have the strength to remain in the job, it is a very demanding job, I had to walk a lot and to accept that I had to tell lies to the client, but I could not do this because the insurance programs were changing all the time and my job was to inform him, not to cheat him, I was always an honest guy, since my client had the right to receive money from the company, I had to help him whatever the cost, that's why I could not withstand all this psychological pressure, my soul and my body could not carry this weight, that's why I fell apart.

As in the case of Hatzidis, honesty is the meaningful theme Diamandis draws upon in order to make sense of his transition from prosperity to downfall. While fraud is the expected behavioral skill insurance brokers have to put into practice in order to be seen as good employees, honesty is what provides him with the sense of sameness as much in the period of abundance (before the collapse of the stock market) as in the period of turbulence (when he experienced health problems). The collapse of the stock market in Greece had as its profound temporal mark the instantaneity whose acceleration, since duration disappeared, incapacitates the actors' ability to process information transfer. In situations in which ccommunicated information loses its location, it follows that ephemerality and transience re-emerge with a vengeance, negating hard-won certainties and stabilities. It is exactly, we hypothesize, the temporal mismatch between the temporality of honesty and the erratic time related to the peculiarities of their jobs that made the informants unable to overcome the fateful biographical moments they faced. What we want to underline by this statement is that informants' temporality of honesty corresponds to a narrative time of the type "things will always be the same" and which binds them to the financial, familial and moral commitments related to previous life decisions. We argue that it is this binding temporality (which is at odds with the social time of finance) that deprived our informants of being protected from the harsh vicissitudes of the transition to precariousness. This process is exemplified in Tzikas' life story. Born in 1965 and a member of a multi-child family, Tzikas, influenced as he had been by his father's life in commerce (he sold clothing), is proud of starting his own business dream as early as in his teen years:

Tzikas: I knew how the job market worked, I learned it 'cause when I was 11I spent my day with my father, I wanted to do what he had not managed to achieve, I wanted to set up my own business, but my business was ruined because of the bounced checks I received from customers, they were not paying me.

Spyridakis: so, you were taking checks as a collateral for the items you were selling.

Tzikas: yes, you ordered stuff worth 2000 euro from me, I sent it to you and you gave me a check, this system of payment worked very well until the early '90s, I started from nothing and I managed to live a life of luxury, I had three cars without taking money from the business, I was just taking my wage.

Tzikas' story is typical of many 'respectable working-class' offspring in Greek society in the 80's who were upwardly mobile through self-employment or small entrepreneurship. By means of his immersion in this field, Tzikas acquired the practical know-how of how to expand his business. However, the Bourdieusian toolkit is not enough for explaining the process of social decline unless one takes into account what we termed the temporality of "things will always be the same". See how this temporality works when Tzikas recounts how he responded to a crisis situation:

Spyridakis: how did you decide to get involved with the child clothing business?

Tzikas: well, in the first years my business had a different orientation, I was selling baby clothing but in the meantime, in 1998, I realized that child clothing was a better prospective, so I started to sell this kind of clothes and things were going excellently, however, while reality was

> changing after 2007 I refused to take heed of its messages, instead of selling clothes in my own stores and of realizing that these stores could be my protection belt, I was still accepting checks, the truth is that I sensed that there was a crisis to come, but I refused to take measures 'cause I was used to this payment, as a result 2011 was the year of disaster.

The cyclical time we referred to in the previous section finds its expression in a kind of temporality which makes Tzikas fearful of taking protective measures against financial crisis. In other words, in experiencing the world of commerce through the prism of "things will always be the same" he developed what in psychoanalysis is called denial as far as the cruel events that took place later in his life are concerned.

> *Spyridakis:* how did you experience all this?
>
> *Tzikas:* I felt too bad Manos, I felt that I lost a child, the reason is that I did not inherit my business from my parents, it was not a car I took from my father, it was something I built part by part, that's why I felt that I lost a part of me, I could not accept this, notice that I have not accepted it even now, I was depressed for six months, I visited my business even after it had closed, that's why I felt I lost a kid, my first kid, a kid I raised for 22 years and suddenly I lost it.
>
> *Spyridakis:* so Yannis, while you were hearing things about the forthcoming crisis, what did you do?
>
> *Tzikas:* business was going well, maybe there was something I had not understood but even at the time I closed I had clients who were ordering clothes from me, you have to underline that these orders were worth 1,000,000 euro, it was a huge number, so since I had no money to bring new arrivals, bank debt started to increase, it was not only this but it was the 20,000 euro I gave to the lawyer for representing me in court all these years, I lost this money too 'cause my clients had gone bankrupt, so I went bankrupt too.

It is important to note that emotions, as happened in the case of honesty, sustain the temporality of "things will always be the same" we describe. It is only to the extent that Tzikas is proud of the past life-decision to enter the business world that he refuses to accept his financial collapse and to further commit to the temporality of "things will always be the same". His pride in treating his business as a child made him more committed to the role of businessman, despite the fact that the new reality in which he found himself demanded of him to adjust to something new and unknown. The line of action which he is committed to is incompatible with the new situation in which his business collapsed. A defining feature of consistent lines of action is that actors reject alternatives even when these actions do not serve the purpose to which the actor chose to commit himself/herself. One way to understand how Tzikas' committed behaviour framed his attitude towards the turning-point experience of the closing of his business is Beckers' notion of "side bet". Becker argues that interests prior to the actions which agents are committed to, make them unable to follow alternatives. Former actions bind actors to life projects from which, in the case where they are proved to be failures, they cannot escape. We believe that the side bets through which actors are committed to a specific line of action correspond to a social time of which the temporal orientation is of the type "things will always be the same". In other words, since Tzikas' side bet is that he devoted a large part of his life to "raising his child" (his business), he develops the temporal orientation of "things will always be the same" which prevented him from taking alternative lines of action which could have protected him from losing his business. One could say that the temporality of the side bet is that the past makes the present resemble something that will last for ever. We could term this temporality "eternal past" in the sense that actors are unwilling to disengage from side bets they made in the past.

Let's sum up our main findings up to now. Although upwardly mobile, our informants faced fateful biographical moments of which the defining mark is a temporal displacement, a mismatch between the cyclical time that characterized the informants' habitus and the erratic time that frames the world of finance. A peculiar feeling structure is tied up with this temporal displacement. Honesty and pride are the two dominant emotions which feed the informants' narrative time and which give rise to the temporal orientation of "things will always be the same". We hypothesize that this temporality binds them to lines of action which are inappropriate for dealing with crisis situations in so far as the defence mechanisms of denial emerge. The reason is that informants are unable or have been incapacitated to commit to alternative lines of action because of the side bets they have made in previous life periods. The more personally important are these past side bets, the more committed the informants are in the present and the more they are engulfed in the temporality of "things will always be the same".

THE TEMPORALITY OF SUFFERING

The passage from normalcy to living on the margin involves two things: first, it is processual in the sense that agents gradually realize their social impotence and, second, narrative coherence is difficult to obtain for those who experience marginalization because of the traumatic nature which is involved in the identity loss which follows job loss. Social impotence and identity loss are the two main ingredients of the kind of suffering we will describe and are expressed in three themes we identified: bad health, stigma related to being reliant on social services and inability to find new jobs. In the remainder we analyze these three facets of the experience of suffering.

By being trapped in the above-mentioned social and temporal vicious circle, informants experience marginalization as a process, in the sense that they gradually realize that the most valuable thing they have lost, beyond their assets and incomes, is their past identities. In addition to the identity of employer, of employee or of family member (most of our informants are divorced) the informants have lost the sense of being healthy persons. While we were reading informants' life stories, we were taken aback by the fact that all of them suffered from some chronic illness. We are not arguing that the financial crisis caused their illness but that their illnesses are indicative of the fact that the gradual turmoil of being downwardly mobile and of falling from grace deteriorated their health status. It would not be far from the truth to say that the temporality we described in the previous section is responsible for making them indifferent to taking measures for safeguarding their health. Repos' life story (he is 62 and the only unmarried informant) is typical of this process.

Spyridakis: so you were telling me that you have no income.

Repos: yes, I need money for my medication, this month I managed to take my medication but last month I could not, I have no pension, my situation is very difficult because I have serious health problems and I can not work, I have a serious problem with my eyes and I also suffer from Crohn disease, it is impossible to deal with this disease without a systematic diet, and I have no money for this.

Repos worked as a lifting truck operator in road and building constructions for 35 years and he devotes the rest of his narrative to the details of the dangers this job entailed and to the risky situations in which he has worked. Repos is one of the informants who had been hit by the Greek financial crisis because it caused a huge decrease in the building constructions sector after 2009.

Spyridakis: until when did you work with the trucks? Before or after the crisis?

Repos: until 2010, since then I have been unemployed, no constructions no job, I went to Cyprus but things were the same too, I tried to find a job but I found nothing, as I told you I have no income at all and I am very anxious about my health, I have put on 20 kilos because of the huge doses of cortisone injections.

Spyridakis: where are you living now?

Repos: In hotel rooms paid for by the municipality.

The reason why we do not succumb to the naïve view that the crisis causes marginalization is that even in periods of affluence (as was the case in Greece before 2009) the job market is structured by means of power relations which the generation of working-class people we researched was unable to combat. Although atypical work has been identified with women, a great many of the male informants had much to tell about working without insurance stamps. Petromichalis (60, worked in construction for 30 years, divorced with 4 children) explains why he did not manage to have a pension after 30 years of work.

Spyridakis: don't you have any insurance stamps.

Petromichalis: yes I have 6,000 but I should have gathered more than 12,000 because I worked since I was a kid in 1974, but building construction did not provide us with insurance schemes, the boss told me that "I will give you only six insurance stamps for one month's work, if you do not like it you may leave", it was blackmail, we were not workers covered by insurance, that is how this sector worked, you worked for three months and you could take 3 X 6 =18 insurance stamps, so how could I have gathered them? I believe that it is bad luck, there are times that I say that God is punishing me because I have done some serious misdeed.

The advantage of the life course approach is that it makes us see the processual formation of narrative time and in our case the details of a temporality formation of those who pass from prosperity into vulnerability are highlighted. In particular, what this passage denies them is the capacity for projectivity, the ability to narrate the past, the present and the future as a whole. All of our informants were unable to talk about the future. John May, the male informant we referred to at the beginning of the analysis, now 56 years old, used to work as a mechanic in a garage for 35 years and has suffered from cancer since he lost his job in 2010. See how he narrates all this past experience:

Spyridakis: how could you describe in a few words the sum of your past experiences?

May: I worked for nothing, I mean I gave all of my life to the job and in the end I said to myself "for what", I took a loan in order to assist my small business but when in 2011 it closed I was deeply disappointed, I had health problems, I was locked in a room and I didn't go out, I was disappointed because an unbearable debt was burdening me, I had never had bank debts, I was very honest but after 2010 everything turned upside down, I could not pay the 1000 euro installment to the bank and I could not help my children, I felt that my life was over, I was thinking that all my life I had worked like a dog.

Beyond the side bet of honesty which gives rise to the temporality of the "eternal past" we described in the previous section, Mays' life story is a trauma narrative which tries to manage the suffering of losing a loved object that is his job identity. It is a difficult task to carry out because the informants' projective dimension of agency has been incapacitated. Instead of distancing themselves from habitual and routine schemes of thought in face of contingent situations, they seem unable to bring to the fore new action orientations and instead of surveying alternative action schemes as hypothetical resolutions to conflictual situations, the informants' grief for the loss of their past life makes them look back and not to the future.

> *Spyridakis:* could you tell me the differences regarding your life plans, before and after the crisis?
>
> *May:* I have no plans now, what plans are you talking about? Everything is unpredictable, my pension is uncertain, this is what I am trying to tell to my son, I am telling him not to make plans and to live his life according to what it offers, when I was young I had various plans and in the end I lost everything, it is the first time after 30 years that I am unemployed, everything is lost, I am obliged to reach 67 in order to take a pension even though I received insurance stamps since 1985, it is like I have not worked at all, all these years are lost.

Grief is the dominant emotion permeating the informants' accounts of suffering and its power is reinforced by the current situation they live in. Being dependent on social services for food, clothing or sleep, they have to deal with two unbearable experiences: first the stigma related to visiting these services and second the weight of filling the time of everyday life (Spyridakis 2018). As to the stigma, see how two of the informants, May and Petromichalis describe their dependence on the social services:

> *Petromichalis:* I have been going through a lot but this is my worst experience that I have to beg the social grocery and the social pharmacy to get by, this is something I have not experienced before, the only thing that calms me is that there are other people like me, the truth is that I feel embarrassed when I go there but I have no choice

and I know a lot of people in my neighborhood who are in a similar situation.

May: since I came to the social grocery I have got involved in offering foods, it gave me a motive to live, my kidney started to function well because I felt I was not a useless person.

All of the informants seem ambivalent regarding their visit to the services for the reason that on the one hand they feel ashamed of being seen as "losers" and on the other hand they gradually obtain the sense of belonging to a community whose members share something (the sense of loss) and who are not the exception but the rule during the crisis period. It is no wonder then that the temporal orientation they develop as to their future is of the type "playing it by ear, wait and see" which is the defining mark of those who are trying to survive. Giorgos and Helena remark:

Spyridakis: how is your life now?
Giorgos: only survival, it is only survival.
Spyridakis: what about your future?
Giorgos: there is no future for me, it does not exist, my future… I am 66.. I am not expecting to start travelling around the world at this age, I am thinking only of the demands of my everyday life, I care about my health because I have had a serious lung operation.
Spyridakis: what about your life from now on?
Helena: no one knows what the future holds, I want my old life back and a house to live in, the most valuable thing is health.

According to Gurvitch's terminology, social times are manifested in conjunction with the degree of relatedness agents develop with others. The relations of withdrawal which characterize how our informants deal with others correspond to a way of life in which commitments are absent for the simple reason that commitment presupposes continuity while their present life is full of incontinuities and contingencies. As long term planning has been annulled for our informants, they are withdrawn from relations demanding devotion, such as work or having a partner. If one accepts the neo-Weberian thesis that individual life chances are framed by specific class situations like job market positions, evaluations made by others and authority hierarchy, then it is obvious that the working class generation we examined is in a disadvantaged position according to all three of these criteria. By being dependent upon the SSI and upon social services, the informants invest in how they will manage everyday life's demands and they are not preoccupied with "colonizing the future" for the simple reason that the future has disappeared from their temporalities because of this disadvantaged position.

Discussion

In theorizing disorder, irregularity and contingency Wagner-Pacifici (2000:2-7), says that they are difficult to handle due to their fluidity and provisionality and that those who live in contingency approach life as if it could be experienced in conditional terms, or in the "subjunctive mood". While for the author the standoff, the par excellence expression of contingency, refers to situations of mutual and symmetrical threat in which parties are frozen, we found that the standoff our informants experience is completely asymmetrical and structured through power relations. We found that this asymmetrical contingency is actualized in two qualitatively different temporal orientations which our informants develop. The first temporality is of the logic "I thought that things would always be the same" and the second of the logic "we go step by step". In the first case informants want nothing to be changed, they feel secure and by projecting the present onto the future they are bracketing it, while in the second they would like things to be different but they are afraid of taking actions, they are imbued with inertia and precarity, the future is what they do not want to be realized (because it is fearful).

In the following figure we present the two forms standing still takes when informants face changes that turn their life upside down, and the period when they were interviewed where they suffer from precariousness. Through this figure we are trying to capture how the informants' temporal orientation is formed throughout their downwardly mobile life course.

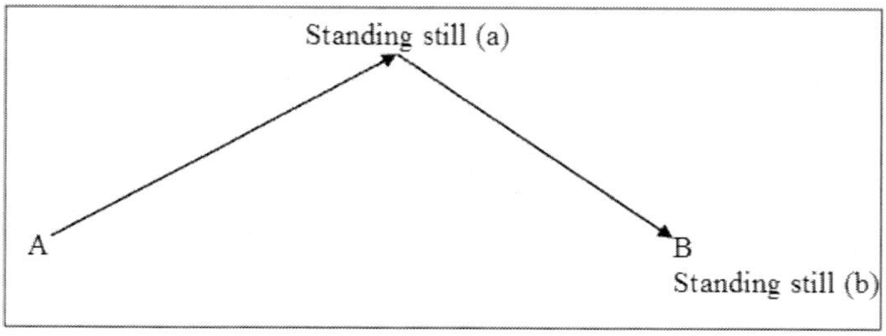

Figure 1. Two life-course phases of standing still.

The common ground of these temporalities is that planning is absent and instead of "future colonization" what dominates is "future bracketing". Our working hypothesis is that the temporal orientation of "future bracketing" is due to the up and down movement of the informants' life course and to the peculiar characteristics it entails. We believe that one could not make sense of the temporality of "future bracketing" unless it is seen through its sequential and processual evolvement within which unequal power relations frame the informants' actions.

One crucial causal mechanism which shapes the temporality of "future bracketing" is the dis-alignment between the social time of financial capitalism and the social time of the working class generation which our informants belong to. The time of financial capitalism is predicated on the logic that fast and short-term decision making actions are more important than the long term strategies of capital accumulation, that human well being is best advanced by liberating individual entrepreneurship and labour markets and by prioritizing private property rights. The social time which the financial acceleration of profit making sustains is both the deceptive time in which unexpected crises and discontinuities between past and present may emerge and the erratic time of uncertainty where contingency prevails. In that way, what matters is only the present and not the past or the future. Business operates in the temporal context of an extended present where focus and orientation rarely endure beyond the next shareholder meeting and the schedule of quarterly results.

In contrast, the social time which forms the movement of the upward and downward mobility of our working-class informants is the temporality of the class situation they have been raised in, that is of the predictability of stable work and of the prevailing of the present over future and past. The consequence of this de-synchronization is that by investing in the logic of financial capitalism the informants enter into a field whose temporality is incompatible with the temporality which structures their time horizons. In that way a lack of fit between the temporal structure of the working class generation we analyzed and finance's social time emerges. As Rosa has stated, social exclusion is related to a specific time inequality in the sense that the chances the unemployed have to catch up with those who run inside the trade mills of late-modern life are extremely low. As he says, they are outside the accelerating system of demands and opportunities. One of the findings our research has pointed out is that temporal displacement produces the temporality of temporal bracketing which is expressed in two forms in our informants' narrative time. This temporality gives shape to a kind of agency which is imbued with fear that incapacitates action.

What is denied those who experience the temporality of "future bracketing" is that they are unable to think of their future in terms of projectivity and to give coherence to the tripartite time organization of living a life. What is more important is that those who come to bracket the future lose the possibility of treating it as a resource for organizing present decisions. Being unable to experience the "not yet" as a present care, they remain stuck in the "always already" emotions which have framed their pasts. Honesty and pride are the emotions that had always structured past decisions and fear makes them remain frozen in the present. In that way, what is expected and what has yet to take place is feared by those who develop the temporality of "future bracketing" because it is their only defense against the vicissitudes which they will possibly face. We believe that these emotions are the informants' way of dealing with the guilt stemming from the accumulated and huge debts they owe to the tax office, to the Public Electricity Service and to the banks. Capitalism is the first instance of a cult that creates guilt, says Benjamin (1999, 145) and by that he means that capitalism turns economic debt into a moral guilt: the perpetuation of debt creates a deficit within the soul that becomes guilt's cause. In other words, in order to combat the sense of being seen as moral failures, our informants are trapped in the narrative time of honesty and pride. The temporality of "future bracketing" which sustains them is unable to overcome the permanence and the power of debt's temporality.

References

Atkinson, Will. 2018. Time for Bourdieu: Insights and oversights, *Time & Society*, DOI: 10.1177/0961463X17752280.

Beck, Ulrich. 1992. *Risk Society*. London: Sage.

Becker S., Howard. 1960. Notes on the Concept of Commitment, *American Journal of Sociology*, 66(1): 32-40.

Benjamin, Walter. 1999. *The Arcades Project,* Cambridge, MA/London, The Belknap Press of Harvard University Press.

Bruckner, Hannah., and Karl Ulrich Mayer. 2005. "De-standardization of the life course: What it might mean? And if it means anything, whether it actually took place?" In *The Structure of the Life Course: Standardized? Individualized? Differentiated?* Edited by Ross McMillan, 27-55, London: Elsevier.

Carmo, Renato Miguel., Frederico Cantante and Nuno de Almeida Alves. 2014. Time projections: Youth and precarious Employment, *Time & Society*, 23(3) 337–357.

Demazière, Didier and Claude Dubar. 1997. *Analyser les entretiens biographiques [*Analyze biographical interviews]. *L'exemple des récits d'insertion*. Paris : Nathan.

Facchini, Carla and Marita Rampazi. 2009. No longer young, not yet old. Biographical uncertainty in late-adult temporality, *Time & Society*, 18(3):351–372.

Furlong, Andy and Fred Cartmel. 2003. Explaining transitions through individualised rationality, in *Youth and Work in the post-industrial city of North America and Europe*, edited by Lawrence Roulleau-Berger, 136-155, Netherlands: Koninklijke Brill NV.

Gabriel, Yiannis, David E. Gray and Harshita Goregaokar. 2013. Job loss and its aftermath among managers and professionals: wounded, fragmented and flexible, *Work, employment and society*, 27(1): 56–72.

Giddens, Anthony. 1990. *The consequences of Modernity*, Stanford: Stanford University Press.

Heinz, R. Walter. 2002. Transition Discontinuities and the Biographical Shaping of Early Work Careers, *Journal of Vocational Behavior*, 60, 220–240.

Iosifides, Theodoros. (2017). "Epistemological issues in qualitative migration research: Self-reflexivity, objectivity and subjectivity", in *Qualitative Research in European Migration Studies,* Edited by Ricard Zapata-Barrero & Evren Yallaz. 113-133, Switzerland: Springer.

Leccardi, Carmen. 2005. Facing uncertainty: Temporality and biographies in the new century, *Young*, 13(2): 123–146.

Muldoon, Mark. 2006. *Tricks of time: Bergson, Merleau-Ponty and Ricoeur in search of time, self and meaning,* Pittsburgh, Duquesne University Press.

Newman, S. Katherine. 1998. *Falling from grace: the experience of downward mobility in American middle classes,* New York: Free Press.

Shirani, Fiona and Karen Henwood. 2011. Taking one day at a time: temporal experiences in the context of unexpected life course transitions, *Time and Society*, 20(1): 49-68.

Spyridakis, Manos. 2018. "'We Are All Socialists': Greek Crisis and Precarization", in *Market Versus Society. Anthropological Insights*, Edited by Manos Spyridakis, 113-132, London: Palgrave Macmillan.

Walther, Andreas. 2009. ""It was not my choice, you know?" Young people's subjective views and decision – making process in biographical transitions", in Ingrid Schoon & Rainer K. Silbereisen (eds), *Transitions from school to work: Globalization, Individuali-zation, and Patterns of Diversity*, 121-45, Cambridge, Cambridge University Press.

Wagner-Pacifici, Robin. 2000. *Theorizing the Standoff, Contingency in Action*, Cambridge: Cambridge University Press.

Weller, A. S. 2012. Financial stress and the long-term outcomes of job loss, *Work, Employment and Society, 26(1):* 10–25.

Woodman, Dan. 2009. "The mysterious case of the pervasive choice biography: Ulrich Beck, structure/agency, and the middling state of theory in the sociology of youth", *Journal of Youth Studies*, 12(3):243-256.

Wengaf, Tom and Prue Chamberlayne. 2013. Biography-using research (BNIM), SOSTRIS, institutional regimes and Critical psycho-societal realism, in *Realist Biography and European Policy*. Edited by Jeffery Turk and Adam Mrozowicki, Leuven: Leuven University Press.

In: Emotions, Temporalities … ISBN: 978-1-53616-203-5
Editors: M. Christodoulou et al.

Chapter 4

IMAGINED WORKING-CLASSES AND WHERE TO FIND THEM: LIFE STORIES FROM SHIPBUILDING EMPLOYEES

Giorgos Bithymitris*
National Centre for Social Research, Athens, Greece

ABSTRACT

In this chapter I explore the hidden components of class identities as manifested through the discourse of workers from the Perama Ship Repair Zone, the largest ship repair and shipbuilding industrial site in Greece. My aim is to examine how the narrativized identities of the workers are constructed through the fundamental precariousness of the field. Focusing on core elements of the personal and collective identities under investigation, we distinguish the various interplays between class as a contingently articulated identity at the micro-level and class formation as a specific configuration of collectivities within a specific set of power relations. In theoretical terms, I draw both from objectivist-relational accounts of class and cultural understandings of how class is manifested in contemporary capitalism.

* Corresponding Author's E-mail: gbithymitris@ekke.gr.

Keywords: working-class identities, class relations, shipbuilding, life stories, nationalism

INTRODUCTION

> "It seems to be the fate of the working classes to become heroes only of the past, never the present," Reay (2017).

The above mentioned remark of Diane Reay, however gloomy might sound, summarizes more than one aspects of both class and class theory: the contested terrain of the end (telos) of the working class struggles ("the fate"); the approach of class as a lived experience subject to change ("to become"); the inherent split of the working class ("the working classes"); the assumed backwardness of the working classes ("heroes only of the past"). I feel that the ongoing debate over classes, or in Crompton's view the persistence of "pseudo-debates" over different definitions of class (Crompton 2010), revolves pretty much around such themes, although the old dichotomy between structure and agency seems to subsume them.

It is not in my intention to defend the analytical category of class here, though I would agree that the report of its death was an exaggeration, to paraphrase Mark Twain's famous quote. In brief, I take for granted that the postmodern critiques on the uses of class as explanans both in terms of validity and relevance (Pakulski 2005, 152) can be theoretically and empirically confuted. Scholars from very different disciplines have convincingly argued why class still matters (Eidlin 2014), although one should be aware of the class concept or approach that fits to the question he/she selects to answer (Wright 2005). The crucial point here is whether there are relevant questions that could not be meaningfully negotiated without invoking class categories. Reflecting on my experience I feel that it would be difficult if not futile to respond to research questions like those I came across when I started exploring the community of shipbuilding workers of Perama Zone, without resting upon one or more accounts of class.

These questions are closely tied to the drives of my study on this formerly thriving working-class community. Perama Zone (hereinafter the Zone), a coastal zone that hosts the vast majority of shipbuilding and ship repair activities in Greece, underwent significant shifts during the recent economic crisis, such as declining employment, deteriorating working conditions and ever-growing precariousness. The socio-economic contingencies have been coupled with stereotyping patterns that cross-cut the public discourse for what regards the surge of right-wing extremism and its toxic shadow. A propos, the Extreme Right appeal to the contemporary working-classes has already been discussed in Europe and elsewhere (Bornschier and Kriesi 2012), within the recurrent (and somewhat misleading) debate on whether this has to do with the culminating social inequalities, or the cultural challenges that globalization pertains to for those feeling more vulnerable.

Departing from the assumption that the electoral gains of the Greek neoNazi party, Golden Dawn in the working-class suburbs that surround the Zone indicate an extreme-right turn of the working-class, I found that a Structure → Consciousness → Action (S-C-A) scheme can hardly be useful for addressing the various interplays at the local level. As E. O. Wright (2000, 185) has exemplarily shown, although class structures are in some sense the fundamental determinant of class struggles, one should also pay attention to other causal factors of considerable potential weight in explaining concrete variations across time and space. Wright's conceptualization of class locations, class structure, class formation and class struggle along with his parsimonious description of micro-, meso-, and macro- level distinction, could be of great importance for the examination of the political attitudes within the Zone's class formation. Nevertheless, this approach usually entails a primary, if not exclusive, concern for intentional practices and consciously determined goals within given class capacities. And this is exactly what I think needs to be supplemented by cultural approaches of class analysis (Devine et al. 2004).

Regardless of what the title of this chapter implies, to unearth the commonalities between a relational-objectivist and a cultural class theorization does not require huge amounts of sociological imagination, or fantasy. But it is not an easy task either. Apart from the above mentioned limitation in the neo-Marxist perspective of Wright, a respective reluctance to deal with the hidden dimensions of class, characterize the neo-Weberian class schemata as well, although it would be unfair to assume that Weber himself was unaware of the role of the non-conscious elements of action (Barbalet 1998, 13). In any case the use of class identities –and identifications- as analytical tools are deemed far more promising, with regard to the three following research questions: a) how relationally determined class locations within a specific class formation are intertwined with dispositions and attitudes both at cognitive and non-cognitive level; b) under which circumstances individuals occupying working-class locations identify themselves with the working-class; c) how nationalism entangles with such identifications.

The use of class identity as core analytical category is not the only point of divergence of this study compared to the dominant schemata in the sociology of class. Focusing on a social grouping with specific occupational and socio-cultural characteristics, as the one examined below, implies a shift from the analysis of class at the aggregate level. As Grusky and Weeden (2001, 203-204) argue, "the great virtue of disaggregating is that the nominal categories of conventional class analysis can be replaced by gemeinschaftlich groupings that are embedded in the very fabric of society and are thereby meaningful not merely to sociologists but to the lay public as well." Therefore exploring social identities at the occupational level gives multiple insights concerning the interconnections between agents, structures and embedded institutional realities.

This is not to suggest that highly aggregated classes are useless, particularly if one is interested in comparing the attitudes of the shipbuilding community with the attitudes of individuals who do not share such a solid occupational identity, or with the attitudes of other collectivities, or other class formations in broader terms. Nevertheless, for the purposes of a micro-level analysis of how a discursively constructed identity of a shipbuilding worker intersects with attitudes and dispositions (both conscious and non-conscious), the disaggregation strategy works well.

Before determining the use of attitudes and dispositions, a better explanation of class identities is needed. The examination of this concept adopts two basic assumptions that are quite common among cultural class theorizations: First, the social class does not exist, nor can be comprehended, outside of its manifestations and relationships in the living world, even if one admits that class structure poses its own limits on class relations. Second, the class and, more specifically, the working class remains a reified concept with little explanatory power if the analysis overlooks its internal splits as they arise in the historical evolution of the technical and social division of labor and as they emerge in everyday life.

Along the same line of argument the approach adopted here tries to surpass the dichotomy between practical and discursive consciousness focusing on narrated versions of the individual and collective self. Concomitantly language is considered as a means both of communication and production that "represents a site of conflict through which a flow of identities, values, beliefs and meanings become established, silenced or affirmed." (Kirk 2004, 145) Starting from the assumption that at the ontological level collective identities are constructed as narratives, namely stories the actors say to understand who they are, which in turn is a precondition of knowing what to do (Sommers 1997), I shall focus on the micro-level of the Zone workers' narrations, to investigate what facilitates, thwarts, or transforms personal, occupational and class identities.

More specifically, I draw from two life stories collected through biographical interviews with shipbuilding employees in order to explore how the narrativized identity is reconstructed through the various interplays between the core agents of the Zone's reality (ship owners, contractors, labor union, workforce, political parties). I am particularly interested in those identifications that could explain collective action (or its absence) in this specific industrial setting. In this respect I suggest a closer look on the affective elements within the discursive construction of the social identities under investigation.

Identification –the foundational and primary component of any identity formation- could hardly be understood as a primarily intentional process in social interaction. Rarely, if ever, working-class members commit themselves to strikes, revolts, or other conflicts, just because they estimate the pros and cons of their action; even more seldom, their decision of taking this or that risk is aligned with a rational evaluation of their broader class interests. Social movement scholars have rendered the old S-C-A ideas obsolete and empirically unsustained, having established a different line of reasoning according to which cognitive agreement cannot lead to action on its own; whereas the "strength" of an identity, even a cognitively vague one, comes from its emotional side (Goodwin, Jasper, and Polletta 2005, 9). It is the broader affective turn in social sciences though, that has enabled a more thorough look at emotions as resources of collective action.

Although the sociology of emotions has been growing massively since the nineties, the literature on the emotional processes that structure and are structured by class relations seems to be attracting a more limited audience. For instance, Andrew Sayer's work on the moral components of class, has paved the way for mapping the emotional dynamics of class relationships (Sayer 2005). The work of Jack Barbalet (1998) is also a great example of how to explore emotions in class formations within a macro-sociological scope. Similar attempts have been assumed at the micro level as well, such as Reay's work on the psychic economy of class in the field of education (Reay 2005).

All of the sociologists of emotions would agree that there is no particular benefit in reproducing a complete, and to a large extent false dichotomy between reason and emotion. Affect, as an "embodied meaning-making" is synergistic with reason in the shaping and negotiation of identities, while, in affective practices, bits of the body get patterned together with feelings and thoughts, narratives, social relations, personal histories and ways of life (Wetherell 2012, 14). With that being said, let me briefly stress some contextual and methodological points.

METHODS

As I have already mentioned, this research focuses on the micro-level of narratives approached as constellations of relationships embedded in time and space and constituted by causal emplotment (Somers 1992; 1997) without overlooking the broader context. In order to shed light on the social network of relationships composed of symbolic, institutional and material practices of the social grouping under scrutiny, my research associates and I (Bithymitris and Koustenis forthcoming) collected and processed a database of 3.279 entries corresponding to the Zone workers who took part in Vocational Education and Training (VET) activities between 2013-2015. I have also collected numerous official and administrative documents (e.g., Collective Agreements), press articles, documentary films, YouTube videos and press releases that refer to the Zone mostly concerning the economic and political implications of the recent crisis.

The social morphology of the Zone and therefore the context within which the life stories were collected and analyzed is of paramount importance in order to make sense of the textual material. Summarizing some basic aspects of this morphology, I would pinpoint: a) the economic significance of the Zone, as the location of the vast majority of high value-added shipbuilding activities in Greece, b) the spatial proximity between workplace and residence, which is a fact for the largest proportion of the workforce, c) the endemic liminality (Spyridakis 2013), which is linked to the inherent flexibility in the organization of work, combined with the effects of the recent economic crisis (informal forms of bargaining, interpersonal job-finding networks, high rate of temporary employment, high mobility within the Zone, strong presence of contractors), but also with a high degree of hazardous labor, d) the local presence of a massive labor union (Trade Union of Metal Workers of Attica and the Shipbuilding Industry of Greece) with a militant profile and communist leadership, e) the local presence of the Extreme Right, which is organized through violence, initially in the broader area of Piraeus, but also within the Zone, though without challenging the hegemonic position of the "Red" union.

It is also worth mentioning that the occupations of the Zone, are male-dominated, while the age group 45-54 is the most populous. Last, but not least, about 10% of the employed workforce has migrant background (mainly in low-skilled and high-risk occupations). In the course of our analysis, we will return to these issues of social and political morphology.

After collecting and organizing my contextual material, I interviewed 14 individuals who a) were either current employees in shipbuilding and ship repair activities in the Zone or have previously been employed there for a long period, and b) live in typical working-class neighborhoods of the broader area of Piraeus (Drapetsona, Keratsini, Perama, and, to a lesser extent, Nikea and Korydallos). I drew a sample out of a pool of 100 trainees whom I met in person during the 2013 and 2015 vocational training programs in shipbuilding and ship repair specialties.[1]

Although a convenient sampling technique was adopted, some criteria to enable comparisons within the sample were applied as well. The first criterion concerns the proximity to the Zone's labor union (active member, non-active member, non-member). As it became apparent during the collection and processing of the contextual material the formal and informal union practices weave a thick web of social relations that affects the positioning of the subjects within the loci (topoi) where the shipbuilding activities take place. Other criteria like expertise and employment status were applied as well, so that interview material is collected from both vulnerable and less vulnerable employees.

The life stories used here (Table 1) are drawn from two cases: Billy is an experienced high-skilled professional, who enjoys a great degree of autonomy at work, he trains and supervises other workers and is an elected member of the Zone's biggest union. Johnny is a medium-skilled welder who works as a salaried employee at a Zone's contractor; he enjoys a lower degree of autonomy at work and is a typical member of his union (he pays his fees, votes and takes part in the union's activities only occasionally). I deliberately selected two informants who, on the basis of their skills, competencies and class positions, are less subject to the field's inherent liminality, so that we can imagine the impact of this fundamental condition on the more vulnerable workforce that constitutes the majority of the Zone's population.

---

[1]Details regarding those two VET programs for Zone workers can be found elsewhere (see below). It is important to stress that a majority of the real population of the shipbuilding and ship repair workers took part and therefore the characteristics of the training population reflect to a large degree the characteristics of the Zone population. A further analysis of the socio-economic profile of the Zone workforce can be found in Bithymitris and Koustenis (in press).

Table 1. Social characteristics of the two narrators

	Trade union membership	Skills	Employment status	Age
Billy (expert)	Yes (elected Member of the Board)	High skilled	Currently self-employed (with a long work experience as a wage-earner)	54
Johnny (welder)	Yes	Medium skilled	Employee	32

The interviewees were asked to talk about their life in general (family life, personal life), their occupational trajectories (expertise, work experience, past and current employment status, acquired skills, achievements, credentials, career prospects), their experiences in the shipbuilding Zone, and their experience of the recent economic crisis.

Although other contributors of the present volume have been engaged with life stories and biographic identities in a much more systematic way than I have (Christodoulou 2016; Christodoulou and Spyridakis 2016), let me briefly explain how this method was employed here. Following a hermeneutical case reconstruction, I approach the experienced life history and the narrated life story as dialectically linked entities that produce each other (Rosenthal 1993, 60) and therefore take both of them into consideration. The narrations are not filtered by predetermined classificatory systems or theoretical schemes, despite the fact that the need of a theory to explain things retrospectively is acknowledged. In this respect I resort to the tradition of a cultural reading of class relations in the end of the chapter. In addition, my conceptual framework is heavily impacted by E. O. Wright's relational understanding of class (Wright 2005; 2000). As already said, we should not be discouraged to combine different epistemological traditions provided that they are not mutually exclusive. If historical events, personal constructions of those events, personal histories, and also collective histories are interconnected (Strauss 1995), then why not approach the social reality of class by using both Wright's analytic categories and biographical methods?

As far as the analysis of the texts produced after the transcription of the biographical interviews is concerned, the adopted analytical strategy enables a reconstruction of the interactional significance of the subjects' actions, or else of the underlying structure of the biographers' interpretations of their lives, which may go beyond the subjects' own intentions (Rosenthal 1993). The latter element is crucial, since the unintentional and automatic aspects of one's evaluations are considered here as the basic component of one's identity. In sum, I attempt to comprehend the entire life of the individual by reconstructing both the narrator's biographical overall construction (life history) and the biographically constructed experiences (life story). I start analyzing each case with a brief note on the context of the interview. Then I provide the interviewee's biographical portrait, and after that I move on to the analysis. The actual names of the respondents are replaced by pseudonyms.

DISCUSSION

Case 1: Billy the Expert

For the "recruitment" of my informants, I consulted the coordinator of the training activities of a VET provider in Piraeus. Among others he recommended me Billy, an expert in the shipbuilding industry, ship inspector and trainer in welding, with a substantive knowledge and experience gained at the Zone's shipyards. I introduced myself as a social researcher interested in the current situation of the Zone's workforce, and we met on 4 October 2017 at a Piraeus local cafe. He gave me the impression of a quite modest person, self-confident, familiar with interview processes, rational and at the same time passionate about shipbuilding in Greece and in the Zone.

Billy was born in 1963 in Monemvasia, a rural area of the West Peloponnese and at the age of 15 he settled in Keratsini (a Piraeus municipality where many Zone workers dwell) in order to study marine engineering and find a job in shipyards. His parents were farmers, his brother is a railway maintenance worker, his older sister used to operate a small garment manufacture, but is currently unemployed and his younger sister is semi-skilled worker in the agrofood industry. Billy started working as a marine engineer in seagoing ships, however quite soon he found himself working as a sheet metal worker and machine operator in ship repair units. He worked in ship repair industry in New York for two years and in the early nineties was hired as a quality control supervisor by "Hellenic Shipyards S.A. (HSY)", the largest Greek shipbuilding company located in Skaramangas (a Zone's neighboring area), where he also worked as a trainer in welding. Billy was dismissed from HSY in 2009 after the company's decision to remove the whole unit of railway material. The next seven years he worked as a quality control supervisor at a Zone's company and since 2017 he has been working as a freelance senior ship inspector. Currently he shares his weekly working time between the West Peloponnese and Piraeus ports. He lives alone, and he intends to return to Monemvasia.

Billy has acquired numerous prestigious qualifications in Greece and abroad. Apart from having a long professional track record he has also been an experienced unionist. He had been elected member of the Board of the HSY's trade union for more than a decade, joining initially the socialist fraction and then an independent one. After his dismissal he was elected as member of the Board of the Trade Union of Metal Workers of Attica and the Shipbuilding Industry of Greece (sector-based union, hereinafter, the union), representing the oppositional radical leftist fraction in this communist-led union. Today he abstains from active trade unionism, but he is still politically active identifying himself with the radical left beyond the left-wing governmental party, SYRIZA.

Billy narrates his past without using idealization techniques, or emotionally charged discursive practices. His rational, positive and evaluative style of narrating seems congruent with his professional identity. Sometimes he uses the third person or passive voice when describing an achievement: "An opportunity appeared to work at HSY [...] I was given the chance to be an in-house trainer of the technical personnel." His positivism reflects his attitudes towards formal procedures validating practical and theoretical knowledge: "In previous decades one could do everything by just declaring 'I am this or that'; today you need the objective proof namely the certification and this is right." Without regressing to nostalgia, he acknowledges that in the beginning of his career, marine engineering was shaping strong and self-confident professionals providing them with economic, social and cultural capital: "There were a lot of job opportunities, the salaries were very good; we used to travel a lot, we were meeting new people and this grew as stronger, we were better off than before." The adversities of his working class background as well as the exigencies of marine labor in general are never explicit, they can only be reconstructed. Unlike other shipbuilding workers, he believes that it is travelling and the positive connotations of his work that acculturated him, not the hardships.

Billy's narration of both the individual and the collective self is shaped from strong evaluative elements that are most of the times based upon solid evidence. He frequently uses verbs like "prove," "show," "document." He evaluates work (both as labor and as a creative task), quality, and security positively. This is apparent when he assesses, for example, a period in HSY during the 2000s "with a lot of works in progress, works with high quality standards that required high specialization and many hours of intensive work [...] it was a golden era, with many people working, a lot of overtime, we had incomes, security."

As to his responsibilities in HSY Billy positions himself at an intermediary location between the shipyard owners, the workforce, and the clients. In terms of Wright's class scheme, Billy occupied a contradictory class location, but this is also subjectively affirmed: "my word, my responsibility was huge; my role was very important [...] I was an intermediary between the company and the clients who trusted me." At the same time he is proud not only for his skills and the organizational resources that he commanded, but also for the prestige of HSY as a "big industrial unit of the country [...] the largest and the most organized shipyard in the south-eastern Mediterranean sea." In accordance with his disposition towards evaluation, and perhaps reflecting his abovementioned contradictory class location, he adopts a very critical tone against company unionism in HSY: "The greatest disaster for HSY lies at the unionists' side. No matter if I stood by them for some years as naïve as I was. When I understood that their role is disastrous I separated myself [...] I insist that they are the first to be blamed for the fiasco."

What is the fiasco that Billy refers to? The "HSY submarines affair" was one of the most debated scandals in crisis-ridden Greece. It involved high-ranking politicians and economic elites of other European countries, such as Germany. As Billy recalls: "The future of the shipyards was bright, until suddenly, the Germans came along in the collaboration with the Ministry of Defense and the unionists [...]. I've got the secret mail exchange [...]. Our unionists had a lot of power at that time." Once again, we witness Billy's judging disposition as he assesses -under the prism of his contradictory location- the company union leaders and the networks of power that they were sustained through favoritism: "Only a few people reacted. I was among them, for I could see the trap behind the cheese [...] technically and professionally I was standing very high, I could stand on my own feet. I didn't need to grovel to the union in order to get a promotion. I was alone, based on my own strength so to speak [...] then I became a target for this racket of unionists. In the course of those events I created a fraction and I disturbed the waters."

Billy argues that his posts within HSY and outside HSY, gave him a clearer grasp of the big picture regarding the Zone's past, present, and future. This becomes explicit when he assesses the Zone's prospects after the HSY downsizing: "Since HSY closed its commercial department, there were no jobs for the workers of the Zone's small firms. Bringing in ships for repair in the Zone was not an option either, since the Perama Zone lacks the big platforms that HSY possesses [...] the neighboring shipyard that attracted ship owners to bring in ships no longer exists. And inevitably Perama Zone collapsed. That's the whole story."

As I reconstruct Billy's narrated experiences after his dismissal and his subsequent entry in the Zone's precarious realm, I observe a shift towards a more personalized tone, a self-assessment that seeks to establish his identity on values such as honesty, independence, and moral superiority stemming from -and reified in- credentials and qualifications, or else his moral coins: "Because I was honest and clean, nobody held me. I spoke my mind openly and I kneeled to no one." Conversely, in Billy's eyes a weak character in the Zone is susceptible to networks of dependence and clientelism, and this is manifested inter alia through the workers' – union bonds: "A technician that stands on his own feet and possesses certifications has no need to enter the union's list of favorites. The guy that doesn't stand on his own feet needs the union, the list; he needs to be attached to them so that he finds a job."

Although he highlights the moments of his active participation in the (Zone's) union and illustrates it as a necessity for the workers, at the same time, he is critical with its leaders, whose perspective is much narrower than his: "The union's leadership is not interested in conditions that provide well-trained and strong technicians with qualifications and that stuff, because this would mean that anybody could make it on his own." Moreover the interconnections between lack of qualifications, moral inferiority, and submissive attitudes explain the cases of those workers who turn to Golden Dawn's right-wing extremism: "Golden Dawn is made of people that aren't strong characters. They believe that they will find a voice of protest there, a reaction."

What is missing in Billy's life story is a class or group identity that would connect his personal fate and the fate of his peers in the shipbuilding Zone. Interestingly enough, when he describes his most recent role as an elected unionist at the union's Board, he acknowledges why the workers of the Zone need unionism and why -given their harsh working conditions- they should not be considered as a well-paid workforce. However, this may be associated with class relations only contingently. And, of course, he hardly identifies himself with the workers, although he represents them.

This is not to suggest that Billy is selfish, indifferent, or irresponsible, on the contrary. He withdrew from his post at the Zone's union when he felt he could not stand up to his duties any longer due to his growing personal needs. The fact that he wants to return to his rural homeland is quite telling of the contradictions that characterize his status as neither a worker nor a boss. His political beliefs draw from these contradictions as well: identified with the pragmatism of the socialist party (PASOK) in the nineties, since the outset of the crisis he shifted to a more left-wing position supporting the party of SYRIZA. After the party's mainstream turn he is adopting a more radical position, supporting a small leftist party. This radicalization seems a bit incompatible with his career path, which in turn, however, has not been translated into economic capital: "Ok, to be honest, today I'm not as militant as I used to be. There are financial reasons that forced me to leave Piraeus. I couldn't make my ends meet. Ok, I participate but I am not running about every day as I used to. "

Billy fails to realize, what means to him the fact that the Zone is a locus of production that inherently lacks the personified class relationship between a more or less stable workforce and a specific capitalist (as for example is the case in the manufacturing industry). Contingent as it is and conditioned upon shipping, the Zone generates a specific habitus that I would call the 'Steppenwolf's habitus': a durable and transposable set of dispositions –to use Bourdieu's (1990, 52) influential formulation of habitus- that transcends the hierarchies of skills and orients the Zone worker towards a hostile, uncertain and meaningless social world. Billy prefers to see himself from an avant garde standpoint that has been reached after years of personal investment in skills and qualifications. Alas! This obstructs him from realizing that he is part of a collective destiny composed predominantly of de-collectivized and fragmented narrations of self and otherhood.

No matter whether a Zone worker ranks higher or lower in the hierarchy of skills, he still exchanges his labor force in a less collectivized way compared to the typical industrial worker. The trend of individualization within this volatile market is balanced mainly through the embedded institutional role of the union, which may shape strong occupational identities but does not lead necessarily to strong working-class identities. The fact that despite his radicalization, Billy never adopted the communist ideology of the local union and its respective class politics has to be considered as well. The implications of adopting communism in the Zone's context lie beyond the scope of this chapter. At the next section I examine a second life story collected at Perama Zone in order to get a better grasp of the dialectics between personal identity, occupational identities, and class identities.

Case 2: Johnny the Welder

I met Johnny in 2015 during the training seminars in Piraeus. I interviewed him on 19 September 2017 in Drapetsona, near the Ship Repair Zone. Johnny was rather tired and a bit hasty, thus the interview was not very long, as in other cases. He is 32 years old, born and raised in Keratsini. He currently lives with his fiancé at her place in Aspropyrgos, an industrial area close to the Zone. His father used to be a construction worker, and his mother was keeping house. His sister works at a factory, the older brother is unemployed, and the younger one works in the Zone as well. After completing his compulsory education, Johnny attended initial vocational education and he graduated as a shipbuilding machine operator. After his graduation he went to HSY's vocational school and he was specialized as a welder. The apprenticeship in HSY's school was quite difficult, but it provided high-standard learning outcomes, while the graduates had the opportunity to be officially certified in welding. Two years ago he successfully completed another training seminar in welding and gained one more certification.

Johnny started working in the Zone in 2004 at the age of 21 and has never been unemployed for a long period. As the majority of his colleagues, he has drifted for years from one contractor (small employers who make ad hoc agreements with ship owners) to another; he travelled to China and Australia for ship repairs and since 2015 he has been working at the same employer who is specialized in yacht repairs. The yacht sector is considered to be less hazardous than other ship repair activities and also requires more sophisticated technical work. Taking also into account that Johnny's monthly net income amounts to € 1.400-1.500 for 35 hours per week, I would place him at the upper medium rank within the Zone's hierarchy of skills, though he lacks Billy's supervising competence and work autonomy. Additionally, unlike Billy, he is not actively engaged in union politics, although he is a union member and professionally networked.

The most explicit element in Johnny's life story is his positive and firm self-evaluation within a volatile and uncertain context, upon which he constructs his positive identity: "I am good; it is not accidental that they keep me in the Zone." This is grounded on his skills, his knowledge of the local labor market contingencies, and his networking, either at the formal (union, training providers) or at the informal level (bonds of friendship with colleagues). Undoubtedly he represents a dynamic segment of the Zone's workforce; he tries to follow the technological changes and innovations in shipbuilding, and despite him being better-off compared to other workers, he realizes how inherently vulnerable the Zone is. Like Billy, and many other workers that I have interviewed, he believes that the union is a necessity: "the guys are running about and whatever claim you may have against the employer you can tell them." As it has been apparent from other narrations, union membership is part of the daily social life (see also Spyridakis, 2013). However, once again, we witness the gap between the ideological and political orientation of the union and the more instrumentalized sense of belonging shared among the Zone's 'Steppenwolves' whose class experience is mediated by the contingent and, thus, impersonal relationship with the contractor: "On the one hand you need the union; on the other, it is a bad thing. It is involved in lots of things, and it messes things up with the contractors… business is spoiled this way, because the unionists are demanding and sometimes in an extreme manner […] partly this is good, but ok, don't overdo it" .

The Zone differs from the manufacturing industry, or the big, organized shipyards (such as HSY), which are characterized by corporatist arrangements, stability in labor relations, and a relative immunity from the market forces (at least in the short term). The Zone's workers are collectivized through the union, the formal and informal networks, the communities located around the shipyards, the relationships of kin and friendship, but their work prospects and hence their life chances, are much more individualized, fragmented, discontinuous, and vulnerable. They share a strong occupational identity, which is not rarely accompanied with feelings of pride and higher self-esteem, but, at the same time, they experience a fundamental condition of alienation: not only do they lack the control over the results of production (exactly like their fellow workers in organized industries); they also lack the control of their skills, which are under a constant threat of become obsolete, or redundant. In other words, I notice a split, which is even more profound within the context of the recent (global, national and local) economic crisis along with its restructuring effects: being a Zone worker and actualizing a positive identity, is a Sisyphean task, even if the level of your skills and your self-assessment tell a different story. Perhaps this could also apply to other class formations too, but it remains to be empirically tested..

Not surprisingly, the inherent split that the Zone workers suffer from is reflected upon their moral sentiments. My interviewees have no trust in politicians and show low confidence in institutions, which is related to skepticism, an unwillingness to presume that political authorities should be given the benefit of the doubt (Cook and Gronke 2005, 785). This disposition ranging from skepticism (the method of systematic doubt, or criticism) to general cynicism (lack of faith in the existence of truth)[2], can hardly be disassociated from the abovementioned radical alienation of the Zone worker. In particular, political cynicism can be an attractive attitude for people with a negative self-esteem and can serve as an identity 'medicine' against feelings of uncertainty and disorientation (Dekker and Meijerink 2012).

When I asked Johnny about the causes of the recent crisis he replied as follows: "I think it is all about politics. Such things are done by the state. I believe the Greeks are better than anyone, in such stuff as shipping. To put it simply, I believe everything is political, everything starts from the state. They are going to sell Greece. Perhaps other countries are involved too [...] How is it possible that Greece is overloaded with work 5 and 10 years ago and then to suddenly fail? This is bullshit to me... everything is fixed beforehand."

The idea that the economic crisis was fixed and Greece was the victim of those powers that envy it, was very popular among the vast majority of the Zone people I have spoken to between 2013 and 2018. This particular attribution of blame, also shared among broader audiences during the crisis,

---

[2]Cynicism could be further distinguished in top-down versus bottom-up versions, or constructive versus destructive versions. In any case, one should be cautious when identifying contemporary cynicism with social and political apathy, although it may lead to that (Demertzis 2013).

tends to overshadow or even deny the inner contradictions of the capitalist markets and the unintended consequences of actions taken long before the crisis began. This should not be unexpected, at least in the case of the Zone workers. Being under the mercy of arbitrary decisions made up on the basis of uncontrollable conditions in global, regional, and/or local shipping markets can easily lead someone to perceive agency as totally missing. Thus, personifying threat aims at making sense of this menacing situation, so that it can be dealt with, at least in the imaginary realm. And when it comes to the imaginary, nationalism rules the game, as is revealed by the following conversation with Johnny:

> Interviewer: Is there any political party in Greece that you would see less unfavorably?
>
> Johnny: I believe they are all the same.
>
> Interviewer: All the same?
>
> Johnny: All of them. There are others behind them. This means that they have pre-arranged what's to come. What if Mitsotakis, or Michalis take the lead? Everything has already been agreed, they have put their signatures to be like this. To be Greece as it is. To reach to such a low point.
>
> Interviewer: Could something change?
>
> Johnny: They are going to make us like Bulgaria, or Romania, working for €150 per month.
>
> Interviewer: Is there any chance for a change?
>
> Johnny: That's it. Politics. If they change (*silence*)... But they don't want Greece to rise up. They don't want it. Because, Greece... well, where could anyone find this climate of Greece?

CONCLUSION

In the beginning of this chapter, I assured the reader that I will keep safe distance from the discussion over the death (and/or rebirth) of social classes. Besides, an empirical material consisted mainly of biographical interviews and some administrative and ethnographic data confines the ambitions of the analysis. I have spent more than five years on the field though, both as a career professional and as a researcher, so allow me to have my doubts on whether a deeper understanding of the attitudes, dispositions, values, and beliefs of social groups such as the shipbuilding and ship repair workers, can actually be concluded without entering the endless (but hopefully not purposeless) discussion about class.

It could be said that the selection of the shipbuilding community as a research area encapsulates, from the very beginning, an assertion regarding the question on whether class, as determined within property and employment relations, has explanatory power when observing inequalities, identities, cultural practices, or political attitudes. I feel I owe an explanation here, on why this particular occupational and social group is still of some importance to social research. Let me first stress the economic significance of the specific industry for modern societies in general. The following argument is drawn from a social history perspective and is quite compelling as to why social scientists should explore shipbuilding as a distinct social formation:

> "[Shipbuilding and ship repair] worksites are an important part of heavy industry, while labour processes at shipyards are much more diverse than labour processes in factories with their assembly lines and standardised production – shipyards combine many different segments of the working class in ever changing configurations. In addition, shipyards bring together large numbers – often thousands – of labourers in one place, thus shaping the culture and social life of the regions in which they are located. And, finally, these huge working-class conglomerations have often played a key role in industrial relations and politics." (van der Linden, Murphy, and Varela 2017, 15).

Undoubtedly the constant technological changes in the global shipbuilding industry, the relocation of the centers of production, and the dominant outsourcing trends have led to tremendous shifts in social relations of the remaining shipyards. However, the demand for fixed-term, contingent, and/or self-employed workers will remain active, particularly in what concerns countries that serve as interregional nodes of the fast-ever-growing global trade. Greece is a good example in this respect. Furthermore, one can assume that the restructuring processes in industry will carry on, reordering occupations and skills in terms of relevance and market utility. Therefore, it seems worth the effort to explore the thoughts, affects, emotions and acts of occupational groups such as the one under scrutiny. The question that follows then is whether we do need class concepts such as class structure, class formation, class identification, class struggle, or not.

As it was shown with the life stories analyzed here, class dialectics construed the workers' narratives without this being realized always. The interviewees talked a lot about themselves as professionals, the occupational realities of the Zone and of shipbuilding in general, the Greek crisis, politics and unionism; they also provided information on the power relations within the Zone and the implications stemming from the contractors' roles, codes of ethics, and bad habits. But class and class relations, even as lay concepts, were absent. In contrast, the signifiers of nationalism were there. I remind you that Billy identified himself with the Radical Left, while Johnny despite his inferred political cynicism, could hardly be considered a supporter of the far-right..

The cross-examination of these and other cases suggests that both workers that occupy relatively privileged class locations and workers that find themselves at the bottom of the Zone's hierarchy of skills, share a common experiential understanding of class relations, which is translated into action only contingently and through the mediating symbolic practices of the union. In other words, on the one hand, structure alone does not suffice to make sense of the individual and collective configurations at the micro- and meso-level; on the other hand, emerging and recurrent acts remain incomprehensible without a parsimonious examination of social reality. With all that said, I would rather argue that not only class-as-relationship, along with its lived effects, determines the deliberations, emotions and acts of the alienated workers, but moreover, class-as-trauma[3] works through its

[3]The traumatizing experience of class has been seminally examined in Sennett and Cobb's sociological work (1972). The effects of the negation of this trauma for individuals with a strong working-class background have insightfully been discussed in psychoanalytical approaches of class. See for example, Botticelli (2007) and Ryan (2014) among others.

negation within the individuals' narrativised identities of the individuals. This process unfolds when the focus of the analysis is shifted towards the massive and recurrent collective actions of the communist-led union of the Zone, at least within the past 15 years.

The Trade Union of Metal Workers of Attica and the Shipbuilding Industry of Greece is perhaps the most militant Greek union, with a long track record of massive strikes, sometimes violent and escalating. Although the communist leadership of the union employs a class discourse with strong anti-capitalist elements, its ties with the approximately 3.000 workers that it represents, are built upon the concrete experience of exploitation within the specific class formation and to a far lesser extend on pure ideological grounds. And while in periods of normality the 'Steppenwolves' barely care for the union's interpellations and the collective cause of the working-class, at moments of intensified class conflict, they entangle themselves in actions that constitute them as a class, however momentary and elusive this may be.

Class identification in the immanently liminal context of the Zone, although symptomatic and contingent in itself, is also vibrant and transformative when it occurs. This has nothing to do with a pre-given working-class identity that supposedly produces class struggles in the form of a calculated, anticipated, and stylized strike activity, with its standard rituals and repertoires (despite the fact that the symbolic universe of the Zone's class conflicts is sometimes fascinating). It is about class identity in the making (or mostly in the unmaking), which is achieved (or is mostly failed) in praxis, against a collective capitalist consisting of contractors and ship-owners in an amalgamation of small employers and very big and thriving business.

The workers in the shipbuilding and ship repair Perama Zone, like their fellow workers in many other class formations in contemporary advanced capitalism, constitute a radically dislocated working class that exists only through its acts, no matter how incomprehensive, sporadic, or contingent such acts may be. Their ambivalent and participative attitudes towards the union are hardly conditioned upon an imputed working-class consciousness or an ideology that the leaders assign to their members. On the contrary, it is the inevitable class struggle inscribed in myriad escapable and inescapable, conscious and unconscious, intended and unintended courses of actions, which allows the possibility for a working class to emerge. As Žižek has put it in the postface of a reprint of Georg Lukács's seminal work titled "A Defense of History and Class Consciousness: Tailism and the Dialectic": "while other classes can still maintain the illusion that 'Society exists,' and that they have their specific place within the global social body, the very existence of the proletariat repudiates the claim that 'Society exists' [...] the universal revolutionary potential is rather inscribed into the very being of the proletariat as its inherent radical split" (Žižek 2000, 169). Along a similar vein, the Zone's Steppenwolves realize the human nature that the class structure deprives them of, not when they are bitten in the Zone's daylight, but when they opt to strike back.

References

Barbalet, Jack. 1998. *Emotion, Social Theory, and Social Structure: A Macrosociological Approach*. Cambridge: Cambridge University Press.

Bennett, Tony, Savage, Mike, Silva, Elizabeth, Warde, Gayo-Cal, Alan, M., and Wright, David. 2008. *Culture, Class, Distinction*, New York: Routledge.

Bithymitris, Giorgos, and Koustenis, Panagiotis. (forthcoming). "Class Identities and Political Behavior: The Case of the Ship-building Zone of Perama." In *The Political Portrait of Greece, Old and New Cleavages,* edited by Christina Varouxi, Nikos Georgarakis, Manina Kakepaki, Nikos Sarris, Angelos Tramountanis, Olga Tsakiridi, Charalampos Tsekeris and Joan Tsiganou. Athens, EKKE.

Botticelli, Steven. 2007. "Return of the Repressed: Class in Psychoanalytic Process." In *Relational Psychoanalysis, Vol. 3: New Voices* edited by Melanie Suchet, Adrienne Harris, & Lewis Aron, 121-134. Mahwah, NJ: Academic Press.

Bornschier Simon and Kriesi Hanspeter. 2012. "The Populist Right, the Working Class, and the Changing Face of Class Politics." In *Class politics and the radical Right*, edited by Jens Rydgren, 1–33. London: Routledge.

Bourdieu, Pierre. 1990. *In other words*. Stanford: Stanford University Press.

Christodoulou, Michael. 2016. "Excluded and Dropped In: Habitus and Biographical Identity in Vocational Adolescents' Life Transitions." *Journal of Vocational Education & Training* 68, 3: 320-341.

Christodoulou, Michael and Spyridakis, Manos. 2016. "Upwardly Mobile Working-class Adolescents: A Biographical Approach on Habitus Dislocation." *Cambridge Journal of Education* 47, 3: 315-335. Accessed February 14, 2019. doi: 10.1080/0305764X.2016.1161729.

Cook, Timothy, and Gronke, Paul. 2005. "The Skeptical American: Revisiting the meanings of trust in Government and confidence in institutions." *The Journal of Politics* 67, 3: 784-803.

Crompton, Rosemary. 2010. "Class and Employment." *Work, Employment and Society* 24, 1: 9–26.

Dekker, Henk, and Meijerink, Frits. 2012. "Political Cynicism: Conceptualization, Operationalization, and Explanation." Politics, Culture and Socialization 3, 1/2: 33-48.

Demertzis, Nicolas. 2013. "On Cynicism, Political Cynicism and Political Marketing." In *Political Marketing: Strategic 'Campaign Culture'* edited by Kostas Gouliamos, Antonis Theocharous and Bruce I. Newman, 11-26. London: Routledge.

Devine, Fiona, Savage, Mike, Scott, John, and Crompton, Rosemary, eds. 2004. *Rethinking Class: Cultures, Identities and Lifestyles*. Basingstoke: Palgrave.

Eidlin, Barry. 2014. "Class Formation and Class Identity: Birth, Death, and Possibilities for Renewal." *Sociology Compass*, 8, 8: 1045-1062. Accessed February 28, 2019. doi:org/10.1111/soc4.12197.

Goodwin, Jeff, Jasper, James, M., and Polletta, Francesca. 2001. "Why emotions matter?." In *Passionate politics: Emotions and Social Movements*, edited by Jeff, Goodwin, James M. Jasper, and Francesca Polletta, 1–24. Chicago: University of Chicago Press.

Grusky, David, B., and Weeden, Kim, A. 2001. "Decomposition without death: A Research Agenda for a New Class Analysis." *Acta Sociologica* 44, 3: 203–218.

Kirk, John. 2007. *Class, Culture and Social Change*. Houndmills: Palgrave Macmillan.

Pakulski, Jan, and Waters, Malcolm. 1996. *The Death of Class*, London: Sage.

Ryan, Joanna. 2014. "'Class is in You': An Exploration of some Social Class Issues in Psychotherapeutic Work." In *Thinking space: Promoting Thinking about Race, Culture, and Diversity in Psychotherapy and Beyond* edited by Frank Lowe, 127-146. London: Karnac Books.

Reay, Diane. 2017. Miseducation: Inequality, Education and the Working Classes. Bristol: Policy Press.

Reay, Diane. 2005. "Beyond Consciousness? The Psychic Landscape of Social Class." *Sociology* 39, 5: 911–928.

Rosenthal, Gabriele. 1993. "Reconstruction of Life Stories: Principles of Selection in Generating Stories for Narrative Biographical Interviews." *The Narrative Study of Lives* 1: 59–91. Accessed February 14, 2019. URL: https://nbn-resolving.org/urn:nbn:de:0168-ssoar-59294.

Sayer, Andrew. 2005. *The Moral Significance of Class*. Cambridge: Cambridge University Press.

Sennett, Richard and Cobb, Jonathan. 1972. *The Hidden Injuries of Class*. New York: W. W. Norton.

Somers, Margaret. 1992. "Narrativity, Narrative Identity, and Social Action: Rethinking English Working-Class Formation." *Social Science History* 16, 4: 591–630.

Somers, Margaret. 1997. "Deconstructing and Reconstructing Social Formation Theory: Narrativity, Relational Analysis and Social Theory." In *Reworking Class*, edited by John Hall, 73-106. New York: Cornel University Press.

Spyridakis, Manos. 2013. *The Liminal Worker: An Ethnography of Work, Unemployment and Precariousness in Contemporary Greece*. London: Ashgate.

Strauss, Anselm. 1995. "Identity, Biography, History, and Symbolic Representations." *Social Psychology Quarterly* 58, 1: 4–12.

Varela, Raquel, Murphy, Hugh, and van der Linden, Marcel. 2017. "Introduction." In *Shipbuilding and Ship Repair Workers around the World.* Case Studies 1950-2010, edited by Raquel Varela, Hugh Murphy, and Marcel van der Linden, 15–46. Amsterdam: Amsterdam University Press.

Wetherell, Margaret. 2012. *Affect and Emotion: A New Social Science Understanding*. London: SAGE.

Wright, Erik, Olin. 2005. "Foundations of a Neo-Marxist Class Analysis." In *Approaches to Class Analysis*, edited by Erik Olin Wright, 4-30. Cambridge: Cambridge University Press.

Wright, Erik, Olin. 2000. *Class Counts*. Cambridge: Cambridge University Press.

Žižek, Slavoj. 2002. "Postface: Georg Lukacs as the philosopher of Leninism." In *A Defence of History and Class Consciousness*: *Tailism and the Dialectic* by Lukács Georg, 151-182. Translated by Esther Leslie. London & New York: Verso.

In: Emotions, Temporalities ...
Editors: M. Christodoulou et al.
ISBN: 978-1-53616-203-5

Chapter 5

TIME, EMOTIONS AND CLASS IN A PERIOD OF CRISIS: LIFE TRAJECTORIES OF SECOND GENERATION ALBANIANS IN GREECE

Eleni Giannakopoulou*
Department of Social and Educational Policy,
University of the Peloponnese, Corinth, Greece

ABSTRACT

This chapter aims to explore the relation between emotional temporalities, class identification and future life plans regarding second generation Albanian immigrants in Greece. By applying the category of time and emotion, I attempt to examine the agentic dimension of their systematic action in order to manage their temporal experience and resist to the external sources of temporal constraint and structure. Fear, shame, resentment but also an inner sense of confidence to their self and individuality shape their action and well designed life projects to transcend class and ethnic barriers and pursue their goal of upward mobility.

* Corresponding Author's E-mail: el_giannakopoulou@hotmail.com.

Keywords: second generation immigrants, life trajectories, temporality, emotions, class, social action

INTRODUCTION

This chapter aims to explore the relation between emotional temporalities, class identification and future life plans as regards second generation Albanian immigrants in Greece. The study approaches a vulnerable youth group transitioning to adulthood, focusing on the agents' strategic life plans in order to escape the growing uncertainties of their working-class milieu and to control their future.

School to work transition refers to an important turning point in one's life trajectory, as it entails a mandatory movement from a likely predictable environment and clearly defined pathway to an often uncontrollable and uncertain terrain (Pavlova 2017, 1). Improving school to work transitions, consists of a challenging way of reducing high unemployment, underemployment and precariousness among youth and therefore, accommodate social integration and progress. In this context, the transition of second generation immigrants from school to labor market is considered as a top priority in most immigrant receiving countries' policy agendas. There are several scholars who speculate that the children of immigrants, being restricted to degraded social and educational environments, undervalued jobs and shrinking economic niches, will experience downward mobility and transgenerational decline, while others postulate "segmented assimilation", in order to describe the diverse possible outcomes of challenging adaptation processes, probably resulting to a typology of vulnerability, which may result in forming a "new urban underclass" (Portes and Rumbeaut, 1996, 248).

Since 2008, Greece is experiencing a prolonged economic crisis which has exacerbated unemployment and precariousness across the entire labor force (Petmesidou and Polyzoidis 2015, 5-6). Young people's unemployment, let alone unemployment of vulnerable categories of population such as immigrant youth, is deeply aggravated by protracted financial austerity, exposing these groups to poverty and long term social exclusion. While the implications of financial crisis on immigrant youth groups seem to be complex and multi parametric (Papadakis et al., 2017), the potential risk of entering a NEET state (young people not in education, employment or training) is considerably high (Liebig and Widmaier, 2009).

In this chapter, I attempt to examine the school to work transition process of the children of Albanian immigrants in the context of the severe financial crisis and austerity: job insecurity and a rapidly changing workplace, precarious employment, increasing risks of poverty and social marginalization, compose the prevailing structural conditions under which second generation Albanians shape their ideas of futurity and make deliberate decisions concerning their life trajectories. By applying the category of time and emotion, I therefore, attempt to examine the agentic dimension of their systematic action in order to manage their temporal experience and resist "to the external sources of temporal constraint and structure" (Flaherty 2011, 3).

Time conceptualization, temporal emotions in future life projection and class identification, are the three main axes on the basis of which I am going to analyze the subjects' transition to adulthood. To this end, first, I will sketch the analytical categories of time, emotion and class in relation to immigrant youth and then I shall explore the worlds of employment and unemployment as well as the strategies which our subjects apply in order to manage their lives and draw their future life plans, emphasizing on the concept of individual action.

Time, Emotions and Class in a Period of Crisis

Time

Since the 1980s, temporal ontology is considered to be fundamental in understanding and in interpreting the social world (Hodges 2008, 406). Eventually, time has come to the fore as a constitutive anthropological category opposed to previous a-temporal models of social theory. The impact of globalization and rapid social change pinpointed the importance of approaching social life existing in a "temporal flow" which facilitates a continuous change in human sociality. Despite the fact that temporalities and temporal regimes have been recently acknowledged in social studies, they have forged new paths in qualitative research, challenging traditional ethnographic methods (Julie Mcleod 2017, 8-9).

However, when it comes to migration, it is framed more as a spatial rather than a temporal phenomenon, either empirically or theoretically, despite recent interest concerning the relation of age/life stage and migration. Migration research agenda clearly demands of a more temporal orientated analysis, if it is to be fully understood, as current heterogeneous and multidirectional migrant flows facilitate new types of migrant agency and migrant subjectivities (Robertson 2014, 3-4). Migration experience, including all generations of migratory subjects, is definitely non linear but open ended, involving diversion, repetition and simultaneity (Collins 2012, 316). As Robertson argues, migration is not to be seen as a single act of mobility *in time* but as a perplex and potentially fragmented process *across time* (Robertson 2014, 4). Thus, temporality emerges as a key concept to a new scholar understanding of migration.

Time is "everywhere and everything" (Robertson 2014, 2) and it is exactly that slippery and pervasive nature that makes it difficult to be captured as a concrete category in a strict theoretical way. As Frederiksen and Dalsgard (2014) highlight in the introduction of their book "Ethnographies of Youth and Temporality", time is both materialized and social, meaning that it may instigate change and deliberate action at any given moment of a person's life course. In this context, the core aspect that underlies our analysis is bringing together the perception of "troublesome time" as it is being experienced in contemporary Greek society and the category of a vulnerable youth group such as young Albanians immigrants who are transitioning to adulthood.

Being at the end of secondary education, young Albanians attempt to negotiate the complex territory of adulthood, taking into account multiple structural barriers.

Focusing on the interplay of structure and agency, we assume that immigrants' children are caught in a temporal situation which demands reflection as well as deliberate action while they are making decisions for their future. Second generation is already experiencing a turning point of transition, deeply shaped by the event of the persisting financial crisis. As precariousness violently transformed the objective and labour market side of migration in Greece, "turning points" connect Albanian immigrant youth lived experiences to their subjective life decisions. Transitions are seen as normative only to the extent that they are practiced by a major part of the population and society expects its members to undergo them. In cases that events happen in a way which undermines this normative dimension of the transition, then one can say that a turning point has taken place (Christodoulou et al., 2018). Such undermining of the transition may refer to economic crises as it is happening in Greece, to which the precariat group of young Albanians is most vulnerable.

Besides perceiving temporality in the form of a turning point, I will also draw at "time tracks" as they were conceptualized by Lyman and Scott (1989). Migration "time tracks" are embedded within biographies involving mobility, physical and symbolic, as well as a number of thoughtful decisions and deliberate actions. In this sense, time tracks not only refer to geographical mobility but to social mobility as well. Time tracks include border crossing of all kinds, physical and symbolic, meaning from settling to another country to moving to another social status. In this sense, borders within the time tracks offer an alternative interpretation of time and space, of "now and then", of "here and there".

Time tracks are products of cultural definitions. They conceive life as divided in temporally specific activities with different qualitative importance. In order to understand the temporal outlook of any social actor, one must comprehend the time period in which the subject is in and how this time track is shaping the subject's futurity. Time tracks divide the life of the subject in different feelings, activities and states, stimulating action or imposing passivity.

Emotions

It is evident that social theory is encountering the development of an appreciation of time as a critical factor in explaining human behavior. Notwithstanding the fact that temporality is involving consideration and deliberate action, one cannot exclude the critical role of emotions in life decisions and trajectories. As Barbalet argues, the category of temporality encourages an integration of the theories of social action and emotions in such a way, as to lead to a reconceptualization of social structure (Barbalet 2004, 183). In this sense, emotions facilitate a deeper apprehension of time which serves as the basis for action. On the other hand, action appears to be what connects temporality and emotions and it is therefore essential to understand it in a temporal way, as the movement to a possible future infused by the experience of the past. Thus, emotion lies in the core of action, shaped by temporal forces.

Emotions therefore, occur within social interaction and within social settings. Research reveals that emotions constitute powerful, pervasive and predictable drivers of decision making (Lerner et al. 2014, 799). According to most sociologists, emotional experience generally results from the meaning that individuals make from social interactions while several sociological theories highlight the relations of emotions and expectancy (Lively 2014, 56-57).

Expectancy is central in the perception of emotions infused by both temporal and emotional elements. As Barbalet argues, expectancy is the apprehension of a possible future but also an interpretation of the past (2014, 184-185). In this sense emotions are orientating action towards the future which is infiltrated by resources acquired in the past. Thus, emotions, stimulate in a way action and shape agency at the same time: without emotions people would be lost in time, while past and future would seem remote or inaccessible. It is, therefore, emotions which give meaning to temporal order of human action.

Going back to the notion of expectancy, it is important to note that understanding futurity is a fundamentally emotional process. Confidence, fear, shame, all deriving from past experience, are the driving forces of a person's future action. As I will show in this chapter, the aforementioned emotions are not only central in the subjects' narratives but they tend to dominate their life plans and strategies. It is these emotions which provide meaningful contexts for each and separate individual course of temporal action. Expectancy could be understood as how these subjects anticipate to be identified by others, how much power or deference they expect to enact or receive, how much of a given resource they expect to attain or, how decisions regarding the allocation of resources like those in the tormented Greek economy and society are determined and how they expect to be treated in the context of their social and interpersonal relationships.

Whereas confidence is not exactly of an emotion such as anger or love, it is clearly an emotional apprehension of the future. The problem of "unknownability of the future" is pervasive in all human societies through time. Securing and predicting future processes and events predominates individual and social action. The subjects of our study are dominated with the desire of holding their future accountable. They struggle to manage the impact of change and temporal disruption which the financial crisis has created, securing in all possible ways their transition to adulthood. Therefore, confidence is inherently entailing anticipation and thus, action stimulated by confidence is based on the subjects' beliefs as regards their capacities to be successfully engaged to their future.

Fear is an integral emotion that influences decision making (Lerner, 2014). In most situations, fear implies that the interests of an individual or a group are under threat. While fear may result to passivity and the avoidance of risk-taking, in many cases it may instigate action, serving as a driving force for individual and social change. In this context, the Greek economic crisis is threatening both individual and social well- being, functioning as an inter-subjective experience in which each individual necessarily contributes to the social experience. According to Barbalet (2004, 153-154), fear may trigger flight or fight. Thus, a sentiment of helplessness is likely to result in flight whereas fight, often fueled by hostility, points against the source which causes insufficiencies of structural power. In both cases, response to fear is a clear ascription of agency.

Apart from confidence and fear, emotions of shame appear either explicitly or implicitly in the subjects' narratives. As Lewis argues, shame is an emotion which helps to maintain the sense of a separate identity, "bringing into focal awareness both the self and the other" with the imagery that the Other rejects one's self (Lewis 1974, 25). Rejection is crucial in Lewis's approach as it is the Other who constitutes the source of shame. Thus, shame serves as a negative emotion which entails negative representations of a self who adapts negative opinions of the others. From a social identity theory prospect, individuals derive a sense of self-esteem from the social groups with whom they identify (Turner and Tajfel, 1986). Stigmatized individuals may employ different strategies in order to manage their tarnished group identities. In some cases they try to engage in social competition increasing the positive value of their identity or disassociate themselves from the group that causes them feelings of shame. The adolescents who took part in our research were tormented by feelings of shame because of their ethnic and class identifications. Most of them, however verified the hypothesis that feelings of shame may instigate action in an explicit or concealed way, so as the subject exit from this emotional environment.

Class

Social class and position shape immigrants' social imaginary, forming their engagement to the social and cultural landscape of the receiving society. As Ainslie illustrates, sociocultural experience is the scaffolding for self-representation across development, playing a crucial role in understanding social change (Ainslie 2011, 560). Moreover, the displacements of immigration into different cultural contexts might also bring previous unaddressed issues of class status, fuelled with various emotions. These temporal and spatial displacements suggest the persistent effects of earlier class identifications and their possible alterations, experienced through family history. New material conditions whether those of aspiration and success, or loss and insecurity are embedded in the centre of representations and evaluations of immigrants and their children.

Analyzing the psychodynamics of class and immigration, Ainslie, (2011, 2009) concluded that pre-existing class experience is usually deeply encoded in the subjects of migration, working in an unconscious way within new circumstances. Thus, immigrants, travel with their social class, whether upwardly or downwardly mobile. Towards this direction, Armitage, on the other hand, highlighted the interaction between real and fantasized class statuses of immigrants (2009). As they are struggling to manage their immigrant lives in Greece, first and second generation Albanians, deeply internalize their low working class positions, forming part of their representations in conscious and unconscious ways. In each participant of our survey, there is a fusion of individual family psychodynamics with a marked embeddedness in a class position along with the conflicts related to the meaning or understanding of their class based identities.

Although these approaches come from the field of psychoanalysis they are revealing as far as the interactive relation of class, temporality and emotions is concerned. This is because class mobility as a process does not happen in a lacuna. On the contrary, it suggests a temporal disruption with the subject's past along with his or hers imaginary future projections, while at the same time entails various emotions such as fear, confidence, shame and resentment.

In the context of social class, resentment is a feeling that according to Barbalet is the most crucial in influencing the "processes of class systems" (Barbalet 2014, 68). Max Scheller, developing an emotional situation described as "Ressentiment", argued that resentment lies in the comparison of an individual with other people on the process of which the individual feels disadvantaged and deprived from social goods and status (Gomez-Garido, 2013). Therefore, resentment could be described as a feeling that someone has unfairly gained advantage and moreover, that an individual is denied access to resources including a superior social status, otherwise available to him. Moreover, resentment as a feeling intertwined with social antagonism is sometimes the result of shame and lack of confidence.

To sum up, in this study we approach class identification of young immigrants in the context of time and emotions. Second generation immigrants locate themselves in working class environments which trigger a variety of emotions: Fear about their bleak future prospects, a concealed sense of shame because of their immigrant origin and low working class environment, resentment for others as they perceive themselves unfairly deprived from resources and opportunities. In this context, young Albanians make future plans shaped by emotions and follow rational strategies in order to implement their aspirations. In this process, time, emotion and class are inextricably connected.

METHODOLOGY

This essay is part of a larger- scale project conducted between 2014 and 2018 in an industrial small town near Athens. Second generation immigrants of Albanian ethnicity were chosen as they constitute the larger population of immigrant origin students in secondary education in Greece (Tzotzopoulou and Kotzamani, 2008). Moreover, since nineties, the social and demographic characteristics of immigrant flows from Albanian to Greece demonstrate patterns of permanent settlements (Kokkali, 2011). Senior high school students were selected as the last years of secondary education in Greece are optional and therefore, indicative of the strategic role that they attribute in education regarding the implementation of their future plans.

Research was mainly conducted on the basis of semi structured interviews as they allow to explore the diverse experience of immigration, approaching in depth the various representations and understandings of the interviewees (Iosifides and Spyridakis, 2006). The students who participated in this research were between sixteen and eighteen years old at the time of the interviews and have been living in Greece since they were born. Interviews took place in the context of the acute Greek financial crisis from which the majority of the respondents' families was seriously affected. I have selected six biographical narratives among these stories which I considered revealing as regards issues of temporality, emotions and class in their life trajectories.

WORLDS OF EMPLOYMENT AND UNEMPLOYMENT

Young Albanian immigrants' narratives concerning employment mostly reflect the experience of the first generation. The struggle of first immigrants for survival, upward mobility and integration in host societies is evident in their childrens' discourse. Indeed, Albanian immigrant presence in the Greek society has undergone significant changes over the decades, mainly in migrants' profiles, demographic composition and sociocultural conditions. Before the crisis, there was a general agreement that Albanians in Greece have shown rapid progress and mobility: Many have moved from rural to urban areas and from agricultural work to employment in cities (even self-employment), especially those employed in the construction sector and services.

However, the economic crisis constituted of a critical turning point in most immigrant families. It functioned as a temporal dichotomy which violently divided life in "then" and "now", leading from a promising and prosperous life to uncertainty, vulnerability and deprivation (Spyridakis, 2013). This sense of temporal rupture is most evident in Fabion's, (17), narrative:

> Before (the crisis) life was different. Everything seemed normal. My parents were planning to buy a house here. They wanted me to study civil engineering and expand my fathers' business (he had a small construction business). Now he is out of work most of the time. I do not see any use in following this career. There are no prospects for engineering here in Greece and my father even discusses of returning to Delvin.

In a similar way, Marianna, (16), highlights the disruptive impact of the crisis on her and her family. Economic turmoil has fundamentally altered everyday normality, creating a deep temporal chasm between the past and the present. Previous certainties are now been challenged, due to structural barriers resulting to an environment of doubt, anxiety and fear:

> My dad used to work in an aluminium construction company. He used to bring money in the house. I was buying clothes and staff and generally we were all happy. When the crisis escalated, he lost his job, the company he was working for almost 12 years fired the majority of the employees. He now works here and there. There are times that he is out of work for a whole month. We owe lots of money to other people. My mother started working a few hours in a bakery. I often feel nostalgia for my previous life. I had everything I needed. Now everything seems to be very hard. It's an everyday struggle. I sometimes feel scared. I cannot answer why it has to be like that. I want to be a physician. But can we afford my private preparatory classes? Before, there were no such problems. I did not have any worry. Now everything is at stake. I might be obliged to postpone my studies and work in order to help. Mum and dad said there is a possibility of going back. I dread to think this possibility.

Crisis has been a violent structural condition which penetrated Marianna's life, casting doubt in what previously was normally planned and anticipated. Her transition process is now revisited by her and her family with a potential rupture of her serial future planning. Marianna is situated in a time track where troublesome temporality triggers temporal emotions of fear and insecurity. Inability to control future and distancing from ideal and carefully planned transitions-mainly to tertiary education- causes young immigrants frustration and blurs sometimes their courses of action.

As we mark in both narratives, fear is also stimulated by a potential return to Albania. This option represents a U-turn for most young Albanians who live in Greece. Almost none is thinking returning to their country of origin despite their parents' wish. On the contrary, a possible resettlement to Albania is perceived as a cancellation of their professional and social capital. Life in Albania is depicted as backward and tedious. Liana (16) is adamant against such a possibility:

> Going back to Albania means throwing away everything I have. My future, my social life which I earned here. I cannot cope with people there, let alone that there is nothing for me to do! I cannot start a new life there, meaning I have different ideas and way of living. Besides, I want to study Drama and this is kind of unacceptable for a woman in Albania.

Apart from fear, young Albanians demonstrate emotions of anger and resentment about this frustrating situation they are in. Interviews reveal feelings of being treated unfairly in relation to what themselves and their families are being through. Integrating in Greek society and accumulating social and cultural capital, sometimes opposed to their family capital has always been a complicated and difficult process. In this context, a considerable number of our respondents have developed a feeling of resentment towards their Greek peers and friends whose life appears to be much more clearly defined in a temporal way. According to Fabion:

> My Greek friends have nothing to worry about. They have their parents' money, a ready job waiting for them. Whereas we have nothing more apart from working hard to achieve what is easy for natives. This is not right. It is so unfair. I mean my best friend, he is Greek, he knows that after finishing school he will join his family business. On the contrary I might be unemployed or end up working just like my father… in a factory.

Immigrants' children seem upset when identifying themselves in a downwardly mobile working class which was previously thriving and gaining status. From the one hand they are experiencing a mobility stagnation which withholds their dreams and aspirations. On the other hand they are noting the income disparities between them and their peers. The difference in opportunities, choices and lifestyles is even galling when expressed in terms of relative toil.

Chris (18) is comparing himself with his "pampered" classmates. Influenced by the hard working ethos demonstrated by the first generation of Albanians he feels devalued and underestimated. This situation causes him a certain degree of resentment towards the host society.

> Every weekend I work in a small tavern. I sweep floors all night for 25 euros. No Greek boy of my age would do that. They are all so pampered and yet life is always rewarding to them. Whereas I have to work so hard just to be always underneath them. This is because I stand alone. I do not have a security net based on my parents' money. It is hard but in a way it is liberating.

Apart from resentment, in many young immigrants' interviews there is often an underlying feeling of shame related to the categories of ethnicity and class. Widespread xenophobia in Greece and the relevant stigmatization of immigrants is obstructing their full integration in the Greek society. In addition, the economic decline of the immigrants' families due to austerity also torments second generation with feelings of shame. Previous prosperity created a climate of hope for most of them as regards upward mobility and integration. The acute crisis which ripped Greek society raised new, insurmountable obstacles for many of them. Therefore, shame is of a dual trigger. First, it appears to be integral to most of the young participants as it is intertwined with ethnicity. It is true that when it comes to matters of ethnicity young Albanians reveal feelings of embarrassment. A considerable number of them avoids discussions about ethnicity at first point. Notwithstanding the fact that Albanians are not used to form concrete ethnic communities in host societies, it could be argued that shame relating to ethnicity is likely one of the very few feelings which they experience as a group, even as an imaginary group. Angela is one of the few who explicitly explains this sort of feelings.

> I am Albanian only to the extent that my parents are Albanians. I do not want any connection with the country and the people who live there. When being asked about my origins I feel so embarrassed to say that I come from Albania. I do not want to do anything with them. They do not exist for me. They make me feel so ashamed for myself. This is because in my few visits in Albania, I saw things which literally disgusted me. I resent those people. It's not my fault that my parents are Albanians and probably is not of a major importance.

In order to manage her feelings of shame Angela attempts to downplay the matter of ethnicity as it constitutes of an unchangeable fact. However, this is not the case when it comes to class. Despite the fact that most immigrants identify themselves with the lower parts of the Greek working class, they still perceive class mobility as possible and achievable and organize strategically their life choices and decisions to this end.

STRATEGIES OF SOCIAL MOBILITIES AND LIFE TRAJECTORIES

According to Feliciano and Rumbeaut (2005), micro-social factors such as life aspirations and plans play a critical role in the successful trajectories of second generation immigrants. Most of our informants had already elaborated a specific life course plan and had crystallized opinions concerning their future careers. Stability, security and financial independence were the most important criteria in the process of choosing a profession. Despite the limited horizons that the crisis has caused, second generation distance itself from the manual professions of their parents. Upward mobility is perceived as one of their top goals in order to attribute meaning and justify their parents' sacrifices so far.

Although temporal feelings of fear, anxiety and frustration predominate the narratives concerning their future lives, the coincidence of their transitioning to adulthood with the structural barriers ushered by the crisis, push them to elaborate clear plans. Moreover, immigrant youth appears ready to uptake risks in order to secure itself from a potential liminality. Towards this direction, most young Albanians declare ready to relocate themselves once again. Their future plans include working and living in Europe. Gabriel (17) reveals her intentions:

> After the completion of my studies I will settle abroad, most preferably in Sweden where my boyfriend already lives. I want to live and work there.

Likewise, Angela refers to her plan

I cannot imagine myself in Greece. No way…there are no chances for me here. I must go abroad. I have a plan, I have already discussed it with my family. I will join my uncle in the UK. I will definitely undertake postgraduate studies there. I want to find a well paid job and probably start a family in a British town.

Life abroad is idealized in young immigrants' imagination. It resembles to their parents movement flow, however their plan is much better designed and secured. My informants are in a process of being well qualified through education and skilled in order to pursue a better life comparing to their parents and finally upgrade their social status. Financial crisis has revealed the agentic dimension of their strategies: young immigrants are being active subjects, taking life in their own hands. Their temporal and eventually spatial rupture with the past does not result into passivity. On the contrary, structural barriers created by the crisis instigate decision making and calculated action so as to facilitate upward mobility. Being in a critical time track these young people are ready to cross actual and symbolic boundaries.

Individual Action

In this context, this analysis finds itself to where it started. Temporal disruption and relevant emotions triggered by crisis, contribute to action and a certain kind of rationality. For the individual actors their decisions and choices provide strategical endeavors of banishing future uncertainties (Dalsgard and Frederiksen 2014, 2). To this direction our informants demonstrate a desire for action in order to implement their goals. Confidence to themselves and their individual skills drives their plans and motivates their efforts.

The participants of our study attribute great importance to individuality opposed to structural barriers. They are emphasizing personality, qualifications and willpower as the prerequisites of success. Their actions are based on a feeling of confidence for themselves and their capacities for successfully engaging to the future (Barbalet 2004, 101). Chris speaks about the importance of being confident to himself

> I know that things are difficult. My parents come from Albania and situation here in Greece is troubled and even more difficult for people like us. However, I am confident to myself and despite the difficulties I will make it. I mean, I put a lot of effort in my classes probably I will study at the university. Then, I am hard working and I will not give up easily. Some people question my future because I am of Albanian origin but I will prove them wrong. I mean. Some people ask me if I will continue my studies, This makes me furious. They ask me because I am Albanian and they expect that I will follow my father's profession in constructions. It drives me crazy, this narrowmindness. Things are tough and sometimes I am afraid and I get lost but I am sure I will find my way, if not here in Greece probably somewhere else abroad. My mother says that when you try, no matter how hard things are, you make your way.

According to Barbalet (2004), time perspective is crucial to make confidence a central affect or emotion for praxis. Human action occurs in time, drawing from a past that cannot be changed and directing to a future that cannot be predicted. The unpredictability of the future undermines the perception of rationality in action and replaces calculated reason with emotion as the basis for action. Time is appearing integral to confidence and subsequently, a necessary condition of action and agency. Therefore, temporality is being introduced in action through confidence in one's self and his capacities to be effective. In this sense Angela who has taken into account her family past experience seems confident regarding her decisions for her future:

I have learned from my parents' mistakes. I know that eventually I will make my own. However, this is who I am and I will not sit here waiting for something to happen to me. I want to live a comfortable life and be respected for who I am. And no matter how difficult because of the situation I can make it.

CONCLUSION

This chapter aimed at exploring the relation of time, emotion and class of Albanian origin students in a period of acute economic and social crisis in Greece. As the qualitative analysis points out all three theoretical categories seem to be intertwined, attributing meaning in the subjects' intent actions. Being at the end of secondary education, young Albanians attempt to negotiate the complex territory of adulthood, taking into account multiple structural barriers. Crisis has caused ruptures in every aspect of their live which our subjects have to negotiate with and rearrange their decisions and relevant life plans. Focusing on the interplay between structure and agency and attempting to shed light mostly on the agentic dimension of their actions, this study primarily emphasized the role of turning points and time tracks. Experiencing liminal situations as a lived experience, young Albanians are ready to cross actual and symbolic boundaries in order to hold their future accountable (Spyridakis, 2013). In this sense, they plan new immigration projects while they are trying to be well qualified and skilled in order to pursue the professions they choose. In this process, emotions play a significant role in orientating the course of action towards a future infiltrated by resources acquired in the past. Emotions therefore, facilitate a new apprehension of time resulting to action. It is therefore action which connects temporality and emotions in a meaningful interplay.

Fear, shame, resentment, confidence as emotional states all based on past experience, are the driving forces of our subjects' future action. These emotions are not only central in the subjects' narratives but they tend to dominate their life plans and strategies and it is exactly these emotions which provide meaningful contexts in their course of temporal action. Time and emotions of young immigrants coincide into action in order to change their precarious present conditions and protect them from future vulnerabilities. Informants are not dragging into passivity but on the contrary, they are the protagonists of their lives. A sense of confidence to their individual characteristics and skills serves as a powerful driving force to change their positions in social hierarchy even in periods of crisis. Thus, overwhelmed with emotions, they seem determined to pursue upward mobility leaving behind working class identifications.

To this aim, second generation Albanians draw their future plans and strategies and seem ready to undertake risks. Liminal situations drive them to bold decisions but well designed life projects. To conclude, despite precariousness and their low social and economic status young immigrants are striving to define their social reproduction themselves.

REFERENCES

Ainslie, Ricardo C. (2009). "Social Class and its Reproductions to Immigrants. Constructions of Self." *Psychoanalysis, Culture and Society*, (14), 213-224.

Ainslie, Ricardo C. (2011). "Immigrants and the Psychodynamics of Class." *Psychoanalytic Psychology*, (28), 560-568.

Armitage, K. (2009). Young, lower middle class and black. Sitegeist: A *Journal of Psychoanalysis and Psychology*, (3), 51-64.

Barbalet, J. M. (2004). Emotion, Social Theory and Social Structure. A Macrosociological *Approach*. Cambridge: The Press Syndicate of the University of Cambridge.

Collins, Francis. (2012). "Transnational Mobilities and Urban Spatialities: notes from the Asia-Pacific". *Progress in Human Geography*, (36), 316-335. doi: 10.1177/0309132511423126.

Feliciano, Cynthia. & Rumbaut, Ruben. (2005). Gendered Paths: Educational and Occupational Expectations and Outcomes Among Adult Children of Immigrants. *Ethnic and Racial Studies.*, *28*. doi: 10.1080/0141987050022440б.

Flaherty, Michael G. (2011). The *Textures of Time. Agency and Temporal Experience*. Philadelphia: Temple.

Frederiksen, Martin D. & Anne, Line Dalsgard. (2014). *Ethnographies of Youth and Temporality. Time Objectified*. Philadephia: Temple University Press.

Gomez-Garido, Maria. (2013). "Hidden Injuries: Class Resentment in Western Democracies." In *On Resentment: Present and Past*, edited by Fantini, Bernandino, and Martin, Moruno, and Javier, Moscoso, 277-294. Newcastle Upon Tyne: Cambridge Scholars Publishing.

Hodges, Matt. (2008). "Rethinking Time's Arrow: Bergson, Deleuze and the Anthropology of time. *Anthropological Theory*, *8*(4), 399-429. doi:10.1177/1463499608096646.

Iosifides, T. & Manos, Spyridakis. (2006). *Qualitative Research. Methodological Approaches and Data Analysis*. Athens: Kritiki (in Greek).

Kokkali, I. (2011). From Scapegoats to "good immigrants'? Albanians supposedly successful integration to Greece. *Quaderni del Circollo Roselli*, 3/2011, 161-173. [Available: http://www.lse.ac.uk/european Institute/research/hellenicObservatory/pdf/ 3rd_Symposium/ PAPERS/ KOKKALI_IFIGENEIA.pdf.

Lerner, Jennifer., Li, Ye., Valdesolo, Piercarlo. & Kassam, Karim S. (2015). Emotion and Decision Making. *Annual Review of Psychology*, Vol. *66*, pp. 799-823, 2015. doi.org/10.1146/annurev-psych-010213-115043.

Lewis, Helen Block. (1975). *Shame and Guilt in Neurosis*. New York: International University Press.

Liebig, Thomas. & Sarah, Widmaier. (2009). "Children of Immigrants in the labor markets of EU and OECD Countries: An Overview". *OECD Social Employment and Migration Working Papers*, no 97. Paris: OECD publishing. https://dx.doi.work/1787/220823724345.

Lively, Kathryn J. & David, R. Heise. (2014). "Emotion in Affect Control Theory." In *The Handbook of the Sociology of Emotion*, Volume *II*, edited by J.E. Stets and J.H. Turner. New York: Springer.

Lyman, Stanford M. & Marvin, B. Scott. (1989). *A Sociology of the Absurd*. NewYork: General Hall.

McLeod, Julie. "Marking Time, Making Methods: Temporality and Untimely Dilemmas in the Sociology of Youth and Educational Change." *British Journal of Sociology of Education*, *38*(1), (n.d.), 13–25. doi:10.1080/01425692.2016.1254541.

Papadakis, Nikos., Antonis, Papargyris., Vasilis, Dafermos., Maria, Basta., Argyris, Kyridis., Maria, Drakaki. & Sifis, Plymakis. (2017). "Youth and NEETs in Greece during the crisis era. Social Vunerability, Public Trust and Political Behavior. *Youth in Crisis Countries. Life situations and Political attitudes of adolescents in Southern/Eastern Europe and North Africa*, edited by M. Herring and Kl. Hurelmann. Chicago: University of Chicago Press.

Pavlova, M., Lee, J. C. K. & Maclean, R. (2017). "Complexities of School to Work Transitions". *Educational Research for Policy and Practice*, *16*, 1. https://doi.org/10.1007/s10671-017-9211-5.

Petmesidou, Maria. & Polyzoidis, P. (2015). What Policy Innovation for Youth in the era of prolonged austerity? The case of Greece. *OSE Paper Series*, *Research Paper*, 20-July, 2015. Brussels: European Social Observatory.

Portes, Alexander. & Ruben, G. Rumbeaut. (1996). *Immigrant America. A Portrait*. Berkeley:University of California Press.

Robertson, Shanthi. (2014). "The Temporaloties of Integrational Migration, Impications for Ethnographic Research". *ICS Occasional Paper Series*, *5*(1), 1-16.doi.org:10/4225/35/57/57a969210fla0.

Spyridakis, Manos. (2013). Work insecurity and Market Economy. The case of the Keranis tobacco industry. *Ethnology*, (15), 5-29 (in Greek).

Spyridakis, Manos., Michalis, Christodoulou. & Eleni, Giannakopoulou. (2019). Intergenerational transformations of vulnerability: Life trajectories of Albanian migrants in Athens, in, Th. Fouskas (ed), *Immigrants, Asylum Seekers and Refugees in Times of Crisis*, European Public Law Organisation, (forthcoming), pp. 1-21.

Spyridakis, Manos. (2013. *The Liminal Worker*. United Kingdom: Francis and Taylor.

Tajfel, Henri. & John, C. Turner. (1986). "The Social Identity Theory of Intergroup Behaviour." *Psychology of Intergroup Relations*, (2), 7-24.

Tzortzopoulou, Maria. & Anna, Kotzamani. (2008). The education of Immigrants Students. Examining the problems and the perspectives of solutions. *Working Papers*, 2008/19. Athens: EKKE, (in Greek).

SECTION 2. CLASS STRUCTURE AND TRADE UNIONS

In: Emotions, Temporalities … ISBN: 978-1-53616-203-5
Editors: M. Christodoulou et al.

Chapter 6

UNIONS AND LABOUR SOLIDARITY: PENDING BETWEEN INCLUSIVENESS AND EXCLUSIVENESS – THE CASE OF GREEK TRADE UNIONS

Christina Karakioulafi[*]
Department of Sociology, University of Crete,
Rethymno, Greece

ABSTRACT

Since the 1980s, unions have been considered to go through a period of decline and retreat, suffering a decrease in union membership, declining rates of unionization, diminishing political power and distrust regarding their public legitimacy. Additionally, the rise of precarious employment and unemployment led to the emergence of an 'insider-outsider' division within labour force and inside unions. The crisis of traditional unionism relates to its capacity and/or willingness to speak on behalf of workers as a whole, and to defend their collective interests and inevitably brings to the

[*] Corresponding Author's Email: chkarakioulafi@gmail.com.

fore the broader question of labour solidarity. Labour solidarity is at the heart of union action and is considered to be one of the main power resources of the unions. Renewal strategies adopted, as a response to this crisis, focused on 'organizing the unorganized'. Nevertheless, central issues, such as working-class labour solidarity and union inclusiveness have often been absent from the relevant debates and strategies and it is acknowledged that the increasing differentiation within workers' interests imposes a re-invention of solidarity and a re-framing of their representation. Greek unions are no exception to these general trends. Facing declining unionization, and a long-term representation and confidence crisis, official unions acted minimally to organize and mobilize non-unionized workers based on a 'working-class solidarity' approach. Hence approaching the most vulnerable segments of the labour force remains a very abstract action. Following, often, an 'insider-outsider' approach, their main strategy and position towards the unemployed and/or the precarious workers is that of exclusion. However, class-oriented identities are not inexistent in the Greek unionism but remain active mainly in the case of new forms of left-wing labour organizations bearing the characteristics of social movement unionism.

INTRODUCTION

Since the 1980s it has been generally accepted that unions throughout the advanced capitalist world have faced multiple challenges, related to a combination of economic, political, industrial and technological changes that, in different ways and degrees, undermined their post-war period foundations. Thus, unions have been considered to pass through a period of decline and retreat, suffering a decrease in union membership, declining rates of unionization, diminishing political and industrial power and distrust with regard to their public legitimacy (Hyman 2007; Richards 1995; Richards and Polavieja 1997). Additionally, labour market changes and rising unemployment have led not only to the emergence of an 'insider-outsider' division within labour force, but also -and by extension- inside unions (Richards and Polavieja 1997). For some, unions *"have become a 'dinosaur' whose justifiable role in the past of protecting vulnerable and exploited low-paid workers has increasingly become irrelevant."* (Darlington 2014, 111).

In this context, gradually, unionists have accepted the fact that traditional union strategies have lost their effectiveness and that unions could remain significant social actors only if they renewed themselves (Hyman 1999). Based on this acceptance, discussions and strategies aiming at their modernization and renewal have been inaugurated (Hyman 1999, 2007). New strategies emphasized (more or less directly) the role of rank-and-file participation or mobilization (Turner and Hurd 2001).

'Organizing the unorganized' and 'hard to reach' workforce became central within unions' renewal strategies (Heery 2005; Martinez Lucio et al. 2017). Nevertheless, focusing on the level of unionization, organizing, frequently, remained a technical issue (Hyman 2007), without a more integrated and radical rethinking of union objectives (Simms and Holgate 2010). Thus, central issues, that are at the core of unions' ideologies, structures and strategies, such as working-class labour solidarity and union inclusiveness have often been absent from the relevant debates and strategies.

Greek unions are no exception within these general trends. Facing declining unionization, and a long-term representation and confidence crisis, official unions did very few things to organize and mobilize non-unionized workers based on a 'working-class solidarity' approach. Nevertheless, the latter is not inexistent, mainly in the case of new forms of left-wing labour organizations bearing the characteristics of social movement unionism.

In the first section of what follows we will examine some issues concerning the ambiguous relations between unions and working-class solidarity, as well as the strategies of inclusiveness (mainly towards precarious workers and the unemployed). Then, we will examine the position and the role of trade unions in Greece within the relevant discussion.

Unions and Working-Class Solidarity: Pending between Inclusiveness and Exclusiveness

During the '80s unions were affected by a twofold crisis. The first one, is a crisis of identity, as a result of the longstanding changes in the internal composition of organized labour, and most particularly the diminishing role of blue-collar industrial workers as the traditional pillar of unionism. The second one, is a crisis of solidarity due to growing divisions not only between unionized and non-unionized sections of the workforce, but also within the ranks of the unionized. Many authors have positioned the problems of organized labour in the much broader context of enduring changes in the class structure of late industrial societies. Thus, the decline of blue-collar unionism is seen as detrimental to the foundations of unionism *per se*, and as vivid manifestation of the wider process of changes in class structure (Richards 2018).

Hence, the crisis of unionism relates to its capacity and/or willingness to speak for workers as a whole, and to defend their collective interests (Richards and Polavieja 1997) and inevitably rises the broader question of labour solidarity. Solidarity, as it is indicated in popular slogans [*'Unity is strength'* (Darlington 2014, 116); *'solidarity forever, for the union makes us strong'* (Levesque and Murray 2010, 136)] is at the heart of union action and considered to be one of the main unions power resources.

However, there is little understanding of how it has been created or in what way it has changed (Heckscher and McCarthy 2014; Hyman 1999). Generally, it is understood in relation to the existence of sufficiently cohesive identities and a unity of purpose that derives either from common collective identities or by deliberative processes where individuality submits to collectivity (Lévesque and Murray 2010). D'Art and Turner (2002) understand solidarity as a community of interests, feelings and actions. While the first refers to the existence of similar material conditions and is based on the idea that these interests can be achieved through collective means, solidarity presupposes also a strong sense of identity and attachment. Solidarity might concern 'real communities' (a worker's immediate work group) and 'imagined' communities, where solidarity also extends beyond the immediate work group.

The reasons on how the increasing fragmentation of the workforce affected labour/ working-class solidarity differ. It is generally accepted that the lines of social differentiation that flow through contemporary society are profoundly changing union dynamics. The underlying hypothesis is that the foundations of the emblematic solidarity for the formation of the working classes, which gave rise to the emergence and institutionalization of large-scale unions, would erode (Lévesque et al. 1998). As Zoll (1998) points out workers' solidarity was based on an egalitarian vision of society. Thus, differences sometimes appeared to be like overwhelming barriers for workers solidarity. The current crisis of workers' solidarity can be interpreted in this perspective. The non-recognition of differences is an imperfection of the workers' solidarity, since urged by the desire to transcend the political and ethnic divisions of the workers, unions made the mistake of focusing entirely on the argument of social equality between workers and thus neglecting obvious differences. Nowadays, the lack of worker solidarity can be interpreted as an imperfection due to its 'mechanical' nature, as it is a solidarity based on equality, resemblance, belonging to the same community and, therefore, not accustomed to differences or to exceeding the community's borders.

Contrary to a dominant perception that related the disintegration of the 'traditional' working class to the decline of labour/working-class solidarity, some authors such as Hyman (1999) questioned class-conscious labour movement, wondering whether the latter is corresponding to an actual situation, to a goal easy to achieve or whether it is an illusory and unattainable objective, not only nowadays but also diachronically. According to Richards (2018), the link between unionism and working-class solidarity has always been problematic.

Stemming from the idea that working class and union divide is not a new phenomenon (Richards and Polavieja 1997) and that the belief in some former golden age of proletarian unity and trouble-free trade-union solidarity can be misleading (Hyman 1992), a number of authors point out the previously existing sectionalism and fragmentations within the working-class and unions (Hobsbawm 1978; Hyman 1989, 1992; Darlington 2010; Richards 2001, 2018), as well as the variety in working class consciousness (Lockwood 1958; Mann 1973). In fact, social divisions have always ruptured workplace and class solidarities, and unionism frequently not only reflected but also underlined divisions and antagonisms within the working class. Even, *"..some of the most conscious working-class movements have been based upon the assertion of white skilled working class masculine identities."* (Moore 2011, 16). Being organizations founded on occupations or industries, each individual union embraced only a segment of the working class; they reflect the divisions inflicted on workers by capitalism (Darlington 2014). Even during their 'golden age', unions often demonstrated both exclusive, as well as inclusive tendencies (Richards, 2018). Exclusiveness has been dominant within craft unionism that safeguarded a restricted access to a monopolized area of work, by controlling entry to the job and putting lines of demarcation often based upon criteria of sexism or racism (Hyman 1989, 1992). This also affected the ways workers identified themselves as members of the working-class: "*Most workers regard themselves, first and foremost, not as members of a general working class but as a clerk or coal-miner, electrician or civil servant, employee of Ford or the health service; and union structure reflects such narrower identities rather than class membership. In embracing particular categories of workers as members and excluding others, each union gives institutional reinforcement to certain perceptions of common interest while presenting obstacles to alternative contours of solidarity.*" (Hyman 1989, 230).

Thus, one must acknowledge the historically contingent nature of labour solidarity (Richards and Polavieja 1997): it is never 'natural,' does not arise automatically but is socially constructed and always contested (Gumbrell-McCormick and Hyman 2015). In that sense, any simple understanding of it in terms of a 'mechanical solidarity' among working class people is and remains imaginary (Hyman 1999).

This also implies the questions of interest representation. Interests, as Offe and Wiesenthal [(1980) in, Hyman 1999] pointed out can be satisfied to the extent that they are partially specified. So, to build union agenda integrating differentiated groups of workers requires a delicate delineation of what interests are represented. Unions must: determine the scope of the population they address or whose interests they are representing; choose the objectives or the interests they are representing; and select the strategies and means adopted to meet interests that will be represented (Heery 2005).

Thus, the increasing differentiation within workers and in interests imposes a re-invention of solidarity and a re-framing of interesting representation. Despite solidarity's historically contingent nature, nowadays building and maintaining union and working-class solidarity is more problematic than ever (Richards 2018).

In most developed countries, full-time workers in long-term work arrangements formed the basis of unions and, as such, they also defined their objectives (Hyman 1999). Frequently, unions have been accused of representing mainly 'insiders,' and not those in the insecure and precarious employment conditions ('outsiders'). At the beginning unions considered the - at that time- rather novel and uncommon forms of atypical employment as unacceptable and claimed its abolition. At the time, this seemed 'logical' since the *"lion's share of their membership"* consisted mainly of 'insiders' (Keune 2013, 6; Durazzi 2017). Exclusion has been driven by an effort to protect workers from insecure employment and existing members from competition within the labour market competition and was often associated with a 'depreciation' of workers who accepted such employment conditions (Heery 2009).

The rise of precarious employment challenged unions' typical ways of thinking and acting. Unions could no longer overlook their often-declining membership among 'insiders' and the increasing number of 'outsiders,' constituting an increasing potential source of membership (Keune 2013). Contrary to their traditional opposition towards atypical employment, most unions acknowledged that *"precarity is a reality that will not go away"* (Gumbrell-McCormick 2011, 297), and understood that their exclusion would weaken unions' capacity to act (Hyman and Gumbrell-McCormick 2017).

Nowadays, unions show variable degrees of inclusiveness and adopt a variety of strategies (Bernaciak et al. 2014; Durrazi 2017). Unions strategies *"range from exclusion through acceptance but in a subordinate position, acceptance on the basis of equal treatment with workers in permanent employment and 'engagement,' characterized by union attempts to represent the specific and differentiated needs of contingent workers. The latter might be conceived of as 'representing diversity,' a union equivalent to diversity management"* (Heery 2009, 430). Although exclusion in not the most common response, it can be regarded as being logical under certain circumstances, as in the case of unions with a 'guild' or 'professional association' identity that may exclude workers from membership, especially if they consider that these workers are undermining regulations of their labour markets (Simms 2010).

Regarding the strategies adopted, these are conditioned by a variety of factors (Gumbrell-McCormick 2011), among whom, unions' identity strongly influences the interests with which they identify, the agenda they follow, as well as the sort of power resources they encourage and put in place (Hyman 2001). For example, class-oriented unions probably will adopt more inclusive strategies towards precarious workers as they are interested in the wellbeing of all workers (Durrazzi 2017).

Nevertheless, in practice 'organizing the unorganized' has proven to be a perplexing task, marked both by successes and failures. In some cases, even if the official union discourse included the representation of 'outsiders,' in reality insufficient resources have been devoted in 'organizing' activities (Keune 2013). Frequently, organizing remained a technical issue (Hyman 2007), a sort of 'toolkit' of practices (Simms and Holgate 2010), applied selectively, without a more integrated and radical rethinking of broader objectives and ways of action (Bernaciak et al. 2014). Focusing on the level of unionization and membership growth, the organizing approach has often been 'de-politicized' (Upchurch et al. 2012), while the question *"What are we organizing for?"* has been absent (Simms and Holgate 2010,157).

The above issues also include the relationship between unions and the unemployed, which is, however, more complex and problematic. This relationship can have a more institutionalized character, through the involvement of unions in unemployment schemes, in the so-called 'Ghent system' countries. There unions seem to to integrate better the defence of unemployed persons interests in their structures and strategies (Ebbinghaus et al. 2011; Faniel 2012; Lind 2009; Van Rie et al. 2011). In non-'Ghent system' countries, the relationship between unions and the unemployed is usually weaker. The inclusion of the unemployed in unions raises the question of whether or not these should be represented within existing professional unions or on a separate basis, assembling all the unemployed regardless of their professional skills. Irrespectively of the strategy adopted, in practice, top-level unions made limited efforts to organize the unemployed and were hesitant to dedicate the necessary resources, even if their bottom-level unions were more open to such strategies (Faniel 2012). Hence, even though unions are *"de facto often indispensable supports"* to unemployed mobilizations, as they are equipped with power resources and the legitimacy of which the unemployed organizations are deprived, they are *"...reluctant to openly support the mobilizations over which"* they do "..*not have total control, which claim for their specificity, occasionally their autonomy, and in any case are beyond the hard core of the working class."*. Despite their concern for the unemployed, unions focus on the struggle for employment and very often have trouble considering the real concerns of the unemployed and transforming them into demands capable of being supported by unions (Chabanet and Faniel 2012, 16). Nevertheless, as we have seen in recent years, the emergence of unemployment movements is not improbable, despite the objective and subjective obstacles (Baglioni et al. 2008; Giugni and Lorenzini 2016).

In the face of acknowledged critics towards traditional unions, and pessimist views regarding their capacity to trigger working class/ labour solidarity actions, there are signs both of union renewal and the emergence of 'alternative' forms of labour organization. Here the dominant question is to what extent, are traditional unions capable of triggering solidarity actions, embracing the most vulnerable categories of workers? Which is the 'mobilizing' cause, 'class (consciousness),' other social identities, a discourse of 'equality' and/or 'fairness' (Moore 2011)? What is the role of new forms of labour organizations? Are they the one and only response in view of the bureaucratization and the retreat of traditional unions? The answers to these questions differ.

As regards 'alternative' forms of labour organization, in recent years emphasis is given to the so-called radical political (RPU) or social movement unionism (SMU)[1], that has often been presented as a universal antidote to union decline and a 'one best way' for union revival (Taylor et al. 2011). SMU is often conceived as external or in opposition to traditional unions. Within the social movement and trade unions' literature, it has been commonplace to distinguish unions with their more bureaucratic and developed formal decision-making structures and procedures from the more spontaneous, 'participatory,' less centralized and often activist-led models offered by social movements (Diani 2017; Hyman 2015). Unions were assumed to enjoy a routine access to policy making, while social movements are mainly regarded as contestants lacking this access (Diani 2017). Thus, their relation was marked by a long history of mutual suspicion (Hyman and Gumbrell-McCormick 2017). Within this dichotomic perception, the new 'alternative,' antibureaucratic and anticapitalist forms of worker organization are considered ***to be*** more relevant for today's workers, since they: are founded on class solidarity emerging in the workplace and the community; oppose to the growth of precarious labour and reformist labour relations; encourage democratic structures; and envision a capitalism-free society. Their origins can be traced to the historical experiences of class-struggle unionism prevalent in the early twentieth century (Ness 2014).

---

[1]According to Moody (1997, 4-5): *"Social movement unionism is one that is deeply democratic, as that is the best way to mobilize the strength of numbers in order to apply maximum economic leverage. It is militant in collective bargaining in the belief that retreat anywhere only leads to more retreats – an injury to one is an injury to all. It seeks to craft bargaining demands that create more jobs and aid the whole class. It fights for power and organization in the workplace or on the job in the realization that it is there that the greatest leverage exists, when properly applied. It is political by acting independently of the retreating parties of liberalism and social democracy, whatever the relations of the union with such parties. It multiplies its political and social power by reaching out to other sectors of the class, be they other unions, neighbourhood organizations, or other social movements. It fights for all the oppressed and enhances its own power by doing so..".* Moody's definition highlights the political dimension and the class-centred action of SMU, contrary to other definitions that, in a certain way, "de-politicize" SMU, omitting questions of unions' political identity and downgrading the role of class as a transformation agent (Upchurch and Mathers 2011). Thus, the concept of RPU is being proposed. While RPU includes the characteristics of SMU, union actions are politically focused and class-centred. It is marked both by an institutional and ideological rupture from social democratic unionism and the party-union nexus (Taylor et al. 2011).

The role of traditional unions within this debate, most particularly in the light of their renewal efforts through organizing strategies is ambiguous. Some authors consider traditional unions as being incapable of triggering solidarity among workers, as they used to do. As Ness (2014, 4) points out, regarding organizing:

> "In the last twenty years, labor historians, social scientists, and union organizers have written countless pages prescribing remedies for rebuilding established unions to the perceived grandeur of the past through devoting greater resources to organizing, making contributions to union-friendly politicians, hiring young organizers from elite universities, and implementing variations of social-movement unionism directed at building alliances between communities and labor organizations. The abject failure of the efforts by traditional unions to apply these formulations for rebuilding labor has rendered these books less pertinent, to say the least, and should caution workers against relying on such prescriptions."

In fact, organizing seems to have resulted in a quite limited set of outcomes in terms of an increase of 'demographic' representativeness, inclusiveness or democracy, while sometimes it became technocratic, bureaucratic, routine focused and disengaged (Martinez Lucio et al. 2017).

To have a transformative value, organising should involve a reassessment of unions' tactics and strategies unions (Bernaciak et al. 2014), a greater sensitivity towards difference, and handling of differences in such a way so as to be able to rebuild workforce unity from diversity through the sharing of common experiences and critical moments for joint action (Martinez Lucio et al. 2017). In fact, the most crucial decision unions must take is whether they are willing to represent precarious workers (Bernaciak et al. 2014; Gumbrell-McCormick 2011).

As unions are often being considered as representatives of vested interest, they must persuade themselves and others that they are the voice of the majority (Hyman 2007). According to Darlington (2014), traditional unions still have the potential to 're-imagine' their interests and to remove from mechanistic solidarities towards more organic solidarities, integrating and promoting broader and diverse interests and identities and uniting different groups of workers. This requests the retreat from the emphasis on workplace-solidarities and the move towards class-based solidarities

> "…with class becoming a 'rallying cry' for understanding, expressing and promoting the commonality of workers' distinct interests in opposition to capitalism. In this fashion unions could assert their identity as a 'sword of justice,' campaigning over broad social and political concerns and contesting oppression, inequality and discrimination in all its forms..." Instead of "..counterposing a supposedly declining, conservative organised working class to the genuine radicalism on the streets or among 'precarious' workers as some commentators have done […], the real task is to bring together the radical energy, creativity and initiative of the young protestors on the streets with the day-to-day struggles and collective power of organised workers in their trade unions." (Darlington 2014, 131, 132)[2].

Nevertheless, if one agrees with the assumption that the legendary working-class solidarity cannot be the dominant mobilizing cause, is it possible that other mobilizing causes or frameworks of action could trigger solidarity actions among workers? In other words, could other social identities and interests motivate collective organization? (Moore 2011). Kelly's (1998, 27) mobilization theory shows that the *"sine qua non"* for collective action is a sense of injustice, meaning the belief that an event, action or situation is 'wrong' or 'illegitimate.'

For individual perceptions of injustice or illegitimacy becoming collective three other critical processes seem to be necessary: attribution, in the sense of blaming an agency (employer) which can be held responsible for their problems; social identification, in the sense of *"distinct group identity, founded on interests that are common to the group but opposed to*

---

[2]Darlington (2014) refers to the dual nature of trade unionism that has been described as a double-edged sword, where the one edge of the sword symbolizes the pursuit of vested interest of their particular members, while the other defined as a sword of justice refers to union action aiming to defend workers from the arbitrary use of managerial power, inspired by a strong sense of idealism and social purpose. This contradictory nature of trade unionism, between conflict (building resistance to capitalism) and accommodation (limiting such resistance within the context of the existing system) is not a fixed proposition in terms of an 'either/or' logic, while the relative weight of each logic is deeply affected by the situation in which the unions operate.

those of the employer and often described in everyday terms as a sense of 'them and us'"; and leadership, who is working on the transformation of a set of individuals into a collective actor (Kelly 1998, 127).

Empirical research has shown that collective identities among workers can emerge, even if these are not directly perceived in terms of working-class solidarity. According to Moore (2011), unionism can also be informed by other abstract ideologies (besides class) based on a discourse of 'equality' and/or 'fairness,' that do not, nevertheless, counterpose to the articulation of a class identity and values. The existence of political ideas and language continues to be important to the creation of identity and the emergence of consciousness.

Whereas union activism presupposes a sort of implicit class identity, factors such as gender, race or ethnicity to changing work relations also affect identity and consciousness. Nevertheless, class identity, does not necessarily imply that form of political class consciousness that is necessary to challenge a class-based society.

Thus, solidarities and collective interests can emerge and articulate "*... even in the absence of a consciously envisioned view of a future society or a 'revolutionary' objective to overthrow a capitalist social order*" (Simms and Dean 2015, 188). This coincides with Fantasias conception of cultures of solidarity, a form of class action that emerges and is expressed during industrial conflicts and actions. These moments of "*explosions of consciousness*" are not "*... "'revolutionary' in the sense that they are designed to overthrow the social order or are capable of doing so in any simple or direct way. But although workers may not be poised to make revolution, they may in certain activities express a consciousness that, though short of the will or capability to make revolution, represents a transformative associational bonding that can shape class relations in significant ways.*" (Fantasia 1988, 6, 11).

GREEK UNIONS AND WORKING-CLASS IDENTITY AND SOLIDARITY

Greek unionism has been going through a structural crisis, which has been further exacerbated during the period of the Memoranda. Most of the problems that Greek unions are facing during the crisis are related to pre-existent dysfunctions of the industrial relations system and labour movement (Kapsalis 2012).

With regard, to "class-oriented" identity within unions, during the first post- dictatorship period, conflict with the state and the existence of industrial sector unionists with a strong class-oriented identity are signs of an attempt to shape a union identity with a very strong class dimension (Bithymitris and Kotsonopoulos 2018). That period was marked by the increase of labour militancy and workers' protest that lasted until the end of the '70's. During'80's unions were marked by the weakening of class identity and the transition to a social-rights identity, where unions focused on shaping social policies. The newly formed social democratic party (PASOK) managed to 'colonize' unions, taking the lead from the communist left (Kanellopoulos 2013). The moderation of the class-political role is consolidated during the 'Europeanization' period, where prevails an approach of 'social consent' and the strengthening of unions' economic functions (Bithymitris and Kotsonopoulos 2018).

Union density has been experiencing a decline, from approximately 37.1% in 1992 to 25.4% in 2011, largely due to a representation crisis and to a distrust and lack of confidence in the existing trade union 'elites' and modus operandi (Kapsalis 2012; Kretsos 2011a, b, 2012). Distrust towards the official unions was linked to a generalized feeling that dependencies and political interests were often placed above the claims and interests of the workers. In addition, the under-representation of trade unions in the private sector and their over-representation in public enterprises and the public sector created the feeling that Greek trade unionism has been a unionism of the 'more protected' workers. Lastly, official unions could be characterized as an emblematic example of 'bureaucratic unionism.' The above factors resulted to 'desyndicalization,' 'asyndicalization' (Dufour and Hege 2010) or even 'countersyndicalization' processes.

Despite evident signs of crisis, no strategic effort of renewal has taken place, and for several reasons. A first set of reasons relates to the available resources (political, financial and institutional). A second relates to objective obstacles, such as weak union presence or even total absence of unions in SMEs and the high number of undeclared workers. Nevertheless, in spite of available resources or 'objective obstacles,' the non-investment in organizing also seems to be a matter of choices and uneven positions towards precarious workers and the unemployed. In reality, organizing and mobilizing the non-unionized workers did not seem crucial and remained a low-priority issue for official unions (Kretsos and Vogiatzogou 2015), which have often adopted an attitude of exclusion towards precarious workers (Kornelakis and Voskeritsian 2018). Trying to overcome the above tendencies, some segments of the labour movement founded in 1999 the All-Workers Militant Front (PAME). PAME opposes the consensual, governmental and capital-friendly goals of GSEE. Officially, according to its constitution, PAME is *"an open, wide, uniting, democratic trade-union front of employees and workers, seeking to have in its lines the most vibrant, fighting forces of the working trade-union movement."* In practice, without being formally linked to the Greek Communist Party (KKE), it mainly coordinates unions controlled by KKE members and leaders. Its strength derives mainly from workers in the private sector (Tsakatika and Eleftheriou 2013, 88) and its foundation is being considered to be important for the maintaining of class traditions within the labour movement throughout the decade of 2000 (and in midst crisis) (Bithymitris and Kotsonopoulos 2018).

Additionally, since the late 1990s, and mainly during the 2000s, unionization procedures of precarious workers in workplaces where flexible work predominated, and/or at the sectoral level, were launched in various sectors. In 2009, primary unions based in Athens founded the Primary Unions' Coordination, as an alternative to the coordination structure of GSEE (Kretsos and Vogiatzoglou 2015; Vogiatzoglou 2014). The Coordination managed to unionize workers who work under precarious conditions and it opposes both the 'governmental' syndicalism of GSEE and

ADEDY and the partisan-controlled syndicalism of PAME. The unions in question are characterised by a strong presence of rank-and-file, left-wing labour activists and bear all the characteristics of social movement unionism (Kretsos 2011a, b). They engage in traditional social movement activities (such as demonstrations and solidarity campaigns) and collaborate with non-labour social movement organisations. Since they operated in workplaces comprising both precarious and non-precarious workers, they chose to relate their work-related claims with a more general setting of working-class struggles (Mattoni and Vogiatzoglou 2014). Regarding their allies, they are much more willing to collaborate with other precarious workers' unions or non-labour social movement organisations, than with official unions, their position towards top-level unions is complex and not unanimous. Generally, they are suspicious towards union elites and bureaucracy. In practice however, some of them participate institutionally in official unions structures and apparatuses, even if their leaders oppose to the top-level confederations' strategies and modus operandi (Kretsos and Vogiatzoglou 2015; Vogiatzoglou 2014).

The recent fiscal crisis, as well as the austerity measures issued in the framework of the Memoranda since 2010, radically changed the landscape for unions. With regard to 'official' trade unions, the crisis constituted a major challenge, while it also brought to light the pre-existing problems. However, even though union officials are aware of the new challenges, they hesitate to proceed to drastic structural changes (Vogiatzoglou 2014). In the middle of the crisis, and lacking a tradition of organizing strategies, official unions have mainly invested in traditional collective bargaining actions and strikes. Nevertheless, despite the extended strike action, with *"...ongoing deunionisation, alienation, bureaucratisation, and subordination to the state's and employers 'will, as well as a gradual loss of the class-based approach to politics [...] it has been difficult for many workers to limit the austerity measures imposed."* (Gialis and Herod 2014, 142). Moreover, not all sectors mobilized equally. The threat of job lossseems to have been the main driving force of the mobilizations, in addition to accumulated organizational resources (number of workers implicated), working-class oriented identity of the union implicated or dominant in the sector/workplace, political opportunities (in terms of employment security) and militant leadership[3] (Papanikolopoulos 2016). Nevertheless, the focus on general strikes and lobbying strategies aiming at influencing major political parties, had limited effects in improving the working situation for the increasingly precarious workforce (Kretsos and Vogiatzogou 2015, 220). In fact, the positions and the rights of the unemployed and those working under precarious conditions were generally not taken into consideration by union confederations, while low levels of unionization in the private sector can be considered to be the Achilles' heel for strike action (Vatikiotis and Nikolakaki 2013).

With regard to precarious workers' unions and alternatives forms of workers organization, during crisis new grassroots unions and initiatives emerged, strongly participating in all anti-austerity protests (Mattonni and Vogiatzoglou 2014; Vogiatzoglou 2014). As research has shown, these labour organizations share a strong working class-oriented identity, discourse and framework of action. As such, they also have a broad perception of solidarity (as in terms of working-class solidarity), and their activity aims not only at protecting and advancing their sectoral and/or professional interests. They understand:

> "Labour solidarity not so much as a solidarity towards the most vulnerable sections of the labour market, but more as a common struggle of the working class, where everyone holds an equal position within trade unions, whether working in the public or private sector, in permanent full-time employment conditions or in contingent work or being unemployed." (Karakioulafis and Kanellopoulos 2018, 139).

However, practice has shown that the unions are facing a series of objective limitations regarding their capacity to act and intervene effectively, most particularly during the crisis period. In fact, economic crisis seems to have had a twofold impact on the activity of precarious workers' unions. On the one hand, the high unemployment rates in some of

---

[3]A typical example of the role of working-class oriented identity of the union and militant leadership is the case of the strike of steelworkers at Hellenic Halyvourgia in 2011-2012, that was the longest strike to take place in post-dictatorial Greece (Bithymitris 2016).

the sectors where these unions intervene, also seem to have a negative effect on unionization, since trade union membership has been reduced, while many of the remaining members became inactive. Additionally, they had a difficulty in providing practical help to the rising number of the unemployed and precarious workers. Moreover, operating mainly in specific workplaces and sectors, they face difficulties in expanding their scope, while their repertoire of action is largely centred on workplace-based activities and their outward-looking actions are limited to participation in protests and strikes. Thus, despite their acknowledged willingness to support labour solidarity actions, they lack the necessary infrastructural, material and political resources to offer practical help, and to press towards the inclusion of precarious and unemployed workers in the system of interest representation and access to labour market regulatory structures. On the other hand, the crisis-related problems also triggered solidarity, since some of these unions were created during and because of the crisis in order to help precarious workers and the unemployed (Karakioulafis and Kanellopoulos 2018; Kretsos and Vogiatzoglou 2015). Additionally, the economic crisis seems to have had a stimulating effect on working- class consciousness and solidarity and even among unions that lost members, this cognitive outcome is considered to be very important (Karakioulafis and Kanellopoulos 2018).

CONCLUSION

The last decades, unions, as it is generally acknowledged, are facing both a crisis of identity, as well as a crisis of solidarity related to the growing divisions within the workforce. At the same time, the capacity and willingness of union in protecting the most vulnerable segments of the workforce has seriously been questioned, since traditional unions often tended to adopt strategies of exclusion and not ones of inclusion, based on a 'working-class' solidarity approach. Even though 'organizing the unorganized; became the focal point for unions, in practice this has proven to be a perplexing task, while the relevant initiatives often lacked a consideration of the broader question of building and maintaining union and working-class solidarity. The aforementioned issues also concern the relationship between unions and unemployed, which is, however, more problematic, since unions, despite their openly declared concern for the unemployed, continue to focus on the struggle for employment and very often have difficulties in transforming unemployed claims in demands capable of being supported by unions. In the face of the above manifold crisis, the assessments as to traditional unions' capacity to trigger working class/ labour solidarity actions differ. Optimist commentators consider that traditional unions still have the potential to integrate and promote broader and diverse interests and identities and unite different groups of workers, if they built solidarities either on a working class-based approach or based on alternative collective identities. Pessimists consider traditional unions to be incapable of triggering solidarity among workers, as they used to do, and consider new alternative labour organizations and movements as more apt to unionize and mobilize workers, and most particularly those who work under precarious conditions.

Greek unions are not the exception from these general tendencies and debates. Within top-level traditional unions 'working-class' oriented identities seem to be in decline, while the unions in question have difficulties in convincing that they are the representatives of workers as a whole and in practice, their solidarity to the weakest and most vulnerable segments of the labour force remains very abstract. Following, often, an 'insider-outsider' approach, their main strategy and position towards the unemployed and/or precarious workers is that of exclusion.

Nevertheless, class-oriented identities are very existent in the Greek unionism but remain active both within precarious workers unions, marked by a left-wing political orientation and the presence of rank-and-fil activists, as well as within unions close to PAME. Even though, the recent financial crisis, as a critical moment, could constitute the opportunity for unions to renew and turn their attention towards precarious workers and the unemployed, this has not been the case. Despite intense strike action, mainly during the first years of the crisis, and the moments of 'explosion of class consciousness' during strike activity, traditional top-level unions remain mainly 'guardians' of vested interests.

References

Baglioni, Simone, Britta Baumgarten, Didier Chabanet, and Christian Lahusen. 2008. "Transcending marginalization: The mobilization of the unemployed in France, Germany, and Italy in a comparative perspective." *Mobilization* 13.3: 323-335.

Bernaciak, Magdalena, Rebecca Gumbrell-McCormick, and Richard Hyman. 2014. *European trade unionism: from crisis to renewal?*. Brussels: ETUI.

Bithymitris, Giorgos. 2016. "Union militancy during economic hardship: The strike at the Greek steel company "Hellenic Halyvourgia." *Employee relations* 38: 373-389.

Μπιθυμήτρης, Γιώργος και Λουδοβίκος Κωτσονόπουλος. 2018. "Μετασχηματισμοί του ελληνικού συνδικαλιστικού κινήματος από τη μεταπολίτευση μέχρι την κρίση: συνέχειες και ρήξεις." Ελληνική Επιθεώρηση Πολιτικής Επιστήμης 44: 99-122 [Bithymitris, Giorgos and Loudovikos Kotsonopoulos. 2018. "Transformation of the Greek trade union movement since the Metapolitefsi up until the crisis: continuities and ruptures." *Greek review of Political Science* 44: 99-122].

Chabanet, Didier, and Jean Faniel. 2012. "Introduction: The mobilization of the unemployed in a comparative perspective." In *The Mobilization of the Unemployed in Europ*e, edited by Didier Chabanet and Jean Faniel, 1-27. New York: Palgrave Macmillan.

d'Art, Daryl and Thomas Turner. 2002. "The Decline of Worker Solidarity and the End of Collectivism? *Economic and Industrial Democracy* 23: 7 – 34.

Darlington, Ralph. 2014. "The Role of Trade Unions in Building Resistance: Theoretical, Historical and Comparative Perspectives" In *Workers and Labour in a Globalised Capitalism*, edited by Maurizio Atzeni, 111-138. Basingstoke: Palgrave Macmillan.

Dufour, Christian, and Adelheid Hege. 2010. "Légitimité des acteurs collectifs et renouveau syndical." La Revue de l'IRES 2: 67-85. [Dufour, Christian, and Adelheid Hege. 2010. "Legitimacy of collective actors and union renewal." IRES Review 2: 67-85.] Durazzi, Niccolo. 2017. "Inclusive unions in a dualized labour market? The challenge of organizing labour market policy and social protection for labour market outsiders." *Social Policy & Administration* 51: 265-285.

Ebbinghaus, Bernhard, Claudia Göbel, and Sebastian Koos. 2011. "Social capital,'Ghent'and workplace contexts matter: Comparing union membership in Europe." *European Journal of Industrial Relations* 17: 107-124.

Faniel, Jean. 2012. "Trade Unions and the Unemployed: Towards a Dialectical Approach" *Interface*. 4: 130-157.

Fantasia, Rick. 1998. *Cultures of solidarity*. Berkeley: University of California Press.

Gialis, Stelios, and Andrew Herod. 2014. "Of steel and strawberries: Greek workers struggle against informal and flexible working arrangements during the crisis." *Geoforum* 57: 138-149.

Giugni, Marco, and Jasmine Lorenzini. 2016. "Quiescent or invisible?: precarious and unemployed movements in Europe." In *Social Movement Studies in Europe: The State of the Art*, edited by Olivier Fillieule and Guya Accornero, 102-117. New York: Berghan Books.

Gumbrell-McCormick, Rebecca. 2011. "European trade unions and 'atypical' workers." *Industrial Relations Journal.*, 42: 293-310.

Gumbrell-McCormick, Rebecca and Richard Hyman. 2015. "International trade union solidarity and the impact of the crisis" *European Policy Analysis* 1: 1-16.

Heckscher, Charles, and John McCarthy. 2014. "Transient Solidarities: Commitment and Collective Action in Post-Industrial Societies." *British Journal of Industrial Relations* 52: 627-657.

Heery, Edmund. 2005. "Sources of change in trade unions." *Work, employment and society* 19: 91-106.

Heery, Edmund. 2009. "Trade Unions and Contingent Labour: Scale and Method." *Cambridge Journal of Regions*, Economy and Society 2: 429–442.

Hobsbawm, Eric. 1978. "The Forward March of Labour Halted?" *Marxism Today*, September 279-286. Available at: http://banmarchive.org.uk/collections/mt/pdf/78_09_hobsbawm.pdf.

Hyman, Richard. 1989. *Political Economy of Industrial Relations: Theory and Practice in a Cold Climate*. Basingstoke: Mc Millan.

Hyman, Richard. 1992. "Trade unions and the disaggregation of the working class." In *The future of labour movements, edited by Marino Regini,* 150-168. London: Sage.

Hyman, Richard. 1999. "Imagined Solidarities: Can Trade Unions Resist Globalization?" In *Globalization and Labour Relations*, edited by Peter Leisink, 94-115. Cheltenham: Edward Elgar.

Hyman, Richard. 2001. *Understanding European trade unionism: between market, class and society*. London: Sage.

Hyman, Richard. 2007. "How can trade unions act strategically?" *Transfer* 13:193-210.

Hyman, Richard. 2015. Austeritarianism in Europe: what options for resistance?" In *Social policy in the European Union: state of play,* edited by David Natali and Bart Vanhercke, 97-126. Brussels: ETUI.

Hyman, Richard, and Rebecca Gumbrell-McCormick. 2017. "Resisting labour market insecurity: old and new actors, rivals or allies?." *Journal of Industrial Relations* 59: 538-561.

Kanellopoulos, Kostas. 2013. "Making the World Working Class." *10th Annual Conference of Historical Materialism SOAS,* London November 7-10, 2013.

Καψάλης, Αποστόλης. 2012. "Τα ελληνικά συνδικάτα στο περιβάλλον της οικονομικής ύφεσης και κρίσης" [Kapsalis, Apostolis. 2012. "*Greek Trade Unions in an Era of Economic Recession and Crisis*."] Available at http://rosalux.gr/sites/default/files/kapsalis_greekfinal_0.pdf.

Karakioulafis, Christina and Kostas Kanellopoulos, K. 2018. "Triggering Solidarity Actions towards Contingent Workers and the Unemployed. The Point of View of Grassroots Trade Unionists and Labour Activists." *PArtecipazione e COnflitto*, 11: 121-144.

Kelly, John. 1998. *Rethinking industrial relations: Mobilisation, collectivism and long waves*. London: Routledge.

Keune, Maarten. 2013. "Trade union responses to precarious work in seven European countries" *International Journal of Labour Research*, 5: 59–78.

Kornelakis, Andreas, and Horen Voskeritsian. 2018. "Getting together or breaking apart? Trade union strategies, restructuring and contingent workers in Southern Europe." *Economic and Industrial Democracy* 39: 357-375.

Kretsos, Lefteris, and Markos Vogiatzoglou. 2015. "Lost in the Ocean of Deregulation?: The Greek Labour Movement in a Time of Crisis." *Relations industrielles* 70: 218-239.

Kretsos, Lefteris. 2011a. "Union Responses to the Rise of Precarious Youth Employment in Greece." *Industrial Relations Journal*, 42: 453–472.

Kretsos, Lefteris. 2011b. "Grassroots Unionism in the Context of Economic Crisis in Greece." *Labor History*, 52: 265-286.

Kretsos, Lefteris. 2012. "Greece's Neoliberal Experiment and Working Class Resistance." *Working USA, 15*: 517–527.

Lind, Jens. 2009. "The end of the Ghent system as trade union recruitment machinery?." *Industrial Relations Journal* 40: 510-523.

Lehndorff, S., Dribbusch, H., & Schulten, T. (Eds.). (2017). *Rough Waters: European Trade Unions in a Time of Crises.* European Trade Union Institute (ETUI).

Lévesque, Christian, Gregor Murray, and Stéphane Le Queux. 1998. "Transformations sociales et identités syndicales: l'institution syndicale à l'épreuve de la différenciation sociale contemporaine." Sociologie et sociétés 30: 131-154. [Lévesque, Christian, Gregor Murray, and Stéphane Le Queux. 1998. "Social transformations and trade unions' identities: trade union institution confronting contemporary social differentiation." *Sociology and Societies* 30: 131-154.]

Lévesque, Christian, and Gregor Murray. 2010. "Understanding union power: resources and capabilities for renewing union capacity." *Transfer* 16: 333-350.

Lockwood, David. 1958. *The blackcoated worker: a study in class consciousness.* London: Allen and Unwin.

Mann, Michael. 1973. *Consciousness and action among the Western working class*. London: MacMillan.

Martínez Lucio, Miguel, Stefania Marino, and Heather Connolly. 2017. "Organising as a strategy to reach precarious and marginalised workers. A review of debates on the role of the political dimension and the dilemmas of representation and solidarity." *Transfer,* 23: 31-46.

Mattoni, Alice, and Markos Vogiatzoglou. 2014. "Italy and Greece, before and after the crisis: Between mobilization and resistance against precarity." *Quaderni* 84: 57-71.

Moody, Kim. 1997. Workers in a Lean World: Unions in the International Economy. London: Verso Books.

Moore, Sian. 2014. *New trade union activism: Class consciousness or social identity?*. Basingstoke: McMillan.

Ness, Immanuel. 2014. "Introduction" In *New Forms of Worker Organization: The Syndicalist and Autonomist Restoration of Class-Struggle Unionism*, edited by Immanuel Ness and Staughton Lynd, 1-17. Oakland: PM Press.

Richards, Andrew. 1995. *Down But Not Out: Labour movements in late industrial societies*. Estudio/Working Paper 1997/112. Madrid: Instituto Juan March de Estudios e Investigaciones. Available at: http://citeseerx.ist.psu.edu/viewdoc/download?doi=10.1.1.604.3365&rep=rep1&type=pdf.

Richards, Andrew. 2018. "The crisis of union representation." In *Can Class Still Unite?,* edited by Guy Van Gyes, Hans De Witte, Patrick Pasture, 13-36. London: Routledge.

Richards, Andrew, and Javier G. Polavieja. 1997. "*Trade unions, unemployment and working class fragmentation in Spain*." Estudio/Working Paper 1997/112. Madrid: Instituto Juan March de Estudios e Investigaciones. Available at: http://epub.sub.uni-hamburg.de/epub/volltexte/2008/1911/pdf/1997_112.pdf.

Simms, Melanie (2011). "*Trade union responses to precarious work: UK report*." BARSORI Report. Available at: http://www.uva-aias.net/uploaded_files/regular/BARSORIReportUK.pdf.

Simms, Melanie, and Jane Holgate. 2010. "*Organising for what? Where is the debate on the politics of organising?.*" Work, Employment and Society 24: 157-168.

Simms, Melanie, and Deborah Dean. 2015. "Mobilising contingent workers: An analysis of two successful cases." *Economic and Industrial Democracy* 36: 173-190.

Taylor, Graham, Andrew Mathers, and Martin Upchurch. 2011. "Beyond the chains that bind: the political crisis of unions in Western Europe." *Labor History* 52: 287-305.

Tsakatika, Myrto, and Costas Eleftheriou. 2013. "The radical left's turn towards civil society in Greece: one strategy, two paths." *South European Society and Politics* 18: 81-99.

Turner, Lowell, and Richard Hurd. 2001. "Building social movement unionism." In *Rekindling the movement: Labor's quest for relevance in the twenty-first century*, edited by Lowell Turner, Harry Katz and Richard Hurd, 9-26. Ithaca, NY: Cornell University Press.

Upchurch, Martin, Richard Croucher, and Matt Flynn. 2012. "Political congruence and trade union renewal." *Work, employment and society* 26: 857-868.

Van Rie, Tim, Ive Marx, and Jeroen Horemans. 2011. "Ghent revisited: Unemployment insurance and union membership in Belgium and the Nordic countries." Eur*opean Journal of Industrial Relations* 17: 125-139.

Vatikiotis, Leonidas, and Maria Nikolakaki. 2013. "*Resistance in Greece.*" In Immiseration capitalism and education: Austerity, resistance and revolt, edited by Dave Hill. Brighton: Institute for Education Policy Studies.

Vogiatzoglou, Markos. 2014. "Trade Unions in Greece: Protest and Social Movements in the Context of Austerity Politics." *WSI-Mitteilungen* 5: 361-368.

Zoll, Rainer. 1998. "Le défi de la solidarité organique: avons-nous besoin de nouvelles institutions pour préserver la cohésion sociale?." Sociologie et sociétés 30: 1-10. [Zoll, Rainer. 1998. "The challenge of organic solidarity: do we need new institutions in order to preserve social cohesion?." *Sociology and Societies* 30: 1-10].

In: Emotions, Temporalities … ISBN: 978-1-53616-203-5
Editors: M. Christodoulou et al.

Chapter 7

THE SOCIAL STRATIFICATION OF FOREIGN LABOUR FORCE IN GREECE

Spyros Sakellaropoulos*
Department of Social Policy, Panteion University, Athens, Greece

ABSTRACT

Greece, especially after the fall of so-called "existing socialism," has been transformed into a recipient country for immigrants. An examination, employing Marxist methodology, is undertaken of the social stratification of foreign workers in Greece before (2001) and during (2017) the crisis. The changes are highlighted and their causes investigated. In addition to this, a comparison is made between the social stratification of the country's total workforce and that of the foreign workers (2017), and an interpretation offered of the differences that emerge. The main parts of the article concern a) an analytic presentation regarding both the demographic – sociographic data and the theoretical framework, b) an analysis of the social stratification of the foreign labour force in Greece and, finally c) a comparison between the social stratification between immigrants and the rest of the workforce.

* Corresponding Author's Email: sakellaropouloss@gmail.com.

Keywords: social stratification, immigrants, Greece, social classes, social disparities

1. Introduction

Greece is a country that for many years (1870-1970) was characterized by significant outward flows of labour. There has nevertheless been a limited inflow of foreign workers dating back to the establishment of the Greek state when foreign nationals began to be employed either as staff in embassies or as specialized technical personnel in a number of different, principally foreign, enterprises. In the formal sense of the term, Greek subjects of the Ottoman Empire living and working in metropolitan Greece could be added to this number.

But the first time that workers at a low level in the labour hierarchy came to Greece was in the 1970s. They were for the most part of Pakistani origin because a relevant agreement between Greece and Pakistan was signed for them to work initially in the Skaramangas shipyards, and they were employed primarily in construction. They were followed in the 1980s by Filipino nationals engaged as home helps.

After the fall of existing socialism citizens of former socialist countries very soon started coming to Greece, first and foremost Albanians, but also Turks and Egyptians.

The following are the reasons why foreign workers are judged to have chosen Greece as a place to settle:

- A number of foreigners use the country as an intermediate stage on their way to a more economically developed European country. This is assisted by the fact that Greece has both land and sea borders and is a crossroads between two continents (Georgarakis 2009, 37).
- The fact that Greece was already a member of the then EEC in the 1980s and since 2002 has been a member of the European Monetary Union has in itself been conducive to attracting immigrants.

- The morphology of the Greek economy itself possesses peculiarities generating key prerequisites for the absorption of a low-skilled workforce: a large number of small and medium-sized enterprises[1], a broad agricultural sector, a developed illegal economy. (Georgarakis 2009, 37-38).

With the exception of a small number of foreign workers who, as in the period prior to the 1970s, were employed in positions requiring occupational skills and a high level of education (working in subsidiaries of multinational companies, diplomatic staff, employees of international organizations), the vast majority of foreigners in 1991 worked in construction (primarily Albanians, Poles, Turks) in the metals sector (Egyptians, Pakistanis) in cleaning and the food industry (Thais, Poles, Africans), but also in other sectors such as trade, health, manual work in industry, etc. (Katsoridas 1996, 6). Three decades later, above and beyond the Albanians who are employed in almost all sectors of the economy, accounting for about 50% of the total number of foreign workers (see below), the relevant 2013 study of the Ministry of the Interior indicated that there are numerous migrant women from Bulgaria, the Philippines, Russia, The Ukraine, Moldova, and Georgia, working as domestic helps, Egyptians employed in the fishing and textile industries, Pakistanis engaged in manufacturing, construction and services, and Indians working in agriculture and stockbreeding (General Secretariat of Population 2013, 33-35).

2. Some Demographic – Sociographic Data

Data from the National Statistical Authority shows that the number of foreigners in the population as a whole rose sharply between 1971 and 2011,

[1]It is characteristic that in 2006 81.1% of foreign workers were employed in a company with up to nine people working in it whereas the corresponding percentage for Greeks was 61.3%. Likewise only 2.5% of foreigners worked in companies employing over 50 wage-earners whereas the proportion for Greeks came to 10.9% (Zografakis, Kontis and Mitrakos 2009, 84).

from 92,568 people in 1971 (1.05% of the total population) to 171,424 in 1981 (1.76% of the total population), to 797,093 people in 2001 (6.97% of the total permanent population) and from there to 911,029 people in 2011 (8.43% of the total permanent population) (Kapsalis 2018, 39).

This is undoubtedly a significant change, highlighting Greece as a host country for immigration, as opposed to its past history, when tens of thousands of Greeks left every year for the US, Germany, Canada, Belgium and other countries. The fact that there is a proportionally large concentration of foreigners in Greece is also apparent from the comparative data (2005) from the Centre of Research and Analysis of Migration where Greece, with 7.3%, is fifth among twenty European countries in the percentage of foreigners in the population, Switzerland coming first with 19.3% followed by Germany with 8.9%, Austria also with 8.9% and Belgium with 8.4% (Robolis 2007, 61).

As for national origins, in 2011 the highest proportion, 52.7%, of the foreigners living in Greece had Albanian citizenship, 8.3% Bulgarian, 5.1% Romanian, followed by 3.7% Pakistani and 3% Georgian. In the second quarter of 2017 the distribution of aliens by economic activity was 21.4% in accommodation and catering, 14.3% in trade, 13.3% in agriculture, 12.8% in construction and 12% in processing (Kapsalis 2018: 84-85).

In the field of individual occupations, in 2008 56% of non-national males were skilled workers, 20.6% unskilled workers, 8.0% operators of fixed industrial installations and machine operators and 8.0% employees in the service sector and sales. Correspondingly, 58% of female foreign workers were unskilled workers, and 26.9% employed in small-scale sales and provision of services (Kavounidis 2012, 90).

Last, but not least, in terms of net monthly earnings of foreign workers in 2008, 32.8% earned up to € 750- or less than the then lowest salary of € 761, 35.3% earned between € 751 and €1,000 and only 12.9% received over € 1,000. Moreover, 14.5% did not respond to the relevant question included in the survey by the Greek statistical authority (Kavounidis 2012, 97).

3. Theoretical Framework

Within the framework of an article focused on the stratification of the foreign workers in Greece it is not possible to refer extensively to theoretical issues of social class theory, which we have analyzed in detail in other work (Sakellaropoulos, 2014). For this reason I will simply mention certain aspects of our theoretical findings, choosing not to embark on more exhaustive discussion, whether inside or outside the Marxist schema.[2]

In my opinion, Lenin's definition is as pertinent as ever in clarifying the multifaceted problem of defining social classes: 'Classes are large groups of people which differ from each other by the place they occupy in a historically determined system of social production, by their relation (in most cases fixed and formulated in law) to the means of production, by their role in the social organization of labour, and, consequently, by the mode of acquisition and the dimension of the share of social wealth of which they dispose' (Lenin 1977, 13). It might be noted that in Lenin's definition there is a co-articulation of three criteria: a) position in relation to the means of production, b) position in the social division of labour, c) means of acquisition of – and level of – income (Bensaid 1995, 203).

The common denominator traversing these three criteria in Lenin's definition is the phenomenon of exploitation. The possessor of the means of production exploits the person who possesses only labour power, because the possessor pays the labourer less than the value of the work. However, in order for this social relation, derived from the possession of capital, to be reproduced (after all, this is why Marx claimed that capital is primarily a social relation), some structural characteristics must be shaped in the production process that will facilitate circulation of capital and create the hierarchical structures necessary for working discipline to become attainable.

Therefore, what is elaborated is an internally intricate but also externally pyramidal organization of production wherein, for the relations of

---

[2]For a recent comprehensive presentation of the basic content of the Marxian and Marxist problematic on the question of social classes, see Atkinson, 2015, 19-39.

exploitation to be implemented, relations of domination are also absolutely essential. In this sense, exploitation and, secondly, relations of domination, especially the way they are articulated into a social structure (Croix 1984, 94), are the agents in the formation and reproduction of social classes.

The conclusion is that the foundations of prevailing social arrangements are situated in the existence of relations of exploitation and domination, yet membership in a particular class depends firstly on who owns the means of production and secondly on each person's position in the division of labour and the amount of social wealth a person extracts.

Nevertheless, it must be made clear that the economic element (relation to the means of production, level of income, etc.) is the most important and decisive, albeit not the only, element. The 'position occupied by individuals' may be determined by reference to both the political and the ideological elements that contribute to shaping the relations of domination. Thus the top echelon of the state bureaucracy: members of government, high-ranking military personnel, etc., belong, by virtue of their position in the machinery of power, to the bourgeois class.

The intervention of capital and the state in maintaining and reproducing relations of exploitation is continuous and embraces all levels of social activity. The reason for this is that capital does not only exploit workers economically but also exercises power over their functioning in the workplace, from the moment that it determines what and how they will produce. At the same time, through the Ideological Apparatus of the State,[3] it integrates them ideologically as the workers accept the terms of their political and economic exploitation as the 'natural' result of the exchange of 'wage' and 'labour power' equivalents. To put it differently, the framework of the relations of exploitation is reproduced by the political and ideological mechanisms functioning, within which capitalist power is also reproduced, not through the realization of surplus value but through reproduction of managerial and executive labour.

It should be stressed that classification of the various agents in social relations is no static, cerebral process. On the contrary, social classes are

---

[3]For the importance of the role of the Ideological State Apparatus see Althusser, 1976.

defined through an antagonistic relation: the class struggle (Balibar 1985, 174), which determines the movement of history. This means that class struggle results in transformations in the positions of social categories and social strata in such a way that there is no one-to-one correspondence between assigned social class and membership in a particular professional category. Nothing is exempt from change (Aronowitz 2002, 56).

With these general definitions as our starting point, we proceed to make some conclusions about the most significant characteristics of the bourgeois class: it is the class that directs the capitalist productive process, and it always, with a view to its own interests, defines the context and the hierarchies of the social praxis dominated by capital (Bihr 1989, 88-89). Its position is based on owning the means of production and subjecting society to its power. At a level of high abstraction, its members are defined as non-productive exploiters/possessors/extractors of surplus labour-cum-organisers of the mechanisms of domination (Johnson 1977, 203).

The working class is deprived of possessing the means of production, but it performs all those practices that are aimed at furthering reproduction of capital and reinforcing social power. It neither possesses control of, nor is able to influence the context of its labour. It simply plays an executive role within the social division of labour (Bihr 1989, 90). In a more abstract away we could define the working class as consisting of exploited/non-possessors/producers/wage-earners enduring the constraints imposed by the mechanism of domination (Johnson 1977, 202-203).

Nevertheless, the existence of the two basic classes of the capitalist mode of production does not mean that there are not other social classes in a society. Only at a high level of abstraction – that of the mode of production – is it possible to speak of only two classes. At the national social formations level, the number of classes is greater precisely because the different historical development of each formation includes more modes of production but also 'a) because there are also more modes of production, that is to say forms of organization of the productive process, which are not based on the appropriation of surplus labour, on exploitation, and b) because some of the class functions of the dominant class are normally delegated to social groups that are not part of the dominant class (are not owners of the means of production)' (Milios 2002, 64). This social class we name the petit bourgeoisie occupies, in the active sense of the term, a position between the working class and the bourgeoisie.

The basic characteristic of members of the petit bourgeoisie is that their income is greater than what is necessary for reproduction of their labour power, irrespective of how this is achieved. Sometimes it is realized through the appropriation of surplus value and sometimes through earnings that exceed the cost of reproduction of their labour power. Above and beyond that a second characteristic is that they are not exclusively subjected to domination by other classes. The traditional petit bourgeoisie exerts power over the workers it employs; the new salaried petit bourgeoisie is subject to the power of capital but *also* exerts power over the working class, whereas the self-employed (who are also to be included in the new petit bourgeoisie) neither exert power nor are subjected to it.

Further refining this line of thought we could argue that the petit bourgeoisie is divisible into the traditional petit bourgeoisie and the new petit bourgeoisie. The traditional petit bourgeoisie includes owners of small manufacturing companies, small family businesses and small commercial enterprises not involved with extended reproduction of capital (that is to say employing up to nine workers).[4] The new petit bourgeoisie is comprised of all those who work as either self-employed professionals or salaried employees engaged in supervising and organizing the work system, realizing surplus value, overseeing the cohesiveness of capitalist operations or, finally, legitimizing the terms of reproduction of existing social relations.

Nevertheless, if the theoretical approach to social stratification is to be comprehensive, it is necessary to refer to cross-class social categories, such as farmers, civil servants and intellectuals, besides the basic class divisions and the petit bourgeoisie.

---

[4]For why more than nine workers are needed for there to be extended reproduction of capital, see Sakellaropoulos 2001, 170.

Farmers fall into the above category, because despite being involved in land cultivation, they differ from each other depending on the expanse of the land they cultivate and the extent to which they employ land laborers.

As regards the *agricultural strata* and small landowners, i.e., those who, in Greece, are proprietors of up to 50 acres, they are the less affluent layers of rural society and do not employ wage labour. Correspondingly, proprietors who make limited use of wage labour in the cultivation of their land, those who in Greece own between fifty and two hundred acres and are engaged in simple reproduction of their capital (Panitisidis 1992) belong to the intermediate rural strata, whereas those who employ a wide range of salaried employees, those who in Greece are proprietors of more than 200 acres, which enables them to proceed with extended reproduction of capital, belong to the wealthy rural strata.

Another stratum that is distinctive for its cross-class characteristics is that of the civil servants, because a civil servant may be employed in very different sectors. A significant sector employed in public enterprises such as processing, energy and water supply, communications, transport and banks, are productive working people (Meiksins 1986, 17), because they are paid less than the value of their work when they exchange their labour power for capital. In that sense individuals in this category are *both* productive workers and people exploited by the collective capitalist and to be included in the working class.

On the other hand people working in education, in cases where education is provided free, and administrative personnel in the various public bodies and ministries are not productive workers but, with the exception of senior and middle-ranking officials in the ministries, the armed forces, university professors and civil servants who are members of the new petit bourgeoisie (engineers, lawyers, doctors) and work in the public sector, belong to the working class for the following reasons:

1) They do not own their means of production.
2) Their surplus labour is subject to extraction.

3) They perform the function of the collective worker (Carchedi 1977, 134).
4) They are remunerated with a salary which is determined by state income policy (Lytras, 1993, 98), which is equal to the value of their labour power, because it correlates directly with salaries in the private sector (Bouvier, Ajam and Mury, 1963, 73) which tend not to rise above the level for reproducing their labour power.

Therefore, civil servants as a collectivity, united essentially by the institution of tenure, are a cross-class entity. The great majority can be classified as working class; the middle-ranking officials in the ministries, public enterprises and the military, and university teachers belong to the petit bourgeoisie, and the heads of administration (political, military, academic) and the managers of state-owned companies belong to the bourgeoisie by virtue of the dominant position they occupy within the collective capitalist known as the State.

Another category of individuals not belonging to a specific social class are the intellectuals. This is not a professional category but a social layer, a large number of which are salary earners. Gramsci, who considered the question in depth, regarded the action of intellectuals as confined to the realm of the superstructure and pertaining to both the 'private sphere' and 'political society'.

Those who are in the private sphere are concerned primarily with the functioning of their hegemony, and in the latter are concerned with the management of their direct domination (Gramsci 1972, 62). There is an internal gradation to their activity. The highest rung is occupied by individuals who have undertaken the formulation, organization and systematization of the dominant ideology (Gramsci 1972, 63) and who belong to the bourgeoisie. The lower levels include executive officers whose concern is the generation and promotion of consent and discipline and who are to be included in the petit bourgeoisie.

Workers who contribute intellectual labour constitute a separate category. They produce surplus labour/value for their employers (e.g., educators in the private sector).

These 'intellectual workers', from whom surplus labour/value is extracted, belong to the working class. They do not count as 'intellectuals' because they are charged not with planning and organizing consent but rather with implementing the terms of its realization.

4. The Social Stratification of the Foreign Labour Force

On the basis of the theoretical framework that has just been presented, we can proceed to an assessment of the social stratification of the foreign immigrants in Greek society in 2017. Above and beyond the preceding theoretical inferences we propose to utilize existing data from the Labour Force Quarterly Data on the mode of employment of the workforce (occupation *and* position in the workplace) in addition to the methodology that has been adopted in a preceding study (Sakellaropoulos 2014) which we cannot present in detail here. The final result for 2001 can be seen in Table 1 below.

It is estimated that the totality of employers (1.2% of the total number of foreign workers in Greece) belong to the traditional petty bourgeoisie because, on the one hand, there is no significant number of foreign employers employing ten people or more and so qualifying to be regarded as part of the bourgeoisie and, on the other there are no foreign landowners also employing farm workers and so, depending on the size of their property, belonging either to the rich or the medium rural strata.

Table 1. Groups of individual professions and positions in the profession 2001

	Profession	1 Managers	2 Professionals	3 Technicians and Associate Professionals	4 Clerical Support Workers	5 Service and sales workers	6 Skilled Agricultural, forestry and fishery workers	7 Craft and related trade workers	8 Plant and machine operators and assemblers	9 Elementary workers	Total
	Total										
Occupation Status	100	2.6	3.3	1.4	2.6	14.4	2.3	38.7	5.3	29.4	100
1 Employers	1.2	0.8	-	~**	-	-	-	0.4	-	-	
2 Self-employed	7.0	0.8	1.1	-	0.1	0.9	0.3	2.2	-	1.6	
3 Salaried Employees	90.4	0.9	2.2	1.3	2.3	12.9	1.7	35.9	5.3	27.8	
4 Workers in a family corporation	1.4*	~	~	~	0.2	0.5	0.3	0.2	-	~	

*marginal deviations due to rounding off.

**negligible percentage.

Source: Hellenic Statistical Authority, Labour Force Survey 2nd Quarter 2001.

The self- employed comprise 7% of the total and can be divided into the following three categories:

1) The first category includes people employed in agriculture (0.3% of the total). They are farmers who do not employ a salaried workforce and they simply manage to subsist, so they belong to the social strata of poor farmers.
2) The second category includes members of the new petty bourgeoisie, that is to say all branches of the liberal professions who do not experience exploitation or domination and who together comprise 5.8% of the total. The third group consists of small entrepreneurs (small traders and small sellers) who do not exceed 0.9% of the total and are to be included in the traditional petty bourgeoisie.
3) The category of *Salaried Employees*, which is also the most populous statistical category (90.4% of the total), consists primarily of members of the working class but also includes members of the bourgeoisie (0.9% of the total employed as managers - 1,619 persons in absolute terms - working in around 350[11] multinational companies operating in the country), and the new petty bourgeoisie (2.2% of the category "professionals" and 1.3% of the category "technicians and associate professionals"). From that point on, the remaining 86.0% are members of the modern working class, with the new petty bourgeoisie class amounting to 3.5% and the bourgeoisie to 0.9%.

Workers in a family business account for 1.4% of the total, primarily consisting of those performing ancillary tasks in trade (0.5% of the total) and secondarily of agricultural workers (0.3% of the total), some as Clerical Support Workers (0.2% of the total) and some (0.2% of the total) who are working as Craft and related trade workers. Therefore, this 0.3% should be included among the poor agricultural strata, and 1.1% among the members

[11]Alevra calculated that 350 multinational corporations had been established in Greece (Alevra 2005, 94).

of the traditional petty bourgeoisie who are not engaged in expanded capital accumulation.

Making the relevant calculations, it emerges that the bourgeoisie accounts for 0.9% of foreign workers, the traditional petty bourgeoisie 3.2%, the new petty bourgeoisie 9.3%, the poor rural strata 0.6% and the working class 86%.

Nevertheless, the question remains of the unemployed foreign workforce, which in the second quarter of 2001 came to 11.4% (Kapsalis 2018, 79). In another study on the calculation of social stratification in the Greek population as a whole I distinguished between the unemployed with a tertiary educational degree who were to be included in the new petty bourgeoisie and those who did not have a university degree and were accordingly classified as working class. In the case of foreigners this is not feasible because, as the relevant research by Lianos and Papakonstantinou has shown, aliens are mostly employed in lower posts within the process of production, even if they are highly educated (Lianos and Papakonstantinou 2003, 153-157). The only exception to this is foreign citizens coming from countries in the developed West who, in the event that they lose their jobs, will not stay in Greece to seek new employment but will return to their country of origin. As a result, 11.4% of the unemployed can be regarded as belonging to the working class.

So, appending the 11.4% of the unemployed to the 100% of workers, an index of 111.4 emerges as a new total on the basis of which calculations of the social stratification of foreign workers in the country should be made. Making the relevant calculation it emerges that the working class is 86 + 11.4/ 111.4= 87.4%, the bourgeois class 0.9/111.4 = 0.8%, the traditional petty bourgeoisie 9.3/111.4 = 8.3% and the poor farming strata 0.6/111.4 = 0.5%.

The conclusion that emerges is that the overwhelming majority of foreign workers belong to the working class. They are people coming from their countries to Greece, their only thought being how they can earn some money themselves and send a sum to their relatives in their homeland. Irrespective of their level of education, which is often high (Lianos and Papakonstantinou 2003, 153-157), they do not hesitate to undertake menial work precisely because of the great need to earn money, which has high purchasing capacity in their countries of origin. A few migrants work as farmers, either as farm hands or by cultivating a small area. There are also a limited, but existing, number of foreign workers who are self-employed. As far as we can see they are people who have managed to acquire a certain basic personal capital that enables them to be something other than wage labour.

An even smaller number, who would be classified as traditional petty bourgeoisie, are in a position to secure enough capital to employ workers, usually of their own nationality, and hired to work in light industry and petty trade. Last but not least there is the small number of foreign workers belonging to the bourgeoisie. They are citizens of countries of the developed West who are executives in multinational corporations, whose life and activities bear no relation to the everyday life of the overwhelming majority of other foreign workers.

Let us see now how things have evolved sixteen years later.

Taking the corresponding data for the second quarter of 2017, one comes up with the following Table 2.

Using the same methodology as that employed for processing the data in Table 1, we draw-the following conclusions:

All the employers (1.6% of the total number of foreign workers in Greece) are to be categorized as traditional petty bourgeoisie, simply because there is still no significant number of foreign employers with 10 or more people working for them. Nor are there foreign landowners to employ farm workers.

The self- employed comprise 8% of the total and, as we have already seen, can be divided into the following three categories:

The first category includes people employed in agriculture (0.9% of the total). They are farmers who do not employ a salaried workforce so they belong to the social strata of poor farmers.

Table 2. Groups of individual professions and positions in the profession 2017

	Profession	1 Managers	2 Professionals	3 Technicians and Associate Professionals	4 Clerical Support Workers	5 Service and sales workers	6 Skilled Agricultural, forestry and fishery workers	7 Craft and related trade workers	8 Plant and machine operators and assemblers	9 Elementary workers	Total
	Total										
Occupation Status	100	0.8	3.7	2.1	6.2	20.9	4.3*	19.4*	5.4	37.2	100
1 Employers	1.6	0.4	-	-	-	0.7	-	0.2	-	0.3	
2 Self-employed	8.0	-	0.8	0.1	~**	2.9	0.9	1.8	0.2	1.2	
3 Salaried Employees	89.1	0.4	2.9	2.0	6.2	16.9	2.8	17.3	5.2	35.5	
4 Workers in a family corporation	1.2	-	-	-	-	0.4	0.5	~**	-	0.2	

*marginal deviations due to rounding off.

**negligible percentage.

Source: Hellenic Statistical Authority, Labour Force Survey 2nd Quarter 2017.

The second category includes members of the new petty bourgeoisie who together comprise 4.2% of the total. The third group consists of small entrepreneurs (small traders and small sellers) who do not exceed 2.9% of the total and are to be included in the traditional petty bourgeoisie.

The category of *Salaried Employees*, which continues to make up the most populous statistical category (89.1% of the total), consists primarily of members of the working class but also includes members of the bourgeoisie (0.4% of the total employed as managers - 858 people in absolute figures – working in the around 300[12] multinational enterprises operating in the country) and the new petty bourgeoisie (3.7% of the category "professionals" and 2.1% of the category "technicians and associate professionals"). From that point on, the remaining 82.9% are members of the modern working class, with the new petty bourgeoisie class coming to 5.8% and the bourgeoisie to 0.4%.

Workers in a family business account for 1.2% of the total, primarily consisting of agricultural workers (0.5% of the total) and secondarily those performing ancillary tasks in trade (0.4% of the total) and some (0.2% of the total) who are working as elementary workers. They are individuals involved in family-run economic activities. Therefore, this 0.5% should be included among the poor agricultural strata, and 0.4% among the members of the traditional petty bourgeoisie who are not engaged in expanded capital accumulation, and there are also 0.2% who belong to the working class.

Calculations indicate that the bourgeoisie account for 0.4% of all foreign workers, the traditional petty bourgeoisie 4.9%, the new petty bourgeoisie 10%, the poor rural strata 1.4% and the working class 83.1%.

But there too the question arises of the foreign labour that is unemployed, amounting to 25.7% of the total in the second quarter of 2017. Following the same argument as was adopted for the 2001 data, it can be postulated that 25.7% of the unemployed belong to the working class.

---

[12]As we have seen, Alevra calculated that 350 multinational corporations had established themselves in Greece. However, the coming of the crisis in Greece has led some multinationals to suspend their operation (Conti Tech, Bolton Group, ILVA, Friesland Campina) and others to restrict it (Coca Cola, Pepsico, Teva).

If one adds the 25.7% of the unemployed to the 100% of the workers, an index of 125.7 emerges, on the basis of which calculations, here too, can be made of the social stratification of foreigners in Greece. It accordingly emerges that the working class comprises 83.1 + 25.7 /125.7 = 86.6%, the bourgeoisie 0.4/125.7 = 0.3%, the traditional petty bourgeoisie 4.9/125.7 = 3.9%, the new petty bourgeoisie 10/125.7 = 8% and the poor rural strata 1.4/125.7 = 1.1%.

The following table is based on the data for 2001 and 2017:

Table 3. Change in the social structure 2001 (2nd Quarter) - 2017 (2nd Quarter) (%)

Class	2001	2017	Change 2001- 2017
Bourgeois class	0,8	0,3	-0.5
Wealthy agrarian strata	-	-	-
Traditional petty bourgeois class	2,9	3,9	+1,0
Medium agrarian strata	-	-	-
New petty bourgeois class	8,3	8,0	-0,3
Working class	87,4	86,6	-0,8
Poor rural strata	0,5	1,1	+0,6
Not classified	-	-	-

It is observed that the bourgeoisie undergoes a significant contraction, attributable to the harshness of the economic crisis which struck the Greek economy, inducing a significant number of multinational companies either to withdraw from Greece or to reduce their activity[13]. At the same time it does not appear that foreigners of non-Western origin are in the habit of establishing enterprises employing more than ten people. This can also be attributed to the severity of the crisis, discouraging any significant degree of financial risk, as well as to repatriation of some of the immigrants, not to mention limitation of the amount of capital obtainable by some of them during their stay in Greece.

---

[13]It is characteristic that whereas in 2001 99.6 thousand citizens of the developed countries of the West were resident in Greece, this number had fallen to 90.7 thousand in 2011 (Kotzamanis and Karkouli 2016, 2).

In contrast the traditional petty bourgeoisie has seen a real increase on account of their acquisition of some basic capital in the first years of their working in Greece, making it possible for them to achieve some upward social mobility. It is in this context that the rise in the number of poor rural strata can also be understood. These are farmers who thanks to their savings have been able to acquire some small portion of land of their own, but they are not in a position to be able to employ labourers.

The marginal contraction of the new petty bourgeoisie is linked to the aforementioned diminution in the presence of multinationals and the fact that such non-Western foreigners as have succeeded in acquiring some capital have chosen to invest it in small businesses, in the hope that this will contribute to further improvement of their financial situation.

Correspondingly the very slight numerical reduction of the working class can be explained by the tendency towards social ascent of a segment of foreign workers, more or less counterbalancing the withdrawal of executive staff of multinational enterprises belonging either to the bourgeoisie or to the new petite bourgeoisie.

5. Comparison of Stratification between Immigrants and the Working Population

Availing ourselves of the results from another of our studies on social stratification in the entire working population of Greece (Sakellaropoulos 2019) in correlation with the findings of the present article on stratification among foreign workers in 2017, we present Table 4.

The data in Table 4 shows that in all social categories, with the exception of the working class, the number of foreign workers is clearly below the national average. And it is indeed interesting that foreign workers are entirely absent from two categories (wealthy and middle-level rural strata). The latter exposes, on the one hand, their financial incapacity to proceed with purchases of medium-sized and large areas of farmland but also that the brevity of the time they have so far been living in Greece precludes the conclusion of inheritances, crop combinations, etc. Which is why they are the proprietors only of smallholdings, and even that by way of exception. Conversely, Greeks are to be numbered among the poor farmers precisely because of the transfers of small-scale ownership in the agricultural sector in Greece.

Table 4. Social stratification of the working population as a whole and of foreign workers (2nd quarter 2017)

Class	Entire working population	Foreign workers	Difference
Bourgeois class	2.8	0,3	+2.5
Wealthy agrarian strata	0.6	-	+0,6
Traditional petty bourgeois class	7.9	3,9	+4,0
Medium agrarian strata	1.5	-	+1,5
New petty bourgeois class	21.4	8,0	+13,4
Working class	59.5	86,6	-27,1
Poor rural strata	6.3	1,1	+5,2
Total	100	100	-

That said, there is an evident correlation between the absence of medium and large-scale property and the low proportion of foreigners qualifying for inclusion in the bourgeoisie. It is very difficult for people having lived for ten or at most twenty years in a country whose economy is plagued by an unprecedented economic crisis to be in a position to accumulate enough capital to establish companies with at least ten employees working in them. As indicated, this meagre participation (0.3%) is not from immigrants coming from countries of Eastern Europe and the Third World but rather from executives of multinational companies that have continued to operate in Greece.

The small difference in the rate of inclusion in the traditional petite bourgeoisie is interesting. For a foreigner it is a sign of upward social mobility to have succeeded in rising above the status of wage labour, joining the ranks of small property ownership. On the contrary, for the Greeks it is a consequence of the crisis and of contraction in the size of many until then larger businesses.

The new petty bourgeoisie is largely associated with the particular functions performed for capitalism by professions such as doctors, engineers and lawyers. In the case of aliens this does not apply: these are people who may not be able to establish their own business but are able to earn a living beyond the framework of salaried employees. That is the reason for this divergence from the national average.

The very significant difference in rates of inclusion in the working class is a reflection, of course, of everything previously mentioned, and at the same time leads to a more general conclusion. The explosion in the number of foreigners in Greece from 171,000 in 1981 to 911,000 in 2011 can be seen from two viewpoints. The former has to do with the significant strengthening of the Greek economy thanks to a highly skilled but low-wage workforce that contributed to the vigorous growth rates observable prior to the crisis. It could also be pointed out that precisely the presence of these people was a factor in delaying the emergence of the crisis. The latter is linked to the way in which the great majority of them have been incorporated into the Greek reality. On the one hand, there was the attitude of the Greek state and a considerable section of Greek society which greeted them with practices of authoritarianism, super exploitation, hostility, contempt - at best with mistrust. On the other hand they themselves were required in a very short time to adapt to the new circumstances, to survive in this hostile climate and in a twofold way to transform their identities: from citizens of their State of origin to migrants, i.e., quasi second-class citizens, and in many cases from people in positions requiring university-level specialization to unskilled labourers.

CONCLUSION

The social history of Greece was characterized by the export of labour for a period of about 100 years (1870-1970). Then, until the onset of the economic crisis, this stopped and a period of limited but real labour inflow commenced. This trend was intensified following the fall of the regimes of so-called "existing socialism." Within a very brief period of time Greeks would have to become accustomed to living with a significant number of their foreign fellow citizens and the foreign citizens to become accustomed to a quite different, and to a significant extent hostile, social environment.

The jobs made available to them were menial, poorly paid and very often without insurance (in the “black” labour market). The result of this was that in their overwhelming majority - about ninety percent - they were included in the working class. One exception to this trend were foreign workers from Western countries who occupied executive positions in the domestic subsidiaries of multinational companies.

This situation was to be modified in the years of the crisis without, however, changing radically. A section of the workforce coming from the West left as the multinationals they worked for underwent contraction or ceased operations. Beyond that, the bulk of the foreign workers from former socialist and Third World states continued to be part of the working class. But there were also limited, but existent, sections that experienced an improvement in their social position, finding a place in the strata of petty proprietors (small shop owners, small farmers).

This trend in no way ran contrary to the overall tendencies in Greek society, where there was a dichotomy between Greek and foreign workers. Among the former the so-called middle strata were very much in evidence. In the latter case the prevailing social identity was working class.

REFERENCES

Alevra, Emilia. 2005. *Multinational enterprises in Greece*. [in Greek.] http://hellanicus.lib.aegean.gr/bitstream/handle/11610/6113/file0.pdf?sequence=2&isAllowed=y, accessed on 8/19/2018.

Aronowitz, Stanley. 2002. *How Class Works. Power and Social Movement*. New Haven and London: Yale University Press.

Atkinson, Will. 2015. *Class*, Cambridge: Polity.

Balibar, Etien. 1985. “Classes” in *Dictionnaire Critique du Marxisme* edited by Georges Labica and Gerard Bensussan, 170-179. Paris: PUF.

Bensaid, Daniel. 1995. *Marx l'intempestif*. Fayard: Paris.

Bihr, Alain. 1989. *Entre Bourgeoisie et Prolétariat* [Between Bourgeoisie and Proletariat], Paris: L' Harmattan.

Bouvier-Ajam, Maurice and Gilbert Mury. 1963. *Les classes sociales en France [*Social classes in France]. Paris: Editions Sociales.

Carchedi, Guglielmo. 1977. *On the Economic Identification of Social Classes*. London: Routledge.

Croix de Ste, Geoffrey. 1984. "Class in Marx's Conception of History, Ancient and Modern," *New Left Review* 146: 94-111.

General Secretariat of Population and Social Cohesion. 2013. *National Strategy for integration of citizens of third countries.* [in Greek.] Athens: Ministry of the Interior.

Georgarakis Nicos. 2009. "Immigration policy. Stances and resistance in the Greek Administration" [in Greek.], in *Views on immigration and immigration policy in Greece today* edited by Christina Varouxi, Nicos Sarris and Amalia Frangiskou, 33-60, Athens: National Centre for Social Research.

Gramsci, Antonio. 1972. *The intellectuals.* [in Greek.] Athens: Stochastis.

Johnson, Terry. 1977. "What is to be known?*." Economy and Society*, 6(2): 194- 233.

Kapsalis, Apostolos. 2018, *Migrant workers in Greece. Labour relations and immigration policy in the Greece of the memoranda.* [in Greek.] Athens: Topos.

Katsoridas, Dimitris. 1996. "Foreign workers in Greece and their living conditions" [in Greek.], *Theseis* 56: 1-16.

Kavounidi, Jenny. 2012. "Integration of migrants into the labour market" [in Greek.] in *Migrants in Greece. Employment and integration into local communities* edited by C. Kasimis and A. Papadopoulos, 69-104, Athens: Alexandreia.

Kotzamanis, Viron and Alexandra Karkouli. 2016. "Migrant inflows in Greece over the last decade: intensity and basic characteristics of illegal immigrants and asylum applicants" [in Greek.] *Workshop for Demographic and Sociological Analysis* 26: 1-7 https://www.tovima.gr/files/1/2016/04/metanaroes.pdf (accessed on 13/10/2018)).

Lenin, Vladimir Ilich.1977. *A Great Beginning*, Peking: Foreign Languages Press.

Lianos, Theodoros and Panaghiota Papakonstantinou. 2003. *Contemporary Migration in Greece: economic investigation.* [in Greek.] Athens: Centre of Planning and Economic Research.

Lytras, Andreas. 1993. *Introduction to the Theory of Greek social structure*. [in Greek.] Athens: Livanis.

Meiksins, Peter. 1986. "Beyond the boundary question," *New Left Review* 154: 101- 120.

Milios, John. 2002. "The question of the petty bourgeoisie. A single class or two discrete class aggregations?" [in Greek.] *Theseis* 81: 59- 80.

Panitsidis, Giorgos. 1992. *Approaches to the class structure of our farm economy.* [in Greek.] Athens: Synchroni Epochi.

Robolis, Savvas. 2007. *Migration from and to Greece.* [in Greek.] Thessaloniki: Epikentro.

Sakellaropoulos, Spyros. 2001. *Greece after the Dictatorship*. [in Greek.] Athens: Livanis.

Sakellaropoulos, Spyros. 2014. *Crisis and Social stratification in 21st century Greece.* [in Greek.] Athens: Topos.

Sakellaropoulos, Spyros. 2019. *Greece's (un) Competitive Capitalism and the Economic Crisis -How the Memoranda Changed Society, Politics and the Economy*, London: Palgrave.

Zografakis, Stavros, Antonios Kontis and Thodoros Mitrakos. 2009. *Migrant steps in the Greek economy*. [in Greek.] Athens: IMEPO (Institution of Migration Policy).

SECTION 3. EMOTIONS AND WORKING-CLASS IDENTITIES: ANTHROPOLOGICAL AND PSYCHOANALYTIC INSIGHTS

In: Emotions, Temporalities … ISBN: 978-1-53616-203-5
Editors: M. Christodoulou et al.

Chapter 8

THE LIVING CONDITIONS OF WORKING CLASSES IN AFRICA: THE CLASS-CONSCIOUSNESS OF WORKERS, AND THEIR POSITION IN THE GLOBAL CLASS SYSTEM

Ioannis Kyriakakis[*]
Hellenic Open University, Open University of Cyprus
Latsia, Cyprus

ABSTRACT

In this chapter I put forward two main ideas: The first is that we cannot maintain national frameworks as the basic researching fields of class-theory, in an era, when class relationships are mainly transnational, and current capitalism cannot be seen in any sense or perspective other than global. The second idea is that the strengthening of the global class-systems, although it does not change the nature of capitalist exploitation, it

[*] Corresponding Author's Email: ioannis_kyriakakis@yahoo.co.uk.

forces the global working-classes into two major transformations. First, exploitation becomes deeper and wider with very low wages and long working hours. Second class-consciousness and class-struggle become extremely difficult for workers for first having their patrons thousands of miles away, and second, for living side by side to an extremely numerous underclass, ready to replace them at any moment at work. The existence of such huge population of underclasses living in conditions of indirect, mass genocide, is the hidden asset, so far unbeatable, of global capitalism. I draw on my ethnographic experience in Ghana, but I also use Ghana's National Statistics, regarding occupational distribution and statuses of employment.

Keywords: global class-system, Africa, Ghana, global working-classes, indirect mass genocide

INTRODUCTION

In this chapter I attempt to shed light into living conditions and social consciousness of working people living in Africa. That is, outside Europe and North America, where the very notion of "social class" was coined, developed and, for a very long time, challenged and debated. The first question this chapter attempts to answer is the following: 'Can we talk of "class" in African contexts?' The question is, above all, methodological: Is, in the final analysis, the concept of "class" a tool for understanding social realities in a global scale in contemporary societies? or it is restricted merely within a, majorly, Euro-American, specific, geographical, historical and social set of experiences, relationships and events, which to a great extent belong to the historical past?

A second question emerges when we take into account the current debates on class-related issues within the Euro-American contexts themselves. The contemporary neo-liberal, de-industrialised socio-political conditions in the North-western part of the globe have almost inevitably weakened the concept of class, at least in its classical Marxist version of the "relationship to the means of production". A specific shift is taking place in favour of new approaches, which emphasise the individual consuming-capacity rather than work- and/or collective ethics, as determinative of social identity (Bauman, 2001). Most of the new approaches regard the classic Marxist schema of class struggle as one of exclusively historical value, essentially irrelevant to contemporary society (Pakulski and Waters, 1996). The second question is then the following: "Can we talk of class and class struggle in the contemporary world in general (and not merely Africa)?" Or it is the world we live in nowadays constructed by sellers, byers and outcasts (who try to penetrate the borders of modern garden of Eden of western consumption-democracies through the illegal migration-routes) as the neoliberal ideology wants it?

I draw on my own ethnographic work in Ghana and the material I gathered there, while searching the relationship between religion and social differentiation for my PhD, as well as, on some statistical data for the entire country of Ghana, regarding the first part of the comparison (Africa). Selected works out of the rich bibliography on the Industrial North-class theories, construct the material for the other part (the "west"). Nevertheless, personal experience and informal discussions during and after my fieldwork remain the major source of inspiration for the ideas presented below. I use the concepts of temporality and emotion as common yardsticks and building blocks of collective identities and social mobility here and there, and in that sense, I meet the problematic of the current volume, upon which I am attempting to add a wider, universal perspective.

SIMILARITIES AND DIFFERENCES BETWEEN MARXIAN AND WBERIAN FRAMEWORKS

According to Wright (2000, 27-34), both Marxian and Weberian frameworks for studying social class, focus in the relational character of social differentiation emanating from social structure built upon unequal relationships. This means that class positions are not just located side by side in an objective social taxonomy, or even rank, according to productive activities and services. On the contrary they relate to each other in such a way that makes productive activities and services possible in the first place.

This relational character of social groupings (be they classes, statuses, nations, genders, races whatsoever) is probably the foundation stone of sociology as a discipline itself. However, Marx and Weber differ in the emphasis they give on the crucial criterion of class-belonging, and in that sense of social differentiation altogether. Marx holds that this criterion is the famous "one's relationship to the means of production", while for Weber what is crucial for placing individuals within social classes is the remarkably similar, or common, set of "life chances" they have got to acquire wealth and pursue their material interests (Wright 2000, 28). Although the two approaches are not mutually exclusive (one can claim that the relationship to the means of production is one of one's life chances), they obviously lead to different methodological and theoretical priorities. Marxian approach leads to prioritizing property and especially property (or deprivation of property) of means of production, while Weberian approach pays much attention to a range of social distinctions other than property, such as status, origin, profession, education, authority, culture and prestige. There is no doubt, to me, that the Weberian perspective is much more inclusive, as well as, in a way, much more operational, methodologically, for social research. If one asks oneself what differentiates oneself from others in a more or less commonly accepted social ranking, the first thing one will think of is one's profession, then income and finally education, with regional and national origin following close. No one will contemplate "oh! What is my relationship to the means of production"?

Nevertheless, despite the advantages of the Weberian framework, in the sense that it is much closer to one's every-day social perceptions, the Marxian framework offers the probability of not just mirroring social reality but also of deeply understand it and change it, like no other school of thought does. The dynamic potential of the Marxian principle of "the means of production", although it does not accord, that well, with every-day experience, offers a unified framework for the entire range of social relationships regardless to one's perception about them. This framework treats society as a system rather than a set of relationships that might, or might not, connect to each-other. Therefore, the Marxian framework does not merely place groups and individuals in specific locations across the social hierarchy, but also reveals the interconnections between these locations, claiming that the interconnections are more important than locations themselves. In simpler words Marxian thought does not merely reveal that the world is made of owners of capital and workers, not even merely that capitalists exploit workers. It also assumes that the workers are workers exactly because capitalists are capitalists and the vice versa. Both positions are intertwined within a system of production, which cannot work without them and especially without the nature of relationships between them. Every change in the position of the one group affects the other, and nothing can change in one's group living conditions without the opposite change within the opposite group: No worker can improve their life without a capitalist giving up some of their luxuries! And no capitalist can increase their profit except a number of workers lose their wages, jobs, homes and in some extreme cases their very lives too. Of course, this is a very strong, almost absolute, assumption of how class-oriented society works. It bears a vast explanatory power, it can motivate huge support within and without academic circles but unfortunately it is too abstract to withstand empirical testing. The problem is that there are so many intermediary groups and vague conditions in the social space between and beside the two basic classes, the so called middle classes, as well as conditions where class belonging is not that clear-cut, such as people studying, young family members, artists and scientists whose relationship to the means of production is far less than clear (if any).

It is in this instance where the Weberian framework gets in in order to facilitate research and measurements. Instead of categorizing people according to class, social scientists, theorists, students, politicians and statisticians tend to use income, occupations, forms of activity (=employer, self-employed, employee), education, etc. in order to see and record whether and how society moves towards social equality or inequality. The result is to use some, not that theoretically elaborated, rather than empirically, de-facto, imposed criteria of social differentiation, such as income, profession and education. Most statistics and researches follow this methodology (see for example, Savage et al., 2013, or visit any national statistics-website anywhere in the globe, to confirm the prevalence of this tendency).

Ownership is also used as a criterion but in the broad sense of total property (including houses and land), not in the narrow sense of "the means of production". Entrepreneurs are treated as a unified category, although differentiation between "big" and "small" is maintained. The idea is that people perform some basic tendencies and exert some fundamental preferences, according to their social and educational background, mixed with their desires, towards big business, small business and regular employment. Despite its operational validity and resemblance to "real-life" observation, this sort of approaches run the risk to treat society as an aggregation of relatively independent locations and positions, positions that do not relate to each-other, nor constitute a wider system, which works towards their reproduction as they are. The social dynamic of conflict, movement and change (other words for "dialectics") disappears in favor of "accuracy" "realism" and "scientific objectivity". Instead of treating social locations as directly affecting each-other, one is led to imagine of a world where a capitalist can increase one's profits exclusively through innovation, cleverness and smartness, without worsening the living conditions of workers. No matter whether intended or not, this tendency within social science and social statistics results in contributing to the maintenance and reproduction of the current system of social hierarchy and exploitation, that is, the capitalist system.

In this chapter I will not challenge the current tendency of sociology as ideological. This does not need to be challenged. It is self-evident. What I will attempt to do is to explain why the "death" of class-division of society (in the Marxian sense) looks so plausible and valid in the traditionally rich countries of the Industrial North, while it was for long held as inappropriate (and still is held so) for studying the societies of the Global South. I maintain that if we take Industrial North and Global South as separate entities culturally, politically and economically, both claims are true. But if we take North and South as parts of one and the same global capitalist system, the Marxian framework of mutually interdepended global classes is the only one with some explanatory strength and validity.

Class in Global Perspective

After the energy crisis of 1970s, most of the manufacturing activities of global capitalism seemed to have preferably moved to the east and south-east of Asia. The reasons for this preference lay in the presence of a fair network of infrastructures (routes, rivers, trains, ports, communication-lines, etc.) a vast reserve of cheap labour consisting in impoverished ex-peasants with cultural and work discipline appropriate for manufacture, and a bulk of governments and politicians, eager to implement measures and legislation in order to force peasants to enter wage-labour. It is well known from the colonial past, how colonial governments pushed peasants and their offspring to enter wage labour (in mines, plantations, ports and railways) by imposing small taxes, which subsistence farmers could not afford. What colonial powers used to do in the past, was now the task of their friendly governments. However, it is not in all parts of the global south that capitalist firms directly exploit workers in (of course harsher in absolute terms!) analogically similar ways they did in the past with the western workers.

According to Wright not all unequal and oppressive relationships fall into the category of class exploitation. It is only the antithetical positions within productive activities (opposite relationships to the means of production) that form class relationships. Wright writes: *"The crucial difference between exploitation and non-exploitative oppression is that, in an exploitative relation, the exploiter needs the exploited since the exploiter depends upon the effort of the exploited. In the case of non-exploitative oppression, the oppressors would be happy if the oppressed simply disappeared."* (Wright, 2000, 11)

The cases when the oppressed simply disappeared are not unknown in history. Genocides are good examples. The genocide of Native Americans by the white colonists stressed the fact that neither the strategy of the oppressors required extended labour force nor the Native Americans were willing to offer it. Committed either for ideological reasons, due to resistance, or for political domination, genocides do not fall into class relationships. However, there is an indirect link between genocides and class-structure as we shall see below. Especially in parts of Africa, as well as, in other fringes of the Global South, due to crappy infrastructures, as well, due to highly unstable political and social conditions, combined with a largely heterogeneous and undisciplined labour force, capitalist firms avoid to invest in manufacturing. Nevertheless, there are zones of very strong interest on the part of Northern (and Australian and South African in that case) multinationals in mining, oil and gas, timber and agricultural raw materials. In these zones capitalist multinationals are interested in their special relationships with local authorities (the state officials and the local chiefs) because land concessions are more important than labour force, which is on plenty supply. Selected semi-skilled or unskilled workers are needed for the mines while timber and agricultural products are supplied through local brokers who deal with local loggers and farmers themselves. Therefore, the demand for *direct* employment by multinationals is pretty restricted. The area in Western Ghana, where I conducted my fieldwork was a gold-mining area. Many of my friends and informants had worked in the goldmines, owned by an Australian company, which leased the land for peanuts. Compensations for destroying farms were also ridiculous. Locals were hired for 1.5 dollar a day for unskilled work. Drillers and other skilled workers were Ukrainians hired by the company and transferred to Africa for work exclusively, directly from Ukraine. They did not trust locals for skilled work.

I will talk about Ghana wherefrom I had personal experience. What I will write, however is valid for many other countries in Africa, as well as in Global South in general. The number of hired local workers by multinationals in Ghana was relatively small as said. Another relatively small number of workers both skilled and unskilled was hired by local capitalist firms in a descent for African standards local chemical and plastics-industry. However, the vast majority of the economically active population engaged with two major categories of activities: Farming and petty trade. A very complex land-rights system did not allow statistics to securely distinguish between big and small farmers. The power over production however lies more with merchants and brokers (state and private) rather than with land owners. There have been steady seasonal migrant currents of workers towards cocoa, cashew-nuts, palm-trees, rubber and copra plantations. These corps are the most important, with cocoa consisting 18% out of Ghana's total exports. Unstable and insecure land-rights (see below) and almost exclusive dependence of small farmers on the fluctuations of international trade, makes a large number of farmers *indirectly* related to the directions and decisions taken thousands miles away in the center of cocoa, nuts and palm-oil markets. A long history of colonial intervention in cocoa production many decades ago, led to deliberate under-development of farming technology, land-rights and infrastructures so that they could keep production-costs as low as possible in favour of local and international brokers and traders (Kyriakakis, 2012). On the other hand, petty trade is a vast, marginal and informal activity saved for the millions of the "underclasses" in Ghana (and in Africa in general), that is all those groups and individuals who cannot find a place in the established economic and political structure.

Although it is not evident at a first glance, one can reasonably claim that the very logic of this structure creates and reproduces the millions, members of the underclass and social outcasts, who are dispensable and invisible both to local elites and their overseas patrons, the western multinationals. What is more important for Ghana's economy and society is exports. From export tariffs and levies the state is financed and functioning. Gold is the major export-good consisting 41% of the total exports and then comes cocoa with 18%, crude-oil with 13% and cashew-nuts with 9% (www.pulse.com.gh/news/business/top-10-exports-from-ghana, 4-3-2018). However, since gold-mining is so narrowly related to the extracting multinationals, and cocoa production to international, related firms in Europe and America, control over production and trade is exerted by global capitalists. Local elites play the role of brokers and intermediate agents serving the interests of big multinational firms. Dependency on foreign support and external trade make the political elites indifferent to popular support, while due to weak democratic control and transparency, corruption and favouritism prevails. Basic infrastructure, roads and bridges in remote areas, connection to power-network for 30 - 40% of the country, health and education facilities, sewage and sanitation networks, hygienic waste disposal sites, telephone landlines and so many other things including justice and descent policing are missing, because of the narrow basis of economy, directed exclusively to export trade. The weakest groups within this system are constantly exposed to risks of fatal diseases, with no social protection and with no chance of organizing collective resistance. Therefore, we can talk about an *indirect* genocide. Since the basic reason for this situation is the profits of the global multinationals, we can speak credibly of a "global class system". Global Capitalists are located far away, in the capitalist center. Local elites, local capitalists and brokers are part of the global middle class (with a very precious privilege, as we will see below, that they can travel abroad, something that the rest of the population cannot do). Workers and the vast majority of farmers constitute the international working class and the rest of the population belongs to the global underclass.

Can We Talk of Working-Class or Classes in Africa?

But apart from the global division of labour and neo-colonial exploitation can we talk of class in the domestic level? Are African countries "structured" according to class difference, class struggle and class exploitation? Or it is the concept of class an exclusively western invention, describing solely North-industrial historical experience? Jean Copans, a researcher, who long ago, claimed that in Africa the relationship to the state is much more important than the relationship to the means of production, writes: *"The exportation of concepts, forged exclusively from European realities, is no speculative and innocent enterprise. It was made possible, and afterwards maintained, through all those processes of domination and exploitation which have linked the south and the north for the last 500 years"* (Copans 1985, 25)

The most misleading and hypocritical concept exported from the west to Africa, was that of "development". The ideology of development had it that African countries should emulate the western industrial countries by taking exactly the same steps they took throughout the past 2 centuries, in order, some-day, to reach the current level of their economic, social, technological and political advancement. Perhaps this is the greatest deceit in human history, since at the same time that theorists of development made such claims, colonial and post-colonial authorities and agencies, both local and international, political and financial, made whatever possible to keep African countries in structural stagnation and permanent underdevelopment. What the colonial government did in Ghana was to stop commercialization of land by maintaining the customary law of allocating community-land by chiefs and heads of clans and lineages to common farmers (Howard-Hassman, 1980, Grier, 1981, 1987, 1993). This first allowed the rural elites to be formed, second kept the number of smallholders very high and third resulted in the very low productivity of land. Average productivity of cocoa beans per hectare in Ghana is 400 kg per hectare, while in Cote d' Ivoire and Indonesia is 1.4 and 1 tone per hectare respectively (Asamoah and Owusu-Ansah, 2017, 4). The majority of farmers manage (but do not own) 2-4 hectares of cocoa farms, while 72% do not possess any legal document proving their relationship to the land (Asamoah and Owusu-Ansah, 2017, 2, 4). Distribution of employment status in Ghana according to 2010 census is shown in Table 1.

Table 1. Employment status of employed persons 15 years and older. Ghana Statistical Service, 2012:10

	Male	Female
Employee	25.3%	11.4%
Self Employed	60%	69.3%
Casual Worker	2.8%	1.3%
Contributing Family Worker	8.7%	14.2%
Apprentice	2.5%	2.9%
Domestic Employee	0.6%	0.7%
Other	0.2%	0.1%

What is of great importance is the proportion of people working under formal and informal conditions. 86% of the economically active people work in the informal private sector! (Ghana Statistical Service, 2012:11). In Tables 2, 3 and 4 we can see the statistical data on occupation distribution, as well as, the economic activities, and specific industry distribution, along with the distribution of employment status. The somewhat contradictory data lies in the fact that in the category "agricultural, forestry and fishery workers" (the largest one) smallholders are included, since, as said, they are not formally land owners! However, in the "self-employment" status, they are also included, as they are really self-employed. The same statistical magic trick happens with petty traders, since the vast majority of them are informal workers, not really owners of capital or self-employed, but usually indebted to a wholesale merchant, or food sellers, or market pariahs! In one statistical category they appear as "self-employed", in another as service workers, and in another as wholesale and retail traders! All three are true depending on the angle from which, one observes them! Statisticians are not famous for their pro-Marxian feelings.

Table 2. Ghana Statistical Agency 2012:74

Economically Active Population 15 Years and Older by Occupation SENCUS 2010		
Managers	2.5%	263,191
Professionals	5.3%	559,455
Technicians and Associate Professionals	1.8%	193,821
Clerical Support Workers	1.5%	153,375
Service and Sales Workers	21.3%	2,227,441
Skilled Agricultural Forestry and Fishery Workers	41.2%	4,319,237
Craft and Related Trades Workers	15.2%	1,594,378
Plant and Machine Operators and Assemblers	5.0%	518,873
Elementary Occupations	6.0%	631,247
Other Occupations	0.2%	18,267
	100%	10,479,485

Table 3. Ghana Statistical Agency 2012:75

Economically Active Population 15 Years and Older by Industry	%	Number
Agriculture forestry and fishing	41.5	4,435723
Mining and quarrying	1.1	115,394
Manufacturing	10,8	1,135,612
Electricity gas stream and air conditioning supply	0.2	16,237
Water supply; sewage waste management and remediation activities	0.2	24,996
Construction	3.1	321,360
Wholesale and retail; repair of motor vehicles and motorcycles	18.9	1,981,290
Transportation and storage	3.5	371,461

Economically Active Population 15 Years and Older by Industry	%	Number
Accommodation and food service activities	5.5	574,671
Information and communication	0.4	43,600
Financial and insurance activities	0.7	72,666
Real estate activities	0.0	4,562
Professional scientific and technical activities	0.9	96,223
Administrative and support service activities	0.7	68,218
Public administration and defence; compulsory social security	1.5	154,559
Education	3.9	409,694
Human health and social work activities	1.2	125,254
Arts entertainment and recreation	0.6	57,997
Other service activities	4.5	476,722
Activities of households as employers; undifferentiated goods- and services- producing activities of households for own use	0.8	80,287
Activities of extraterritorial organizations and bodies	0.0	2,959
	100	10,479,485

Table 4. Ghana Statistical Agency 2012:78

Economically Active Population 15 Years and Older by Employment Status	%	Number
Employee	18.2	1,904,039
Self-employed without employees	60.0	6,282,509
Self-employed with employees	4.9	509,061
Casual worker	2.0	210,087
Contributing family worker	11.5	1,206,935
Apprentice	2.7	282,618
Domestic employee (House-help)	0.6	66,570
Other	0.2	17,666
	100	

If one takes seriously Table 2, one will conclude that working class in Ghana is 85% of economically active population! However, when one looks at Table 4, working class seems to shrink into 20 to 22%. Although both images are true according to the angle of view one employs, as said, considering income, property-rights and precarious conditions of existence of farmers and petty traders one will place without doubt the vast majority of working people in Ghana in the working classes, that is, all the classes that are deprived of the ownership of means of production. However, this is not a sufficient condition for labelling Ghana society as a class-divided society. A class divided society requires also a social and economically distinct bourgeoisie, that is, owners of means of production who derive their profits from the direct exploitation of the working classes. Despite the development of a domestic industry of plastic, chemicals and textile manufacturing as well as some plants of spare-parts for computers and laptops with majorly Chinese support (Cheru and Obi 2010, Alemayehu, 2017), the numbers of domestic bourgeoisie are quite small. Out of the 4.9% of employers in Table 4 more than 60% employ 1-9 employees, while state firms take the lion portion of large enterprises (Ghana Statistical Agency: 2015).

Therefore, one can credibly claim that the privileged classes in Ghana are not as much the owners of factories, as the owners of strategic positions within the customary institutions, the state, and civil-administration apparatus. Because it is these strategic positions, which secure a stable and permanent superiority in Ghana's social hierarchy. Chiefs and politicians, judges and superior police officers, as well as directors of various civil services and state enterprises are more likely to accumulate wealth through bribes and commissions. These are the true ruling classes in Ghana and in Africa in general. This condition is highly desirable on part of the global capitalists, since there is no real domestic competition. In conclusion African countries and societies are not class-divided in Marxian terms, despite the vast inequalities within them. They are subjected as a whole to the domination of global capitalists. That is why the Weberian perspective seems (and largely is) more appropriate for studying them. Because the exploiters are thousands of miles away. The same is true for the (post-) industrial North. Everybody looks like middle class, since the real working and underclasses are thousands of miles away! What a brilliant planning for such a mean cause!

THE ETHNOGRAPHY: THE LIVING CONDITIONS OF THE WORKING CLASSES IN AFRICA

When I was doing my fieldwork in South-western Ghana back in 2004-2005, searching for the connection between social differentiation and religious affiliation (this was the topic of my PhD), after a dead-end in my endeavour to find links through interviews and life-histories, I decided to conduct a survey with the help of my local friends and assistance. I was living in a middle to big size village of approximately 1,700 inhabitants, located 5 km from the Atlantic coast, neighbouring to gold-mining areas. Most people were farmers, cultivating coconut-trees in a former wild-forest region, but occasional legal and illegal mining was also very popular, especially among young males. The distribution of occupations in the village of my fieldwork is shown in Table 5.

Table 5. Distribution of Occupations/Economic Activities in fieldwork village (April 2004)-Kyriakakis 2012

Occupation	individuals	percentage
Farmers	340	32.5%
Teachers	43	4%
Craftsmen (carpenters, electricians, masons, mechanics, smiths, drivers)	49	4.7%
Craftswomen (seamstresses, hairdressers)	24	2.5%
Shopkeepers/Entrepreneurs	14	1.5%
Workers and Apprentices	32	3%
Food Sellers (all women)	47	4.5%
Market Women and Petty-traders	151	14.4%
Miners	10	0.9%
Students	193	18.5%
Unemployed	140	13.5%
Total	**1043**	**100%**

One can see the striking similarities with national statistics. The relatively large number of “students” and “unemployed” (more than double from the national average) hid the fact that gold-mining was not merely occasional but also illegal.

An illegal mine was established near the village on stool (that is, communal) land, which a few years later the local chief along with state-officials leased to an Australian gold-mining multinational. Therefore, no-one could declare "I am illegal miner". What I was most interested in, at that time, was social inequality. I tried to make a lot of demographic questions, and in the end, I had a full demographic profile of the village. But I also tried to elicit information on social differentiation and inequality.

One of the questions of the survey was the following: a//*If we divide the village residents in three categories, which category you place yourself into? Upper? Middle? Or Lower?* b//*Due to your condition regarding money? Land ownership/property? Housing? Origin? Education? Profession? Age? Gender? Marital status? Other?* In the first part of the question, although the majority of 547/52% placed themselves in the middle stratum (as expected for a rural area), another very significant 375/36% regarded themselves as lower stratum and only 102/10% said they were the upper stratum. 19 respondents (2%) did not reply to the question. With regard to the second part the highest criterion for placing oneself in social hierarchy was by far "profession" (275, 27%), with education (199, 19%) and money (189, 18%) following after it. Land and other properties ownership comes fifth with just 78 responses (7%). Therefore, the respondents of my questionnaire were certainly Weberian!

The most important issue for villagers was income and money because after the IMF coming to Ghana in 1983, everything, even education with school fees, and health with national insurance-contributions and medicine, became financially burdensome (Guifford 1998, Hutchful 2002). Let alone fertilisers and pesticides for farmers. Everything was subject to the markets. Local and international. Local farmers gave their crops to a local coconut-oil-processing factory but pests and diseases was a constant threat for crops and one must had money to face the threat. Therefore, what colonialists did with taxes, neo-colonialists (IMF and World Bank) did with markets. Everything went to the market, even social policies. Everything? Oh! No! Not everything! Land remained communal! Other problems were the lack of running water, the lack of roads and bridges, the lack of any telephone land-line network, the badly maintained power network, which resulted in everyday long-hours power disruptions, the lack of public toilet facilities, the lack of medical doctor. 50% of the villagers were illiterates and only 25% could speak fair English, which is the official language of the state. This means that most people cannot contact any state agency without help.

What impressed me was some of the demographic data I gathered. Almost half of the girls between 16 and 20 years old, were single mothers. Almost half of the couples were divorced, most children lived with only one of the parents or grandparents, and 1/4 of all men were temporarily living elsewhere working or seeking for jobs. Families and households were literally disintegrated. National data regarding infrastructures were not that different. According to Ghana Statistical Agency, only 2.3% of households in Ghana are connected to land-telephone lines! 7% of people have pc's and laptops and 45% mobile phones. This means that the vast majority of the population are excluded from communications. There are "telephone centers" in every village with satellite phones, but that's all, and that's expensive too! Only 15% of solid waste and only 10% of liquid waste of Ghana's households are disposed in a hygienically safe way! The rest are disposed in open gutters and open waste sites beside slams, houses and markets. (Ghana Statistical Agency, 2012: 84, 88-91). The entire Ghana and the entire Africa looks like an open-air dump site. Only one, who has lived in Africa knows how disturbing all that is. In that sense living conditions of the working classes in Africa today do not differ much from the living conditions of the working classes in Europe in the 18th and 19th centuries, the centuries when global capitalism achieved its first great accumulation of profits. The culprit now and then is the same, the global capitalist class and the political agencies, which serve their interests. Do, however, African workers realise that this is the main cause of their problems? What is, in other words, the African workers' class consciousness? This is the last issue I will be engaged with, in this chapter.

Temporality and Emotion in the Global Class System: The Politics of Self-Guilt

According to Wright and Shin (1988) in one of their articles on temporality and social class, workers adopting a more or less structural approach to class identities, tend to look towards the past for forming, explaining and reproducing their identities, cultural preferences, social networks and political references. On the contrary, workers who adopt a more or less "processual" approach to class, tend to look towards the future. The former tendency emphasises tradition, the latter mobility. Olin Wright and Shin define "structural" as this approach, which takes social structure as determining social relationships. Structure exists before individuals and workers fill the pre-existent positions destined for them by the capitalist mode of production. An orthodox Marxist tradition has a lot in common with such approach but also workers in countries with a strong trade-unionist history tend to adopt this approach without being necessarily Marxists. "Processual" on the other hand is the stance of workers, who believe in life-course individual trajectories, which may lead workers in a better social position in the future. One would have no difficulty to identify this stance with a more or less Weberian theoretical predisposition, and a more or less, North American social ideology and experience.

Psychologist Antony Manstead in a very well-known article titled "The psychology of social class: How socioeconomic status impacts thoughts, feelings and behaviour" (2014), observes that members of the working class tend to blame external conditions and circumstances for life misfortunes and misconducts, while members of the upper classes tend to emphasise individual responsibility, neglecting totally external factors in personal behaviour. Manstead explains how a whole range of behaviours stems out of these two basic tendencies. Both Manstead's and Wright's and Shin's articles are based on specific empirical researches, the findings of which, the three scholars elaborated and analysed. The issue is that these researches were conducted in countries of the industrial North, USA and Sweden in one case and United Kingdom in the other. What, however, happens in Africa?

What is the stance of African workers and African elites? Can the implementation of similar categories of analysis (structural-processual class stances and working and upper class feelings towards misfortune respectively) in Africa, prove the existence of global tendencies, and consequently, class analysis universally valid? Or are things in Africa radically different?

I cannot claim that I conducted any sort of empirical research on the issue, during my fieldwork, as it was out of my focus at that time. However, in hundreds of discussions, formal or informal, almost every day during my 14 month-long fieldwork, the issue of "class-consciousness" that is the self-knowledge of what exactly brings misfortune and limited life-chances to my interlocutors, emerged more frequently than any other. To be totally honest about that the tone on that issue was not given neither by workers nor by elites. It was given by the underclasses. Because it was the underclasses, who massively joined, followed or even established local Christian Churches in the Pentecostal and Charismatic genre, which promised to cast out evil and help people avoid the evil forces of local gods and their African past. A dominant ideology that the basic reason for structural underdevelopment in Ghana, as well as in Africa in general, was the tradition, and especially the religious tradition of the past was gradually orchestrated by elites based on old missionary messages and new popular ideologies of salvation. Various social groups benefited from this ideology, unemployed graduates who became pastors, local and national authorities who diverted social protest, international religious agencies, who found in Africa their privileged playground for missions and conversion. But above all, the ideology of blaming the religious past and the evil gods and spirits of traditional religion was a huge metonymy from traditional land-rights to traditional land-gods and spirits.

It does not seem to exist any collective expression of "structural" approach in Ghana. No-one can discern the structure that makes underdevelopment permanent. Underclasses give the tone, because there are so many workers who find themselves in the risk to become underclasses, every year, every month, every day. Statistics give 5% unemployment! This is ridiculous in an 85% informal economy! Only this fact is sufficient to discard statistics altogether. Elites, government and administration along with IMF and World Bank struggle to show a success story, there, where only devastation and poverty prevails, despite the newly found oil and gas reserves, and despite the steady growth of GDP. Both Olin Wright and Shin and Manstead presumptions seem to be confirmed in Ghana, but in an unexpected and dramatic way. Processual approaches constitute the only choice, regarding temporality. All workers are looking towards the future, and their only hopes are to live this future either in Europe or in America! Migration is the only hope of the working classes, but migration-chances are also divided by class par excellence (Arthur, 2014)! On the other hand, it seems that not only workers but all classes seem to blame external conditions for their misfortune and this definitely impacts their thoughts, feelings and behaviour. Although inequality exists and ruling elites exploit their middlemen-position to make fortunes, the fact that elites are even more religious and god-scaring than commoners, proves that there is no real upper-class mentality among elites. For the simple reason that they are not real upper-class in Marxian terms! Generalised blame on the external conditions however, has deep consequences for class-consciousness, because external conditions in that case are Africans' own cultural past, that is, they blame themselves for their misfortunes! Neither capitalism, nor neo-colonialism, not even local elites! Elites blame the underclasses and underclasses blame the witches, the spirits and the gods in stones, streams and bushes! Global capitalism could not imagine a more ideal condition to loot and destroy an entire continent untrammeled.

CONCLUSION

In this chapter I attempted to show that class analysis and class theory is still operational within social science, provided that we follow the changes that have occurred in the world during the last four decades, at least. I claim that not only Weberian but also Marxian perspective on class is valid today, but we have to follow the development of means of production, the global division of labour, and the new forms of global capitalist domination in order to be able to see this validity. Restricting researches and theoretical elaborations within the borders of the countries of the industrial North, without taking into account what happens in the rest of the world, seems to be rather a political and by no means an academic choice that serves the system of global capitalist domination.

REFERENCES

Alemayehu, Mariam G. (2017). The Chinese Neo-Colonialism in Africa. *Pambazuka News*, 7-9-2017. https://www.pambazuka.org/global-south/chinese-neocolonialism-africa, accessed 9-1-2019.

Allen, V. L. (1972). The Meaning of the Working Class in Africa. *The Journal of Modern African Studies*, Vol. *10*, No. 2 (Jul., 1972): 169-189. Stable URL: https://www.jstor.org/stable/159961.
Accessed: 17-10-2018 13:33 UTC.

Arthur, John A. (2014). *Class Formations and Inequality Structures in Contemporary African Migration: Evidence from Ghana*. Lanham, Boulder, New York, Toronto, Plymouth UK: Lexington Books

Asamoah, Mercy. & Franc, Owusu-Ansah. (2017). Report on Land Tenure & Cocoa Production In Ghana. Accra and Washington DC: A CRIG/WCF Collaborative Survey, February 2017.

Bauman, Z. (2001). The Individualized Society, Cambridge: Polity Press.

Brautigam, Deborah. (1992). "Land Rights and Agricultural Development in West Africa: A Case Study of Two Chinese Projects." *The Journal of Developing Areas.*, Vol. *27*, No. 1, (Oct., 1992), 21-32.

Charlesworth, Simon J. (2000). *The Phenomenology of Working class Experience.* Cambridge: Cambridge University Press.

Cheru, Fantu. & Cyril, Obi. (2010). *The Rise of China and India in Africa. Challenges, Opportunities and Critical Interventions.* London, New York: Zed Books.

Copans, Jean. (1985). The Marxist conception of class: political and theoretical elaboration in the African and Africanist context, *Review of*

African Political Economy, *12*, 32, 25-38, DOI: 10.1080/03056248508703612. Accessed 18-10-2018.

Frimpong-Ansah, Jonathan H. (1991). *The Vampire State in Africa. The Political Economy of Decline in Ghana.* London: James Currey, Trenton NJ.: Africa World Press.

Ghana Statistical Service. (2012). *2010 Population and Housing Census. Summary Report of final results*. Accra: Ghana Statistical Service, May 2012.

Ghana Statistical Service. (2015). *Integrated Business Establishment Survey. National Employment Report.* Accra: Ghana Statistical Service, September 2015.

Gifford, Paul. (1998). *African Christianity: its public role.* Bloomington Indiana: Indiana University Press.

Grier, Beverly. (1981). Underdevelopment, Modes of Production and the State in Colonial Ghana, *African Studies Review*, Vol. *24*, No 1, 21-47.

Grier, Beverly. (1987). Contradiction, Crisis and Class Conflict: The State and Capitalist Development in Ghana Prior to 1948, in *Studies in Power and Class in Africa*, 27-49. Oxford: Oxford University Press.

Grier, Beverly. (1993). Pawns, Porters and Petty Traders: Women in the Transition to Export Agriculture in Ghana, in *Pawnship in Africa*, edited by Paul E. Lovejoy and Toyin Falola, 159-183. Boulder: Westview Press.

Hann, Chris. & Hart, Keith. (2009). *Market and Society. The Great Transformation Today.* Cambridge: Cambridge University Press.

Howard (-Hassman), Rhoda. (1976). Differential Class Participation in an African Protest Movement: The Ghana Boycott of 1937-1938, *Canadian Journal of African Studies*, vol. *10*, No 3, 469-480.

Howard (-Hassman), Rhoda. (1978). *Colonialism and Underdevelopment in Ghana*, London: Croom Helm.

Howard (-Hassman), Rhoda. (1980). Formation and stratification of the peasantry in colonial Ghana, *Journal of Peasant Studies*, vol. *8*, No 1, 61-80.

Hutchful, Eboe. (2002). *Ghana's Adjustment Experience: The Paradox of Reform.* Geneva: United Nations Research Institute for Social Development in association with Oxford: James Carrey, Portsmouth NH: Heinemann and Accra: Woeli Publishing Services.

Kimble, David. (1971). *A Political History of Ghana: The rise of Gold Coast Nationalism 1850-1928*, London: Oxford University Press.

Kyriakakis, Ioannis. (2010). *Christian Pluralism and Social Differentiation in an Nzema Village in Southwestern Ghana.* Doctoral Thesis, University of London.

Kyriakakis, Ioannis. (2012). "Free Market", Society and Capitalism in the Ex-Colonies: The Case of Ghana. *International Journal of Anthropology.* Vol. *27*, n. 3, 167-181.

Manstead, Antony S. R. (2018). The psychology of social class: How socioeconomic status impacts thought, feelings, and behavior. *British Journal of Social Psychology*, *57*, 267–291.

Pakulski, J. & Walters, M. (1996). The Death of Class, London: Sage.

Savage, Mike. (2010). *Identities and Social Change in Britain since 1940. The Politics of Method.* Oxford: Oxford University Press.

Savage, Mike., Fiona, Devine., Niall, Cunningham., Mark, Taylor., Yaojun, Li., Johs, Hjellbrekke., Brigitte, Le Roux., Sam, Friedman. & Andrew, Miles. (2013). A New Model of Social Class: Findings from the BBC's Great British Class Survey Experiment. Published online 2 April 2013, *Sociology.* DOI: 10.1177/0038038513481128. Accessed: 18-12-2018.

Sklar, Richard L. (1979). The Nature of Class Domination in Africa. *The Journal of Modern African Studies*, Vol. *17*, No. 4, (Dec., 1979), 531-552.

Stable URL: https://www.jstor.org/stable/160739.

Accessed: 17-10-2018 13:39 UTC.

Wright Olin, Eric. & Kwang-Yeong, Shin. (1988). A Comparative Study of the Effects of Class Trajectory and Class Structure on Class Consciousness in Sweden and the United States. Temporality and Class Analysis. *Sociological Theory*, Vol. 6, No 1, (Spring 1988), 58-84.

Wright Olin, Eric. 2000. *Class Counts. Students edition.* Cambridge, New York, Melbourne: Cambridge University Press.

Yeboah, Eric. & David, P. Shaw. (2013). Customary land tenure practices in Ghana: examining the relationship with land-use planning delivery. *International Development Planning Review*, *35* (1), 2013, doi:10.3828/idpr.2013.3.

In: Emotions, Temporalities …
Editors: M. Christodoulou et al.
ISBN: 978-1-53616-203-5

Chapter 9

Working-Class Adolescents' Identities through Internet Use: A Psychoanalytic Perspective

Nikos Papachristopoulos[*]
Department of Philology, University of Patras, Patra, Greece

Abstract

The present study is to show the ways in which the changes in the structure and the function of the family create new class-based types of symptoms, instantiated not only in the role of the family, but also in the function of wider social mechanisms, such as the school. These changes are the result of (a) the redefinition of the Oedipal identifications and especially the weakening of parental models for identification; and (b) the use of the Internet, and especially Social Media by adolescents as the modern form of communication and socialisation. In the case of working-class families, in particular, two factors are mostly responsible for such a change: (a) the parents' lack of a mechanism to comprehend and evaluate their children's use of the Internet; and (b) the absence of cultural stimuli

[*] Corresponding Author's Email: papachristo@upatras.gr.

within the family environment, owing to increased professional commitments, which ultimately lead to the children's unchecked use of the Internet.

Keywords: internet, unconscious, family, working-class adolescent

INTRODUCTION

In the annual series of seminars for the year 1996-1997, Z. A. Miller and E. Laurent, psychologists of the School of the Freudian Cause, introduced the issue of 'The Other Who Does Not Exist' (Miller and Laurent 1997). This thesis marks the new concept of the register of the subject in the social bond, as it shows precisely how the nature of new symptoms and the shape of the individual identity are constructed beyond the notion of prohibition and the authority of the One. Or, to put it differently, beyond the undisputable principle of paternal authority and its symbolic associations.

According to the Freudian hermeneutics, the register of the subject in society is dictated by the inevitable withdrawal from the instinctive pleasure-seeking: the subject relinquishes the most vital part of its pleasure to the civilization's Other in order to allow it to experience pleasure in the community (Freud 1908). The Oedipal coordinates, and the symbolic position of the father, in the form of the civilization's Other, retain all their magnitude. The subject desires, but the symbolic Father of the cultural coexistence prohibits. The acceptance of this prohibition, the sacrifice of the larger part of the instinct also ensures acceptance by the Other, a necessary condition for harmonious coexistence with it. This is the foundation of the symptom, born out of the withdrawal from instinctive pleasure, on the one hand, and the excessive prohibition of the social Other, on the other.

The Oedipal Other prohibits and accordingly determines the conditions for participation of the subject in the social norm. This is also Lacan's version in his initial theory. The decline of the paternal imago causes a series of dysfunctional situations for the subject, according to Lacan, too (Lacan 1938). As a result of the weakening of the paternal figure and the symbolic balance that the family enjoyed with its head, the mechanism of identifications is disrupted as is the quest for new signifiers in the cultural Other, especially in scientific discourse. Much like the development of the Freudian neurotic symptom in relation to the demands of the civilisation, the symptom is encompassed within the prospect of the symbolic prohibition of the Name-of-the-Father, the dominant Other (Lacan 1998).

Gradually, however, the cultural environment changes and affects the former symbolic equilibrium, the mechanism of the symbolic balance between the subject and the demands of the civilisation (Brousse 2005). The civilization's Other is no longer so dominant, as it lives in a regime of symbolic dysfunction: no longer one, but many. The Name-of-the-Father becomes plural, the Names-of-the-Father and reverses the entire rationale for the development of symbolic limits within civilisation: the paternal imago is in decline. It is the time of the reconstruction of the relation between the subject and the Other: the Other who does not exist, the Other who does not desire to impose prohibitions, the Other who is not interested in putting any limits on pleasure. In theory, he permits everything, but, in reality, he prohibits everything, except for the safeguarding of the universality of the superficial things and a facade of pleasure. In such a context, the inexistence of its own structure, the inconsistence of the Other, causes more problems than it purportedly resolves. This is when the civilization's Other, instead of nothing, demands everything. Such a directive exceeds the subject's capacity to respond adequately, thus increasing the distance between himself and the ideal Ego. Inevitably, new types of anxiety emerge that generate new symptoms: the subject is invited to designate limits to his pleasure in order to define its own coordinates of its symbolic equilibrium (Laurent 2004).

THE CASE STUDY

The present case-study deals with the use of the Internet as a means of bullying at school by a group of working-class pupils, attending a degraded downtown school in a large provincial city of south-west Greece. This study reveals new aspects for the reception of the relation of the self with the Other, on the basis of the analysis of the statements provided by three fourth-graders, namely pupils in their third year at Secondary school. These kids created a Facebook page, retained their anonymity, and posted abusive comments for their schoolteachers. In addition, the interconnectedness between the self and the Other in relation to both the perpetrators of this act those directly involved or affected, i.e., family and school will be thoroughly examined.

These new aspects are dictated by complete confusion regarding what is imaginary and real, private and public, permitted and banned, in short, by the complete dismantling of the notion of 'limit' in relation to the way in which the subject is registered in the social bond. This dismantling is diffused across all levels of the manifestation of social roles: between child and parent, pupil and teacher, agent of a lawful action and agent of an unlawful action. In addition, they are directly linked to the social classification of the family environment and the everyday functioning of the family – in this case, parents from working-class background with limited engagement and participation in their children's upbringing.

The present case refers to an incident dealt with by the Counselling Services Centre for Secondary Education in the region of Peloponnese. The Centre, headed by the author in his capacity as its Director and Chief Psychanalyst, provides support to all the educational community in the municipality of south-west Greece, coordinates the research carried out in approximately 200 schools, and maintenance of sound counselling provision to address both emergencies and chronic incidents befalling the community. In particular, among the Centre's other actions and activities one may mention school visits following an invitation from the school headmaster to address issues, related to occasionally extremely serious incidents, for instance the murder of a pupil by another pupil. Besides visits, the Centre systematically provides counselling sessions to pupils, parents, and teachers, held in its own facilities.

On one occasion, Mr. P., a secondary school headmaster, visited the Counselling Services Centre, after an incident of bullying, which had received wide public attention, in his school: the victims were a number of teachers and, in particular the maths teacher, while the culprits were four pupils, who posted abusive comments anonymously on a Facebook page.

The page operated for a week, until it was discovered by the maths teacher himself, who – after reporting the matter to the headmaster —filed a case against any responsible party for abusive language and defamation. The Facebook page immediately stopped operating and was subsequently deleted from the Internet. The administrators of this Facebook page were revealed following the headmaster's persistent and extensive efforts and only when the pupils began to fear that they were likely to be considered legally liable for their abusive behaviour. Until then, they had retained their anonymity, under the false impression that they were involved in some sort of 'game', without legal consequences.

What is interesting in this case is the viewpoint of those not directly involved in this incident:

1. The pupils. Despite their claiming to having been unaware of the identity of the administrators of the Facebook page, they, in fact, subscribed to its activity, by 'liking' each post. An indication of their approval is the fact that 280 out of approximately 400 pupils 'liked' each post. Their main concern was, basically, whether they themselves risked facing legal action.
2. The teachers. They exhibited a wide range of contradictory reactions to the incident. Some of them (four out of twenty-two) suggested that legal action should be taken immediately against the culprits. Others (three out of the twenty-two) held a somewhat neutral view to the effect that immediate action in response to the incident should be avoided, while the remaining fifteen teachers essentially subscribed to the pupils' claims: they understood the pupils' lack of awareness of the severity of their offence, going so far (six of them) as to blame the maths teacher, who had taken legal action against any legally liable party, instead of leaving the matter to be dealt with within the school community itself.
3. The parents of the four pupils. They acknowledged the seriousness of their children's behaviour, yet all failed to understand its legal implications. They believed that their children 'were joking' and

since they had apologised to their teachers and admitted that their action was inappropriate, they should receive lenient treatment.

4. The culprits. They were absolutely confused in relation to the issue of limits on their actions. In each case, the content of their statements reveals a clear weakness in relation to their symbolic identifications with their parents and most of all, the complete lapse (conscious or unconscious) of parental authority itself in their symbolic associations.

Discourse Analysis

What follows is an analysis of selected statements from the four pupils who were involved in this incident, with particular focus on the description of the structure of their family relations and their own interpretation of the incident in which they had participated in.

Pupil A

Dimitris is the oldest of the group. His father is a taxi driver (employee, not the owner of the taxi), his mother is a sales person in a clothes store, with inflexible working hours. The children are looked after by the maternal grandparents.

Dimitris' statement regarding his routine reads as follows: 'When I finish school, every afternoon, I meet the other kids in the square and we do various things together. I stay there until five. Then I return home, because I am hungry, I eat something, play games on the Internet, and at about eight o' clock we meet up at the quay, in the cafeteria. There, we play various games and we often stay until late. Then our parents come to look for us and take us home. My parents always complain that I don't study, that I'm always on the streets and that I waste my time surfing on the Internet. But I cannot stay at home not even for a minute! And when I stay, I always want to play games'.

Dimitris said as much about the incident: 'We wrote the comments about the teachers for fun. I would hear some catchwords in the stadium, I would slightly change the wording and thus I would create some lines of "fine poetry"'.

The central aspect in the adolescent's narrative was the absence of shared time with his parents, which led to the complete weakening of the parental models as points of reference for the development of his symbolic identity. The adolescent has entirely equated the notions 'time at home' and 'time outside home', since the transition from the one situation to the other does not undergo any intra-family process.

His parents – due to their demanding working schedules – are not only absent but also seem not to understand the importance of a strict system of control regarding the scheduling of the time which the adolescent can spend outside home. As a result, he gets involved in activities inappropriate for his age, such as his participation in a sports fan club. As a result, he occasionally acquired a leading role in hooligan behaviour, ultimately developing this particular system of symbolic self-representations beyond any parental control.

Transition of authority from the family to the group was central to the adolescent's speech. The group values in such cases are the point of reference for any symbolic identification. These values, however, are dictated by a purely circumstantial framework, since collectivities of this sort require only a rudimentary and group-specific evaluation scale. In his narrative, the pupil describes an easy transition from one group to the other, since he does not develop a bonding with, or commitment to, a single group. His parents, to whom the pupil speaks selectively about his involvement, appear to be completely ignorant of the existence of some of these groups.

As far as the offence of defamation is concerned, he does not appear to have realised its severity, considering it a kind of joke, like the jokes he used to make with one of his groups, with which he created a Facebook group, in which they exchange vitriolic comments with each other, in a somewhat jocular way. His parents appeared not to have realised the consequences of such an incident either, not only in relation to the development of their son's value system, but also in relation to the legal consequences of the action, maintaining that their child was simply joking and that the mechanisms of institutional control should refrain from exercising extreme severity in this case.

Pupil B

Pavlos who is his family's only child. His father is employed in a pharmaceutical company, his mother a housewife.

Pavlos's statement concerning his routine reads as follows: 'My mother is very oppressive. She is always trying to make me study for school. She is really repressive. But I don't need to study so much. I can get by with little effort. And if my grades are fine with little study and I progress to the next class, why should I try harder? I like singing very much; I rehearse in front of my mirror and record various videos. I then upload them onto YouTube – I have my own channel. When I grow up I want to become a professional singer'.

Pavlos said as much about the incident: 'I had no idea about this Facebook page. I had a big problem with the maths teacher. He always insulted me – he knew I was the school representative on the student council and I could turn many pupils against him – and as a result, he embarrassed me in front of my girlfriend'.

In this pupil's narrative the development of the Oedipal identifications on the basis of a strong image of the mother and a weakened image of the father is pretty much evident. The mother's continuous invilvement with her son has completely degraded any symbolic identifications with the father. As a result, any kind of reaction on the part of the son is not addressed to the father but to the hyperbolic maternal model, as the son sees it. In this case, too, the amount of time necessary for the development of a healthy evaluation system for the adolescent appears extremely sparse. The father, due to his professional commitments, essentially fails to follow his son in his symbolic quest for identification, while the mother, who lacks any professional activity and is limited to housekeeping expresses her (possibly suppressed) desire through her identification with her son.

Pavlos' narcissism, his narcissistic enclosure, and his large Ego are clear stand out prominently here. Adopting models for identification outside his family environment and school, which is considered the ultimate authoritative form of socialisation, he is developing an individual evaluation system of his act, in which the evaluation of his ideal Ego relies on his acceptance or not by the Internet community, as expressed by the 'views' on his YouTube channel. This, in combination with his popularity in the wider school community – since he is the head of the student council – and his expertise in the use of technology contributes to the complete weakening of the family's role in establishment of limits his behaviour. The family is unable to limit his behaviour, because it fails to interpret it, while he himself, through his expert use of technology, appears to prevail in his confrontation especially with the paternal authority.

Pupil C

Manolis is his family's second child (he also has one older sister), a child of divorced parents. He lives with his mother, who is a nurse in a central hospital. His father, a carpenter, lives in a city 500 km away and has another son from his second marriage.

Manolis' statement about his routine reads as follows: 'Nothing in the school stimulates me. Useless knowledge. They always talk about old things, which are found in these old-fashioned books. For me, what matters is the image, live information, Internet games, people with whom I can share my problems anonymously, without us knowing each other. I stay in front of my computer day and night, and in the morning, I am, of course, sleepy and I cannot go to school. I have reached the limit of the number of accepted absences at school. At first, my mother tried to lure me away from my computer. At some point she grabbed the cables and unplugged all my electronic devices. But then she realised that this is my life and now she hardly says anything about this situation. She simply brings me food in my room, when I don't feel like leaving it.

Manolis said as much about the incident: 'I don't understand why they are making such a fuss about something so insignificant. I don't know what the rest of my fellow pupils had in mind. They simply asked for my help on a technical matter to ensure that their identity would remain private. I simply don't care whether they punish me or not. Actually, it is better to be punished, so I may not need to go to school'.

In Manolis's narrative the family, and especially the father, is entirely absent, as if he never was a child. He always speaks of the potential that technology offers, which is linked with his enjoyment and his expertise, or his communication with the Others. The pupil completely abstains from any extra-curricular activity and, in general, any extra-curricular interest. He completely relies on the use of his computer (verging on addiction), having developed remarkable skills in programming. At times, he earns pocket-money from small-scale illegal activity, such as 'breaking' passwords upon request, very selectively and without turning this activity into a profession, for the time being.

The way he perceives his relations with the wider community, not just the school community, is revealing. He has excellent knowledge of English, having developed a network with individuals around the globe; he sees himself as a member of a wider Internet universe, to such an extent that, in his own words, he needs 'no social relations whatsoever with his fellow pupils'. As a result, school as an institution is an old-fashioned institution, 'a useless waste of time and energy', which he prefers to spend on computer programming and, in general, exploring the potential of his computer.

In addition, the denigration of family relations is obvious in his words, as his relations with his family are almost non-existent. There is a significant 'gap' between parents and child, as the parents completely fail to comprehend or evaluate their son's action. On the one hand, the weakening of family structure itself, as a result of the parents' separation, and on the other hand, their complete ignorance of the dangers of unreasonable use of technology, create a symbolic vacuum in the adolescent which he himself is happy to fill, reaching the limits of clinical abuse, at times, that is, depressive isolation.

DISCUSSION

Our analysis of this incident provides support to the aforementioned problem with regard to the Other who does not exist and the emergence of other symptoms within a given social environment: working class families, with children attending school with a mass population, in a degraded area of a big provincial city. The social aspects of the case are suggestive of the substantial dimensions of the issue. Its origin lies in the absence of a symbolic framework which arises from the role allocation within the family and, essentially, from the inability of the paternal model to construct the symbolic law (Cottet 2007) and its replacement with the symbolic order of new signifiers, such as knowledge and science, in general. (Leguil 2006) There is an absence of systematic development of the Other which is linked with the weakening of wider symbolic identifications in a social environment, since the role of old-fashioned forms of social control is now taken over by the personalised, and essentially narcissistic, reflection of the image of self in the Internet community. (Laurent 2017) The parents' prolonged working hours combined with their failure to acknowledge the need for constant and systematic involvement in the management of household matters contribute to the development of a gap in the child's moral and intellectual development, which is subsequently filled by the child itself. Thus the child resorts to substitute mechanisms to acquire his symbolic identity, such as the Internet and Social Media. That is why the child fails to acknowledge the existence of 'the rule' as a milestone in the shaping of his behaviour: the rule has no defined content, it has a precarious origin and, most significantly, it has no recipient.

As this case-study shows, a need for intervention emerges, within an established institutional framework, so that such a dysfunctional situation may be addressed. An issue in relation to the role of the school and that of the wider context of education, and its supporting mechanisms also emerges, when the family environment reproduces dysfunctional forms of socialisation for the child. Accordingly, the actions suggested by the Counselling Services Centre in this particular case are primarily concerned with an effort to highlight the significance of the incident: namely, the clear realisation by all parties involved of the severity of an action, which shows explicit criminal elements and is potentially subject to legal punishment. Furthermore, the illustration of the clinical foundations of such an action, which may not point directly to a clinical semiology, reveals, however, a weakened family bond and, as a result, the need for its reconstruction. A prerequisite for such a development is the meaningful participation of all members in common family life. For this reason, the systematic clinical support of the whole family is considered essential. Finally, the need for serious reflection on the role of the school emerges, in cases where the symbolic identifications within the family environment are weakened, that is, when the family fails to limit its members' behaviour both symbolically and practically. What is particularly interesting in this case is the social status dimensions, as they are shown in both the family and the school environment: these are working class families and the school has a mass population of pupils and is located in a degraded city centre. To conclude, the development of carefully planned strategies, which require collaboration between school and family, through a series of actions, both in the school environment and outside the school, are necessary to address such cases. These strategies will reveal the role of the community, which is invited to fill as far as possible, the symbolic gaps, caused by the defective structure of the Other in the civilisation in all its manifestations.

References

Brousse, Marie-Helene. 2006. "Fatherhood: a neologisme of modernity", *The Freudian Cause*, 60: 113-117, Brousse, Marie-Helene. 2006. "La parentalité: un néologisme de la modernité, *La Cause Freudienne*, 60:113-117.

Cottet, Serge. 2007. "The family novel of family", *The Freudian Cause*, 65: 39-47, Cottet, Serge. 2007. "Le roman familial des parents", *La Cause Freudienne, 65:*39-47.

Freud, Sigmund. 2007. [1908]. "The cultural-sexual morality and modern neuroses" *Complete Works. VIII,* 195-200, Paris: PUF, Freud, Sigmund.

(2007). [1908]. "La morale sexuelle culturelle et la nervosité moderne". *Œuvres Complètes. VIII.* 195-220. Paris: PUF,

Lacan, Jacques. 2001. [1938]. "The family complexes within the formation of individual". *Otherwise Written,* Paris: Seuil, Lacan, Jacques. 2001. [1938]. "Les complexes familiaux dans la formation de l'individu". *Autres Écrits.* Paris: Seuil.

Lacan, Jacques. 1998. *The Seminar. Book V. The formation of Unconsciousness,* Paris: Seuil, Lacan, Jacques. (1998). *Le Séminaire. Livre V. Les formations de l'inconscient.* Paris: Seuil.

Laurent, Eric. 2004. "The society of symptom", *Quarto, 85:*18-23. Laurent, Éric. 2004. "La société du symptôme". *Quarto, 85:*18-23

Laurent, Eric. 2017. "The pleasure of Internet". *The Cause of Desire*, 97: 11-21. Laurent, Éric. 2017. "Jouir d'internet". *La Cause du Désir, 97:*11-21.

Leguil, François. 1996. "The bond which separates" *The Small Giraffe*, 24:7-15. Leguil, François. 1996. "Un lien qui sépare". *La Petite Girafe*, 24, 7-15.

Miller, Jacques-Allain. and Éric, Laurent. 1997. *The Other who does not exist and her ethical commitments.* Miller, Jacques-Allain. and Éric Laurent. 1997. *L'Autre qui n'existe pas et ses comités d'éthique.* Available at: http://jonathanleroy.be/wp-content/uploads/2016/01/1998 -1999-LAutre-qui-nexiste-pas-et-ses-comit%C3%A9s-d%C3%A9 thique-JA-Miller.pdf.

In: Emotions, Temporalities …
Editors: M. Christodoulou et al.
ISBN: 978-1-53616-203-5

Chapter 10

THE UNDERCLASS LIFE EXPERIENCES AND THEIR EMOTIONS TOWARDS TIME: THE PRISONERS OF THE CORRECTIONAL INSTITUTION "KORYDALLOS" IN ATHENS

Kalliopi M. Orfanaki*
Hellenic Open University, Patras, Greece

ABSTRACT

The purpose of this paper is to present life experience and emotions regarding time of prisoners, as part of the sub-proletariat, in contemporary times. The data used, which was produced by a qualitative research carried out on a randomly selected representative sample of 235 prisoners during the period 2007-2016, present the way prisoners deal with labour and leisure time during imprisonment, examining their feelings, activities and the meaning of time for them in prison. The prisoners are viewed as agents of action and this research seeks to understand and present how prisoners perceive labour time and how this shapes their subjectivity, as well as how

* Corresponding Author's Email: pepiorf@hotmail.com.

they manage leisure time and what kind of disciplinary impact this produces.

Keywords: underclass, sub-proletariat, dangerous class, prison, linear time, circular time, labour time, leisure time

INTRODUCTION

There is a sociological element to time when it is linked to identity, reproduction of social cohesion and formation of society. In particular, the social perception of time is a social parameter (Durkheim, 1978), which is interdependent with the formation of a system of structures, while time management practices are associated with the strengthening of class contradictions and social and cultural distances among different social groups and strata (Christian Lalive d' Epinay, 1996). In this context, this work attempts to highlight aspects of how prisoners experience time in Greece in the 21st century, from the point of view of cultural criminology. The factual material of this work derives from a field survey conducted by the author from 2007 to 2016 in the Greek prison of Korydallos, which is located in a residential area in Athens and numbers approximately 1800 inmates.

The chapter is divided into three sections. The first section rests upon the bibliography and presents the conceptual content of underclass and sub-proletariat as analytical categories, with data giving the social background of the Korydallos prisoners and a brief overview of empirical research on how prison time impacts the prisoners. The second section gives a summary of the methodological framework of the research and finally, in the third section there is a shift from analysis to prisoner narrations regarding time and their time management techniques during their imprisonment.

SUB-PROLETARIAT VS UNDERCLASS

In the 70s, much of sociology focused on the structural and class dimension of socially marginalised subjects. The focus of the analysis was the concept of the underclass, intended to define the lower working class consisting of people who are not part of the labour force, either because they are unable or because they are reluctant to join the labour market (Morris, 1996).

This term, formulated in 1963 by Gunnar Myrdal, evolved into a fluid (Silver, 1996, 106, 121-122) and particularly controversial concept by a number of researchers. The criticism centred on the belief that the concept of the underclass was too vast, including an overwhelming number of heterogeneous categories of socially disadvantaged people, and as a result, it stigmatized entire social groups, cutting the welfare expenditure corresponding to them (Wacquant, 2008, 3-47,). Factors such as being financially disadvantaged, institutionally isolated, lacking employment opportunities, being racially or culturally different and a spatial concentration of poverty, were all presented as components of the gravely poor, whose suffering was attributed to a lack of working ethos and social disadvantages that posed obstacles to their smooth integration into the labour market.

This critique led to the reconstruction of the Marxian concept of the sub-proletariat as an analytical tool for the study of the social marginalisation. The concept of a multilevel and historically produced sub - proletariat, also referred to in terms of social stratification in the lower - lower class, has a different content from that attributed to the underclass concept (Aloskofis, 2003). The difference is lying in the fact that in the first case the phenomenon of poverty is not represented as a consequence of the characteristic disadvantages of the poor, but as a structural derivative of the system of production and distribution of wealth and social isolation (Wacquant, 2008).

In the case of the penal population, every study of the prison culture is also a study of the sub-proletariat. International empirical data maps the living conditions and family relationships characterizing the pre-penal past of prisoners and demonstrates through a number of perspectives (parental work, level of education, housing conditions, place of residence, kind of family relationships, relations with the labour market) that the majority of them belongs to population groups that have the characteristics of the lower social classes (Vidalis, 2017, Wacquant, Skarðhamar, Torbjørn, 2003). In addition, since the 1930s, G. Rusche and Mr Kirchheimer (1939) have emphasized the importance of the labour market in the over-convict of social class outside or at the margins of the labour market. The class origin of the prisoners is also empirically confirmed by the class selectivity of the penal mechanism, which ensures that perpetrators will primarily come from the constantly growing and "dangerous" sub-proletariat of the cities (Waquant, 2001). Ideologically, the prison as a place of surplus workforce is linked to the choice of the hegemonic elites to confront the global economic crisis and the changes in the labour market by strengthening the means of repression and making use of an aggressive repertoire against the working class groups. The treatment of the sub-proletariat as a dangerous class was accomplished by the cultivation of moral panic (Melossi, 1999, 41, 2006) and led to the increasing use of prison. In jail, the living standard should be low, similar to that experienced by the lowest social class in the free society, so as to act as a deterrent to crime (the principle of less eligibility) (De Giorgi, 2006, 13, 311-326). As a result, the real problem in prisons was not over-crowding (Maculan, Ronco, Vianello, 2013) but excessive poverty and the management of the misery of the working class that has now been subject to criminal custody (Irwin, 2005).

The Social Status of Prisoners in Greek Prisons

As per official data provided by the Greek Ministry of Justice in the period 2007-2016 and on the basis of the available quantified data concerning the profession, the employment and the working portrait of the criminal population in Greek prisons, it would appear that most prisoners correspond to a working age-group, they are urban residents with limited education and come from the lower socioeconomic classes (Aloskofis, 2003).

At Korydallos Prison, which is the largest prison in Greece and, based on official Prison data corresponding to the period 2007-2016, amongst a total number of 1800 prisoners, Greek nationals represented the majority, though representing only 25% of the total population of inmates. The remaining prisoners came from 71 other countries, but most were of Balkan origin. The Korydallos inmates are mostly young men (average age being 33.8 years old), either married or unmarried and have children (31.5% reported being married with children, while 723 inmates or 60% reported being umarried with children). A big number of Korydallos prisoners has a low level of education compared to the overall prisoner population (35.1% are primary school graduates or attended some grades of primary school), most are Muslim (46.2%) and of working-class origin with large numbers of unemployed ones. Observation of the social origin of the detainees is an institutional regulation that allows the Prison Administration to provide the necessary representative clothing and footwear to the prisoners (Article 33 (2) of the Correction Code), to establish a fund of financial support for the time prisoners are released (the EPANODOS of Article 81 Correction Code) and to fund Donations for the support of low-income detainees (Article 45 of the Correction Code).

REVIEWING PRISON TIME

In the period of global crisis, along with the increase seen in the criminalization of social groups (unemployed, immigrants, drug addicts, etc.), there appeared the phenomenon of "criminal diaspora" (Cohen, 1979, 341-36). It should be noted that criminal diaspora has not only impacted with increased incarceration rates, but also impacted with the appearance of more "economical feasible" forms of punishment, especially ones that directly interfere with the self (Foucault, 2011). Such a form of punishment may be found in the management of prison time. Time-management by the Prison in the penal field involves "concentrating and reproducing - under its own terms - a whole range of social relationships" (political, ideological, economic, legal and other), which "do not only influence or mould or pressure penal practices, but operate within them and are an integral part of them" (Garland & Young, 1983, 1-36). Thus, in later modernity, prison time is used as a strategic and technical tool to impose authority. The organization of time in prison is a cheap and efficient means of ensuring that the execution of an activity impacts and controls the self. Time penetrates the body and is followed-suite by the exquisite controls of authority (Foucault, 1989, 174).

Very few studies have dealt with the question of empirical investigation of time in prison. A major investigation was conducted in 1967 in the Durham High Security Prison, investigating the impact of long-term imprisonment on prisoners' perception of time (Cohen & Taylor, 1972). In this study, researchers investigate the prisoners' attempt to survive in prison and find that recourse to linear time calculation, which occurs when there are event-stations, is impossible since the expectation of conditional dismissal is not stable and given. The consequence of this inability is that prisoners adopt personal time measurement techniques (education, work and gymnastics) to avoid the adverse effects of dead time on their mental health, while prison administration uses time as a mechanism to control detainees.

Another more recent research is that of T. Meisenhelder (1985). In this research, the researcher argues that prison time has two characteristics: waiting and burden. Waiting refers to the expected duration of the sentence and burden, to the torturous non-passing of time in prison. The monotony of prison time imparts a temporal uniformity in the lives of prisoners, resulting in the development of coping techniques such as daydreaming, group gatherings, working, sleeping, etc. In the same direction, Brown's work (Brown, 1998) demonstrates that the extensive presence of long-term punishment distorts the sense of the past and the future, as does M. Cunha's study in female prisons where the experience of time is represented as non-real, while the past and the future only make sense outside the prison (Cunha, 1977, 59-68).

METHODOLOGY OF RESEARCH

This survey is based on qualitative data that was collected during semi-structured group and individual interviews, as well as on-the-ground participatory observation. The gathering of material from the group interviews corresponds to the total number of participating prisoners, that is of 80 men and 35 women prisoners who attended the Second Chance School (SCS) at Korydallos Prison, during the academic years 2007-2009. In the remaining school years (2010-2016), the empirical material was collected through individual interviews and observations on a randomly selected sample of 235 inmates. As to the characteristics of the sample, the majority of participants belong to the middle classes of the social organization of prisoners- society of captives (Sykes, 1958). In the context of society, however, they would belong to a part of the population considered to be "dangerous sub-proletariat" (immigrants, addicts, single-parent families, unemployed, manual workers), (Nikolopoulos, 2001, 52-57).

The methodological change from the whole to the random representative sample was due to informational abundance, which was made available via the collective interviews during the first period of the research. The random representative sample of the research which was conducted between 2010-2016, was chosen with the aim of achieving informational saturation (grounded theory). The study of the empirical material was done with the method of content analysis based on the inductive way of forming conceptual categories, taking into account the research questions and the purpose of the research. The issues of the analysis described in this chapter are as follows: (a) the life experience of prisoners as regards time (b) prisoner time management techniques and, (c) time as a tool of political controversy and political demand. For this, three methodological tools were used: interviews, on-the-ground observation and written and visual evidence (data). The goal of the research is to highlight the ways in which prisoners interpret and recreate time while serving their sentence, and how this makes the disciplinary function of the prison visible.

RESEARCH FINDINGS

Time and Confinement

The prison is a time environment in which two major categories of time are distinguished: the institutional time of the prison sentence (the time of execution of the prison sentence and the distribution of time by the internal regulation of the prison) used to control the prisoner's behaviour, and the prison time, which is shaped by routine, monotony and isolation (Cohen & Taylor, 1981).

In these juxtaposed timeframes, it is sometimes the linear and sometimes the cyclical perception of time that prevails. In Korydallos Prison, the first form of linearity is located in the representation of time through two stages: before and after imprisonment. As such, the time of imprisonment becomes a point of reference for the past, the present and the future. The second form of linearity is found while the subject is in custody awaiting the court hearing (Liebling and Maruna, 2005).

During this period, the days pass slowly, the nights are filled with stress and lack of sleep, and the court adjournment will either crush or relieve the person sentenced. Once the prison sentence is imposed, the perception of time is replaced by a different form of calculating the passing of time. The prisoner stops counting the days and begins to count the anniversaries of imprisonment, like the birthday of a new-born. First, by counting weeks, then months, then years. This cyclical perception of time is also confirmed by calculating time from the changing of seasons (summer, winter), the repetition or occurrence of events and practices of the prison community (visitor days, festivities, etc.). With the circular conception of time, social time becomes "frozen time", where time does not pass, leading to the distortion of its perception.

Simultaneously time acquires a special symbolic value, as an evaluation criterion and social positioning of the prisoner in jail. Inveteracy or life imprisonment are criteria for inclusion in the upper social strata in the society of the inmates. Time is extracted from the crime and the isobutene proves through his sentence that he is not an "insider scum", gaining him/her respect and prestige within the prison community. Thus the time of punishment becomes an element of a new identity.

Following the imposition of the sentence, the prisoner must make some decisions regarding the management of the present. As such, the prisoner develops techniques to help him/her cope with prison time at a lower cost (Goffman, 1984). These time techniques aim to reduce the prison sentence time, or to avoid engaging in clashes and avoid disciplinary penalties that will lead away from the beneficial calculation of sentencing days.

Regulating Time in the Prison

The Correctional Code defines a regulating time frame that specifies the exact time at which cells open and close, the inmates wake up and turn in, food is served, visiting hours, work hours, outdoor hours, library operation, ecclesiastics, etc. Consequently, the division of time into small time units produces an "institutional routine". In the long term, this routine is torturous, because it creates prison monotony and frozen time. Yet, at the same time, it fills up the day, making time in prison go by less painfully. However, the prison imparts a binary character to institutional time. The feeling of security experienced by the prisoner through the prison program is accompanied by a certain flexibility in the management of institutional time. As such, the prisoner has a work schedule but is not forced to go to work, to wake up or go to sleep. Prisoners can meet in one cell under certain conditions and the prison warden shows discretion when opening and closing cell doors. However, this tolerance, is in fact a policy leading to non-action, which in turn enhances the monotony of inactivity for the prisoner. It is thus not intended to increase prisoner liberties, but used as a disciplinary tool to intensify the prisoner's suffering through time that does not pass. It is a disciplinary tool consciously applied to impose punishment at a fairly low cost and consequences for the Prison.

> Dimitris: *"Here you sit and rot, you decay. You have nothing to keep you busy. The mind starts to work strangely. 'Idleness is the root of all evil'*

is what the Ancient Greeks would say. It really is unbearable to have nothing to do and just sit [...] personally, it upset me! I feel like I'll burst!"

The Prisoner's Reaction to the Routine

The first piece of advice given to a newly arrived inmate is to plan a schedule of activities, allotting prison time. Organising a program of activities is protection against the detrimental effects of time. A typical piece of advice often given by convicts with life sentences is: "*learn how to kill time so that time doesn't kill you*". (Cohen & Taylor, 1981).

A prisoner's program regulates activity time gradually giving a chronological form in prisoner behaviour where there is exhaustive use of time. The prisoner will thus attempt to fill his daily program to the utmost, so as to prevent it being empty, stagnant and meaningless. This self-regulation has the positive impact of increasing the individual's self-confidence, since carrying out these activities is proof of personal choice and initiative, (i.e., working, going to school, etc.) and it also helps to replace in a way the "lost" socialization that existed in the outside world, setting off a new social clock that will safeguard the prisoner against boredom and prison routine.

This defence mechanism against the torturous time in prison does not however lack discipline. One such example is prison labour. Korydallos Prison has a work program offering 600 jobs to approximately 1,800 prisoners, defined by a ministerial decision. Inmates will be placed in a certain post initially for three months, based on the Labour Council decision, who will meet again to decide whether or not the inmate will continue to occupy that post for a longer period of time or not. These paid jobs, the so-called "merokamato" help to reduce the prison sentence and thus prison time. Prison labour thus plays a major role in a prisoner's personal program, but sadly, the limited number of jobs, which are either manual (such as kitchen, blacksmith, printing shop, prison garden, cafeteria) or non-manual (detox programs, school), are given to only a minority of prisoners.

Labour in prison does not only offer material benefits, but it also has a substantial psychological impact, in that it helps to pass time in prison.

From an ideological perspective, prison labour forms a work ethos that helps to shape the prisoner's obedience and adjusting to prison life. On one hand, prison labour creates a kind of an artificially individualized system of policing, whereby one knows exactly where a prisoner is to be found, on the other hand prison labour operates like a disciplinary machine, by rewarding or sanctioning accordingly. The reward for a prisoner's good behaviour can be getting a better job, and a better job means better wages. And on the contrary, any fault can be punished with reduction in wages (Goffman, 1994), which works as a deterrent for slips. Globally, the limited number of jobs, better wages for some of them than for others, the fear of losing a job or the wages and the hope to be placed in a better job, all result in the prisoners' behaviour conforming to the requirements of the system.

Ultimately, prison labour may be seen as "productive", not so much in the sense of actual quantity of production, but in that it occupies much of a prisoner's time and keeps him/her out of the cell. It does however also incorporate a power relation. The reward for labour is not so much the fee, as much as a reward for good behaviour; there is thus a corrective value, subordinating the prisoner to the penal mechanism (Foucault, 1989). Prison labour is thus a means to keep order and eurhythmy. The physical work in itself keeps the body and mind busy, it keeps away turbulences and distractions, imposes a hierarchy and supervision that influence behaviour and, no doubt, also impacts on the prisoners' social identity.

The Drama of Leisure Activities

While the time spent doing labour activities is, during imprisonment, a way to make believe time goes by faster and it provides for a faster release, leisure time is perceived as abundant, compulsive, flat and tortuous.

> Romney: *"Someone who is not a prisoner cannot come near to understanding prison routine. He cannot understand this closing of the*

door at 8.00, or the sound of the key turning with the shutting of the door that strikes you straight in the heart. Even now, even though I've been in jail for so long, the striking does not cease..."

In order to manage empty and frozen time, a prisoner will develop activities, which will in the short term help to distract him/her from prison reality, but in the long term "kill him" (Goffman 1994, 78). Some of these distracting activities are collective (i.e., sports, gambling) whereas others are purely individual (handicraft, television). Some are compliant with prison regulations, whereas others are in actual fact forbidden, such as the use of social media, alcohol consumption, etc.

Regardless of their nature, these leisure activities reflect the cultural model existing in the prison and the corresponding social values; for example, the hegemonic masculinity. There is also a show of power behind each activity, determined by the social environment of the prison. Consequently, the social dimension of the leisure activities will depend on what impact they have within the prison culture.

And with activities being publicly known within the prison, the prisoner will tend to take on activities that are socially accepted, encouraging this system of social cohesion. There are thus activities that are susceptible to in-prison social reaction (i.e., a male prisoner knitting) and others that are socially acceptable. Acceptable leisure activities are mostly limited to watching TV, handicrafts, gymnastics - weights or boxing, drawing, listening to music, praying (which is seen as a duty for some religious groups) and even gambling.

Kosmin: *"Each day things are better. Okay, I've found my way; I come to school, I work out, I cook, I meet friends, we sit, we talk ... To survive. Otherwise, I will not survive. I'm still vulnerable."*

In the prison's monotony, the possibility to feel intensely pleasant feelings is largely limited. For most detainees, there is nothing new, nothing sensational in prison life, which is why in leisure-time they seek activities that might move them. Many times their need to feel emotion leads to illegal transactions (the so-called "ntaraveria" or "alisverisia")[1]. The introduction and trafficking of drugs, mobile phones, gambling, usurer lending, alcohol making, tools, making improvised weapons, all these replenish the lack of goods or offer a counter satisfaction that they beat the system.

Further on, I present a small sample of inmate leisure activities that indicatively, stood out during the research.

TV and Social Media

All cells have a TV set that operates 24 hours a day. In many cells there is a separate TV set for each prisoner, and there is also the possibility to acquire a special TV network subscription for prisoners with an income. The most popular TV shows are news broadcasts, reality shows and products reflecting contemporary folk culture. Television is for the prisoner a window to the outside world and current affairs it is also a way of coping with isolation and "dead time".

Social media are an ideal means of self-preservation. Through Facebook, the prisoner has the ability to impersonate different roles or adopt different identities, especially when in contact with the opposite sex. This pastime strengthens the gendered identity and the sense of continuity of life in prison. At the same time, the use of social media reflects the prisoner's status and prestige, since to be a smart-phone owner, which is a prohibited good, requires a certain purchasing power and influence.

Crafts

Prisoner crafts have a special style and character from a morphological and visual perspective. The theme (prison scenes) but also the materials used (wood, bread, etc.) determine their style and form. Craftsmanship (lighters,

---

[1]In the prisoner idiom, ntaraveria or alisverisia are illegal transactions of phones, drugs, tools, weapons ect.

ashtrays, paintings, cushions, beaded jewellery, etc.) express personality and emotional-state. At the same time the craft is a personal gain for the homo faber prisoner. The lighter may be exchanged for a phone card or tobacco, and will yield double benefit to the creator. The prisoner feels important through his/her craft, transforming leisure time into a kind of non-institutional working time.

Handicrafts are the only items to which the prisoner attributes gift value. The prisoner will gift to a loved one an item that she/he has manufactured in prison, or purchased by an inmate in exchange for a much valued quantity of tobacco or a telephone card. The existence of these objects thus contributes to maintaining the system of social relations and alliances, both inside and outside the prison walls. It is not long, however, before the immense continuity of prison life weighs down on the prisoner who then abandons this craft activity. Repetition will tire the prisoner unless s/he becomes a professional manufacturer, but even that is hard to achieve within the restrictive prison environment, where it is hard to obtain the material required for the manufacturing. The prisoner thus turns to his/her cell bed.

Life Goes by with Sleep

> Bartull: *"I would like to sleep and wake up only when it's time for me to get out of here. I wish I could do that: To sleep non-stop. To make time pass, as there is no other way to make it pass in here."*

Sleep becomes a technique of preserving the mental well-being of the prisoner. During imprisonment, the prisoner looks forward to sleep time, which allows him/her to escape the torturous "dead time".

The prisoner's desire to fall into deep sleep, to reach the point of disconnecting from his/her milieu, is simultaneously linked to a desire to awaken into an unexpected new reality. But excessive sleeping can be tricky in that it has negative side effects. Many prisoners suffer from insomnia. Then constant daydreaming takes over, allowing the prisoner to create the time and space of his/her choosing. Daydreaming and inactivity modify the sleeping hours that are thus reversed - sleeping in the morning and being awake at night, thus creating a subjective present, in which the prisoner mentally frees him/herself from the detention restrictions and prohibitions.

The Use of Prohibited Substances

A large number of prisoners use toxic substances, mainly Indian cannabis, as a strategy to combat institutional time and escape from the gloomy prison reality. Other forms of distraction are the illegal production and consumption of alcohol.

There is a small number of prisoners, mainly of Balkan origin, who make tsipouro[2] from fruit peels in their cells, and then consume it in group meetings or sell it for tobacco or telephone cards. The production and consumption of tsipouro in the prison is of course forbidden, since alcohol consumption is associated with manifestations of violence and other troubles in the prison. Although prisoners verbally express a desire to drink alcohol, most of them believe that banning alcohol is legitimate insofar as it avoids troubles in the jail.

In Greek prisons there is a fairly large number of prisoners who take heroin or prescribed psychotropic medication; substances with a calming effect that suppress any need for action, making the bodies senseless, immobile, sickly. In these cases, the prisoner's time-management technique becomes dependant on obtaining these substances and on creating the necessary social network that will enable him/her to obtain the substances. The prisoner user will thus become involved in a complex network of trading and trafficking of substances that define time within the prison. The drug user starts to "*borrow*" from the prisoners who control the drug trafficking in the prison and obtains a social position of dependence. This social position is associated with depreciating images and negative characterizations such as the "junky" or "bedside table"; the drug user is ultimately treated with contempt and exclusion.

---

[2]Tsípouro is a strong alcoholic drink which is produced by the peels of soma fruits (ex orange, grapes).

The drug use is a time-management technique that takes place within a prisoner's cell and is thus seen as a choice; an action that takes place with a certain level of autonomy. Nonetheless, drug addiction can then be seen as self-enclosure. Some prisoners regard drug use as an encouraged means to suppress detainees, to prevent them from protesting and to preserve a peaceful environment in the prison.

The Worry Beads ("Koboloi")

Playing with worry beads is a typical pass-time, or time management technique used by prisoners. The worry beads are a prisoner's companion, his/her music, an object of his/her prisoner identity. A prisoner's bond with his/her worry beads, is one of the strongest. The prisoner will play with the worry beads all day long; in the cell, in the wing, in the corridor, or in the courtyard. The prisoner stands, kneels and walks playing with the "koboloi" (the worry beads). When not playing with it, the prisoner will put it away in a sweatshirt pocket, or wears it around the neck.

Prisoners make improvised worry beads out of wood or bread. Others obtain the beads from visiting family and friends. The size of their "koboloi" is larger than the average koboloi used by middle-class Greek youth. The beads are large and resemble a garland in length and shape. They are positioned on a string, loosely tied in a circle, though there can be variations.

A "koboloi" is not only an object of personal belonging; it is also a symbol of social values and recognition. As such, the number of beads symbolizes the prisoner's sentence time, "*the years I heard in court*". It is therefore not only a leisure time management technique, but also an object representing the prison value system. It moreover symbolizes masculinity, machismo and it is associated with honesty, having no negative connotations. A "magas" is a cool guy, the long term convict who respects the rules of the prison and moves in the wing with the koboloi calmly confronting any difficulties.

> *Angelos: "The beads are a prisoner's guts. A lot of beads signify a lot of guts. That's why the koboloi must not fall to the ground. If it falls down, so do a prisoner's guts."*

As a sacred object, the koboloi is almost fetishlike. Hardly ever will a prisoner lend his worry beads to another prisoner. It is as if it has magical qualities that will determine the length of stay of the prisoner in the distressing prison environment.

> Babis: *"If you drop your koboloi, it's bad luck... If you drop it and it breaks, they say the number of beads that fell off will be the number of years you will be sentenced by the court."*

CONCLUSION

Prisoners as part of the sub-proletariat, present their life experience and emotions regarding time. Prison shapes the subjectivity of the prisoner and the time is a tool of "economical feasible" forms of punishment which affects the class identity. The concept of time is perceived differently for the prisoner before and during imprisonment, whilst the duration of the sentence impacts the perception of the main categories of time; the past, the present and the future. Time is initially experienced in a linear form, and with the imposition of the imprisonment sentence it becomes circular. The "frozen time" of punishment is distressing for all prisoners and thus they develop time-management techniques as a coping mechanism. These techniques aim at avoiding the sentence being prolonged and to make the sentence time feel like it goes by painlessly and fast.

Furthermore, the duration of the prison sentence is one of the criteria for social assessment by the prison community. The fragmentation of prison time into beneficial labour time and tortuous leisure time creates social differentiation and influences the time-management techniques. A good prisoner is one who has a long prison sentence and is placed high in the social prison hierarchy. The "wise" prisoner is the one who, through the provision of prison facilities (i.e., work and wages), creates a daily routine with activities that will help him/her get through the "frozen time" in prison.

However, feelings of inaction, the slow passing of time and the sense of a wasted life are so intense that, despite all these time-management techniques, the time spent in prison is experienced as a "anchyloses of time", weighed down by the routine and monotony that the prisoner experiences. As incarceration distorts the prisoner's perception of the present, it can be taken as proof of how prison authority interferes even to the point of reaching the last recourse of the psyche, it touches on the body and penetrates the subject's actions.

Globally, the prison operates like a huge machine that recreates and reconstructs time. It overturns time correlations, bringing the past to the present, catalysing reality whereby prisoners start to confuse their lies with the truth, and simulating myths with reality. There may be a prison program, institutional time, and the creation of techniques for the management of frozen time, yet it is the "anchorage time", the non-time, which has a disciplinary effect, through a policy of inaction and through the granting of positive and negative sanctions, rendering any authoritarian enforcement by the jail unnecessary.

REFERENCES

Aloskofis, William. (2003). The social Profile of the prisoners and the needs after disposal, Athens, *Epanodos*, *l*, 2-4 (in Greek).

Brown, Alyson. (1998). Doing Time: The extended Present Of the Long Term Prisoner, *Time and Society*, Mar (7), 93-103.

Christian, Lalive. & d' Epinay. (1996). Time: social dynamics and social diversification in *The Sociology of Leisure Time* Edited by Alexandra Koroneou, Nisos: Athens (in Greek).

Cohen, Stanley. & Taylor, Laurie. (1972). *Psychological Survival. The experience of long term Imprisonment*, 2th ed. Harmondsworth, England Middlesex: Penguin.

Cunha, Manuela. (1977). Suspended Time, Rythms and Duration in a Portoguese Prison. *Terrain, 29*, 59-68.

De Giorgi, Alessandro. (2006). *Re-Thinking the Political Economy of Punishment: Perspectives on Post-Fordism and Penal Politics*. London & New York: Routledge, Taylor and Francis.

Durkheim, Emile. (1975). *The Roles of Sociological Method*, Athens: Gudenberg (In Greek).

Foucault, Michel. (1989). *Discipline and punish: The birth of the prison*, Athens: Rappas Publ (In Greek).

Garland, David. & Young, Peter. (1983). Towards a Social Analysis of Penality. In David, Garland & P. Young (Eds.), *The Power to Punish: Contemporary Penality and Social Analysis*, 1-36. London: Humanities Press.

Goffman, Erving. (1994). Asylums, Trikala: Evrialos Publ. (In Greek).

Irwin, John. (2005). *The Warehouse Prison: Disposal of the New Dangerous Class*. Los Angeles, CA: Roxbury.

Liebling, Alison. & Maruna, Shadd. (eds). (2005). *The Effects of Imprisonment*, Cullompton, Devon: Willan Publishing

Liebling, Alison. (1992). *Suicides in Prison*, Routledge: London

Maculan, Alessandro. & Ronco, Daniela. (2013). *Prison in Europe: overview and trends*, in the European Prison Observatory. Detention conditions in the European Union, Antigonis: Rome (www.prisonobservatory.org/upload/PrisoninEuropeOverviewandtrends.pdf).

Meinsenhelder, Thomas. (1985). *An essay on Time and the Phenomenology of Imprisoment in the Deviant Behavior*, *6*, 39-56, New York: Wiley.

Melossi, D. (2006). Penal Practices and Governance of the Marx and Foucault Populations, in the Koukoutsaki Afrodity (Ed), *Prison Images*, Athens: Plethron (in Greek)

Melossi, D. (1999). The social theory and the changing representations of the criminal in the Koukoutsaki Afrodity (Ed), *Prison Images*, Athens: Plethron (In Greek).

Morris, L. (1996). Dangerous Classes: Neglected Aspects of the Underclass Debate. In the E. Mingione, *Urban Poverty and the Underclass*, (160-175). Urban Research Publications Ltd.

Nikolopoulos, George. (2001). *State, criminal power and European integration. A Criminal Approach*. Athens: Kritiki (In Greek)

Pitch, Tamar. (1995). *Limited responsibilities. Social movements and criminal justice*, trans. J. Lea, London – N.York: Routledge.

Penitentiary Code. http://www.opengov.gr/ministryofjustice/?p=8630 (in Greek).

Rusche George. & Kirchheimer, Otto. (1939). *Punishment and Social Structure*. New York: Columbia University Press

Sykes, Gresham. (1958). *The society of captives: A study of a maximum security prison*. New Jersey: Princeton University Press.

Vidali, Sofia. (2017). *Beyond the limits. The crime policy today*. Athens: Nomiki Vivliothiki (In Greek).

Wacquant, Louis. (2001). *The prisons of misery*. Athens: Patakis (In Greek).

Wacquant, Skarðhamar Torbjørn. (2003). Inmates' Social Background and Living Conditions, *Journal of Scandinavian Studies in Criminology and Crime Prevention*, Volume *4*, Issue 1, (39-56).

Wacquant, Louis. (2008). *Urban Outcasts: A comparative Sociology of Advanced Marginality*. Polity.

In: Emotions, Temporalities … ISBN: 978-1-53616-203-5
Editors: M. Christodoulou et al.

Chapter 11

"A Hope for a Better Life for the Children": Women of Migration, Domestic Work and Emotions

Konstantina Bada*

Department of History and Archaeology,
University of Ioannina, Greece

Abstract

Given that emotions make for a dynamic and complex field that impacts on social relations and on the formation of social and cultural identities, in this chapter we explore the role of emotions in the everyday life of Ukrainian and Bulgarian women, who work as domestic workers in Greece. The analysis of ethnographic material consisting of oral testimonies and life stories of Ukrainian and Bulgarian immigrant women, shows that the role of emotions is important in redefining a) one's identity as a migrant domestic worker, b) the forms of sociality—developed in conditions of precariousness, non-formal and low-profile work and social inequality—and c) their relationship with their place of origin and family.

* Corresponding Author's Email: konbada@gmail.com.

The constant care they invest in improving the lives of their underage or adult children and the parental relationship that they often develop with the children of the employers' family, gives meaning to their everyday lives as immigrant domestic workers and helps them to establish an identity as mothers and good women.

Keywords: immigration, domestic work, emotions, emotional practices/policies gender, family, identity

1. Introduction

Eighteen years ago, through a job center, Olia made her way from Athens to Agrinio, using the intercity bus service (KTEL), to take on the personal care of my father, a cancer patient. Olia was Ukrainian, around 52, she had no residence or work permit in the country, but she had already worked in a similar position for two years in Athens, three in Aigio, one in Nafpakto, and six months in Agrinio, where she looked after my father. She lived with him and was responsible for his care, the house, the groceries, everything. She grew up and lived in Rubizne, a small city in Ukraine. Before making her way to Greece, she was a skilled worker in a glass factory. There she lived with her family, her two children, her parents and other close relatives (a married brother and two of her uncles). After leaving, her parents took care of the children, a boy of 19 and a girl of 17. With their father, who lived in another city and had another family, she had separated two years prior to her journey. The decision to emigrate was primarily defined by the need to take care of her family. The loss of her job at the factory, now shut, as well as everything else that came with the collapse of the socialist regime, combined with her inability to respond to the political and economic circumstances of the time—or even to basic family obligations, the encouragement from a friend already living and working in Athens as a "nurse" in a home, shaped her decision to temporarily (as she believed) migrate. She reached Greece with a tourist visa in 1997.

There was no need to look for employment in agencies because her friend found her work in Athens immediately, in a home in which she looked after an elderly, ailing man. With him she became proficient in Greek (he was a professor in literature), and after two years she moved elsewhere, through an agency, and then to Aigio where she was paid well enough and no longer had the asphyxiating obligation of looking after his children. When she arrived in Agrinio, she took on the care of my father and all the other family obligations around him. Her situation, that of an immigrant with no residence or work permit—an internal and single domestic worker—seemed to be experienced in fear, though not without stoicism or adaptability.

Meanwhile, she appeared to overcome her own situation through a sense of self-sacrifice for the sake of her family. After leaving them, she had not visited her children once for fear that she would not be able to re-enter Greece. In the room where she lived there were always small items that we offered as gifts or that she purchased; every so often she would pack them and through her own people send them to her children. Once a week she would talk with them on the phone, and once a month she would go with my brother to send a remittance to her own people in Ukraine. Frequently, however, she would show photographs of her children and her house, and she spoke of both with immeasurable affection—her son was already in university and her daughter was finishing high school and wanted to be a civil engineer; she would stress with pride that she had children and lived for them only.

In the context of my own difficult family moment, I was not acting as a researcher. I had only cared on a human level to learn of her life there, here, her hopes and expectations. But I had noticed that her self-perception and identity conflicted with her role as a mother who loves, cherishes and suffers for her children. This feeling was, I would say, a moving force, as was her interpretation of her difficult workplace and mundane social life. The latter was experienced through her own, separate spacetime, defined by mental and emotional attachments with the home, her children, and the greater family she left behind.

I looked her up five years later, and this time, in my function as a researcher, interested in the lived experience of the transnational migration of women from Eastern Europe to Greece, and those employed as domestic workers. She was older, more fatigued, she no longer had that old fear in her—she had secured a temporary residence and work permit—she always did the same job, moving from place to place and from one environment to another.

The prolonged period of time during which she had been exposed to the experience of migration and servitude, had increased and altered her emotional baggage. I noticed that she had internalized and accepted her position as a foreigner and worker in domestic work; she seemed indifferent and unable to alter her prospects in life, though she had now set a little money aside, she had a partner and had formed some social relations. Her sense of joy and satisfaction manifested only when speaking of her children, when she said that she had succeeded in creating a good life for them. Yuri had completed university and was already working in a large foreign company. Valentini was in the fourth year of her studies and was trying to work out what she might like to study at a postgraduate level. She had renovated the house, and her family would obtain some residence permit and visit her here and there using their own finances.

Olia remained in Athens and stayed "in the same job," until 2014 when she returned to her home country. Although her intention was to stay "for as long as her hands were good for the job," the economic crisis in Greece galvanized her decision to leave. Her expenses were significantly reduced, her daily life in the house as a supplier of services over the past few years was dictated by terms of strict frugality: food, utilities, shopping, everything. In addition to all of that, her work was once more informal and uninsured, at least since the time her employer gradually ceased the payment of her already limited daily work stamps. As she said tellingly, "the crisis struck her head first," and that of her "circle," a reference to other Ukrainian workers in the same job. "Now that I too would want to set something aside for myself, for my old age, now I can't do that."

I met Olia shortly before she left, and this time her feelings of bitterness, disappointment and a manifest angst, almost overshadowed the joy of returning to her family. Bitterness and disappointment, because "I am forced to leave, though not of my own accord, and because I live here for so many years, I was cut off, a stranger... And I did not have the time to look after Olia a little too." And angst at the imminent reception by her family but also the broader community, her adaptation to its circles. "I don't know what to expect. The children are now independent and have other people by their side, they have dreams to go elsewhere, my parents are no longer alive… who now remembers Olia…"

2. Theoretical and Methodological Axes

Olia's migration and work experience, the meanings, the definitions and the interpretations that she attributed herself to her experience, to her value system, to emotion too, was for me the impetus for the search for visible and invisible aspects of female migratory experience and domestic work. To be more precise, a search for the experience of women who had migrated alone, autonomously, and who worked for several years as internal domestic workers. My point of view was shaped, I would say, both through my contact with the social subjects of migratory work, but also through an effort to understand the lives and experiences, through the application of approaches to migration that heed the micro-level, the level where people are, people whose migratory and work choices are defined based on their personal stories, social relationships and identities, though without suggesting that their positions or choices are not affected by the broader structural factors of the modern capitalist system.

The particulars of narrative lives allow us to understand migration from an insider's perspective, and to emphasize the multi-faceted nature of the migration and domestic work process. Through therefore the analysis of the interviews of immigrant domestic workers and the analysis of the ethnographic data, it is exanimated how the specific work experienced acquires meaning and is interpreted by migrant domestic workers, what emotions it gives rise to and how the image of the self and their identity is shaped.

2.1. Analytical Categories: Gendered Migration and Emotions

The analytical categories used in the present text, and the themes tied to the former, revolve around the gendered character of migration and work, the meaning of work, understood as not only an economical, but also a social cultural meaning with a particular reference to salaried domestic work, which is by and large the arena in which gendered, class and racial inequality is reproduced; they also revolve around emotions, which in the context of integration of salaried work in the space of reproduction, give rise to new dimensions of work, work practices, and work identity.

2.1.1. The Gendered Aspect of Migration

Anthropological research on migration and on its gendered dimension in Greece is limited, though the country has been receiving for 30 years a large number of male and female immigrants from several countries (Vermeulen 2004: 178-79). Additionally, the modern phenomenon of migration displays features interweaved with globalization as it happens in the shaping of transnational social fields and networks that connect two different societies—that of origin and that of settlement of immigrants who traverse borders of origin and residence, and develop and maintain several relationships (family, economic, social, religious and political) (Ventoura 2009: 32–36; Nitsiakos et al. 2019).

The interest in researching immigrant women has been by and large associated with the informal type of labour, and in general with the unequal, informal and invisible work of the female gender. Meanwhile, the main features of modern immigration are strongly identified with informal economic migration, informal work practices, and the tension of the feminization of immigration. In Greece the percentage of the female immigrant population from certain countries is particularly large, greatly surpassing the male population. Women, say, from the Philippines, make up

80% of the total immigrant population from the same country. This rate is at 78.8% for Ukrainians, and approximately 60% for Bulgarians and Georgians. In general, the countries of Southern Europe (Italy, Greece, Spain, Portugal) which up until 1973 were lands of emigration and were perceived as such, also became countries of immigration, illegal immigration in fact, lands of informal work (Castles and Miller, 2009:113-115, 240-242), but also countries with an increasing tendency towards the feminisation of migration (Maratou - Alibrandi 2007: 26 - 27). Although women were never absent from immigrant flows in the past, the increasing tendency of female migration and the important role they played in gender-specific networks of labour migration, made them more visible both as social subjects and subjects of social research, highlighting a defining, dynamic role in modern transnational migration (Bauer and Thompson 2004). In addition, from the 1980s onwards, female migration to other countries in particular, had contributed to the lifting of the silence around the immigrant woman, around the system of dichotomy that paired woman with immobility and man with mobility. Therefore, men and women migrants experience and comprehend differently both their departure from the place of origin and their life in the place of settlement (Green 2004). In this reading, the new research of international migration has approached it not as a common and homogenous experience that defines all immigrants in the same manner, but also as differentiated, on the basis of gender ethnicity, culture and experience. Women from Bulgaria, aged 40 and above, migrate by and large on their own, leaving family behind and tending to it with the money earned from their work, mostly as domestic workers (Nikolova 2010: 257 – 308; Angelidou 2010: 157-188). A corresponding practice of immigration is implemented by a large number of Ukrainian immigrants in Greece (Nikolova 2015), whereas Albanians move in the context of family or relative circles (Boeschoten 2015). As mentioned earlier, immigrants are active subjects with a role in decision-making and a plan for their migration, a plan not determined only in family strategies or economic processes, but one that involves complex negotiations of identities and gender relations, both at the starting point, during the journey, and in the place of arrival and among all related social networks.

2.1.2. Emotions

Emotions, as early as 1980s, have been treated as products of a historical, social and cultural context (Abu-Lughod and Lutz 1990). Recent historical-anthropological studies seek to identify the indirect ways in which emotion is conveyed and finds its place between people, objects and situations, thus affecting the means of taking in and interpreting experiences of the past and their mnemonic manifestations. For instance, studies on collective trauma, social pain, social, economic, and cultural crisis, etc., show that these situations disturb time, uncontrollably blend the past with the present, and the future with memories and traumatic experiences that are brought to the surface in ways and terms that are not necessarily logical, since the empirically lived sense of time and past do not agree with what we call history, or the linear perception of its chronicity. The tendency of emotions, such shame or and guilt, to form the identity of holocaust survivors, is determined by chronicities that are confused but inscribe also an aspect of history, perhaps defined by the uncanniness as noted Paul Ricoeur but still an aspect of history (Ricoeur 2004:303), while integrating additional feelings through the social, cultural context that creates them and gives meaning to them, we may identify the politics of emotions, their entanglement in social and economic asymmetries, and finally their highlighting as dynamic and multi-faceted fields of formation of social and gendered relations of power and resistance. Thus the turn of scholarship towards the world of emotions and their meaning-attribution by the acting subjects, especially subjects found in conditions that make them invisible and mute, highlights their role in human, personal and collective action, in history and in the process of shaping social identities, giving meaning to the integration of the perspective of emotions in the study of, e.g., female migration and in particular to domestic work. It also highlights their importance as means of manipulation, internationalization, and legalization of social relations of power, of discipline and social inequality. Recent studies, such as those investigating domestic labour and the construction of the serving labour force, heed the importance of emotions on the processes of internalization of servitude and social inequality (Hantzaroula 2012; Psimmemos 2013: 29). The approach, more analytically, of salaried domestic workers as embodied social subjects with desires, feelings, and interpersonal relations on the one hand, gives rise to the possibility of expressing their subjectivity in a different manner, and on the other calls for readings that highlight different dimensions, contents and meanings in domestic labour. While the latter is connected by and large to the space of reproduction (the family and the home), it reproduces, especially when it is provided over a long period of time in the same space, ties and feelings that lead the individual domestic worker, deprived of her own family, to a voluntary and selfless identification with roles of a family nature, feelings, interests even in the controlling practices of the employing family. It is, as highlighted in recent sociological studies, a form of relations of "pseudo-familial" character with their employers, which result in the blurring of boundaries between salaried and non-salaried work, a blurring that contributes catalytically to the trapping of immigrant women in the specific employment. Trapping, in the sense that they are forced to endure the security of a home and in the context of a family that is not their own (Xypolitas 2012; Psimmenos 2017:54-59). There is also another dimension, equally salient, in what is the forced (in the context of their labour) expression of specific emotions towards the employer. The so-called "emotional" labour is, more analytically, a process of instrumentalization, management or professionalization of specific emotions such as joy and compassion, patience, enthusiasm, and support that the domestic worker is expected to express towards the employer to create satisfaction (Hochschild 1979:561). It is perhaps the heaviest and most exhausting burden of their labour, as noted by most women.

> "In the evening I feel empty inside… I do not mind manual labour, I am strong, I can withstand it, but constantly smiling, or feigning enthusiasm with what is said and what takes place around me, kills me, I feel like a rag" (Nikoleta, 62, Bulgarian, interview in Agrinio, 2009).

In contrast, the motherly feelings of compassion and love towards their own children or family, for which they migrate in difficult and humiliating circumstances, are expressed with particular vigour. These emotions, great, honest or magnified, are converted into a dynamic field of action and influence on the process of identity-formation of the female domestic worker.

2.2. Women from Ukraine and Bulgaria, Live-in Domestic Workers

The research material consists of twenty five migratory and work histories of 12 Ukrainian and 13 Bulgarian women who migrated alone, leaving their families behind, from approximately 1998 to 2008, to work as domestic workers/helpers. Given that their ethnicity to a great extent appears tied to domestic work in Greece (Nikolova 2013; Nikolova 2015:9, 28-29), both in urban centres and in the countryside, I chose to focus my interest on immigrant domestic workers in the rural setting. It must first be stressed that Greece was one of the first countries to which Ukrainians[1] travelled to work in the informal market, between 1994 and 1998 in particular, while a key feature of this migration was its female character. Meanwhile, senior women mostly worked in domestic labour. It is indicative that of the 25 domestic workers that I approached only three (two Ukrainians and a Bulgarian), decided to return to their countries (Xypolitas, Vassilikou, and Fouskas 2017:90-93). Even by investing their own financial resources in building or repairing a house back home, to house the family there in a modern domestic environment, they continue to postpone their own return, for when they can no longer work.

The immigration of Bulgarians to Greece begins in 1989, but the largest wave arrive between 1997 and 2001 as a consequence, by and large, of the economic crisis in Bulgaria (Hatziprokopiou and Markova 2015). It is

[1]Migration from Ukraine to Greece took on a mass character between 1994 and 1998. Entry was secured with a tourist visa, and workers then remained in the informal labour market after its expiry. From the early 21st century Ukrainians became "visible" (their status was formalized), especially in Southern European countries such as Portugal, Italy, and Greece, as a result of amnesty programs (Nikolova 2013). More generally see Migration 2008: National Statistical Institute. URL: http://www.nsi.bg/ EP DOCS/ Migration08.pdf, accessed 20.9.2011. According to the analysis of the Bulgarian National Bank published in 2011, the number of post-socialist Bulgarian (long-term) migrants is estimated to be at 618,430 (Hatziprokopiou and Markova 2015).

highlighted that immigrant men and women from Bulgaria, after the integration of their country in the European Union (2007), have secured better conditions for their stay in Greece. Their opening e.g., to the job market from 2009, with the free access granted to Bulgarian citizens, which allowed the legalization of the formerly informal (for several reasons) domestic activity, the facilitation of the process of issuing a residence and work permit, the collaboration of the two countries for the recognition of the time spent working and the transfer of their pension rights etc., constitute significant changes in their migration history. However, these changes do not seem to have brought about significant improvements in the terms of labour of domestic workers from Bulgaria, and neither have they opened, as it may appear, a prospect for professional mobility between them. As is discovered through the testimonies of these women, though they have now secured a residence and work permit, they did not experience some improvement in their lives, though insofar as work is concerned long-term domestic workers remained in essence in an informal and illegal labour regime. And this is because having for many years worked either entirely or partially uninsured, they themselves remained indifferent to the few work stamps that would not be enough to secure, even if they were being insured regularly over the past few years, a right to a social security and pension.

3. Data Analysis

The biographies of the 25 immigrant domestic workers were recorded in different times and places: three were held in Athens, five in Nafpaktos[2], five in Agrinio, four in Arta, six in Yiannena and three in Igoumenitsa. To these women these were places of temporary residence, a short or long-lived stop before continuing on their journey to another city. The interviews were held over several years (2004-2015) and for the study of their daily lives and embodied emotions, it was necessary to engage in an ethnographic,

[2]The interviews of immigrant domestic workers living in Nafpakto were held by postgraduate student Theodora Varveri, as part of the course titled "Identities and gender in Modern Greece (2009)." The interviews were submitted as part of an assignment on female migratory labour.

observational research. The latter, however, was limited due to the fact that entering the workspace and the daily life of the domestic worker was nearly banned. To the extent that it was made possible, it was a result of my personal contacts with the employing family.

It should be noted from the start that no noticeably differentiated work experiences or relations appear. The work culture and the identities of the domestic workers of the two ethnicities mean that they are later referred to as immigrant domestic workers, without reference to their ethnic background. The discovery of a common trajectory of domestic workers who come from different environments highlights the existence of forms of a common, non-cohesive with ethnicity, work culture, from immigrants domestic workers. The potency of a by and large ethnocentric, perhaps ideological taxonomy of domestic workers is significant. In this light, Ukrainian and Bulgarian women, like other workers from around the Balkans or Eastern Europe, integrate in the domestic labour market at a position found low on the preference range of employing families. In large urban centres, for instance, Philippinos are selected for domestic work or childcare. In contrast, Bulgarian or Ukrainian women are selected to provide personal care to geriatric or ailing parents, though not to look after children.

> "I wanted to look after children, I wanted to do this because I saw that this job was like taking care of my own children, but I was accepted nowhere. I didn't understand why. I happened to be a kindergarten teacher in my home country and I knew the job. I told them that I was able to do it, that I had my own children, I don't know if they were reticent but they didn't accept me, perhaps it was because I arrived here on my own, perhaps they were afraid of other things—see, the Bulgarians are like this, they're like that, they wouldn't take me. I found a job only when I said that I could look after the elderly. I don't know, perhaps they saw us as physically resilient women, as hardened women. I didn't want this to be my job, but I decided it would be. After two months I went into a house and looked after an old grandpa. I stayed there three years because he got used to me too, so I learned too. I have change three homes in the fifteen years of my work, I became good at my work, I was never laid off. I just go somewhere else

when the grandpa or grandma dies. You know, it hurts with death." (Nadia, 59, Bulgarian, interview in Yiannena, 2012).

The aforementioned fragment shows once more how the important role of gender and ethnicity in the context of any diverse categorization is strengthened by the power of hardened stereotypes and perceptions that concern the female gender and its role, its social rank too, in poverty and its penalization, even in body type. All the interviewed immigrant domestic workers are beyond regulatory standards: they migrated alone—leaving the family and country of origin behind—yet this autonomous move without the family becomes the cause for expressing reservations, suspicion, and isolation. They are also the subjects of poverty and difficult living conditions in the home country; for this reason they are weak and incriminated. They have, in other words, all the features that put them in a position of inferiority in the domestic labour market in Athens or in any other large urban setting in Greece. In these circumstances, of the 25 immigrants only one remained and worked in Athens from the beginning, the others moved, though this may not have figured in their original plans, towards the more rural urban centres where the 23 remained, out of choice or necessity, always providing, in their function as domestic household workers, services of care to the old and ailing.

In providing their own interpretation of their move to Greece, the immigrants themselves relate it initially to historical and socio-economic factors and transformations that took place in their countries of origin which pushed them to look for work overseas (Christou and Michail 2018: 70-86). Meanwhile, it is noted that the subjects, through the post-socialist representations and mnemonic reconstructions of the past there, are re-familiarized and symbolize elements of the social and cultural character of their countries (such as guaranteed employment, good education, cultural life accessible to all, including theatre, music, etc., as well as intercultural relations), and make this past, activated in the present, a field of action that is part of the process of building their identity as a set of values of respect and honor of working women.

"In the socialist past, we all had jobs in factories, hospitals, agriculture everywhere, but we all had work, a good life, education, not a luxurious life, but a tranquil life, without stress. Then there was the collapse, the wars we fought amongst ourselves, they closed the factories, nothing stood standing. We were good before, at everything. We had a good healthcare system, order, equality, and all the children were taken care of by the state. Daycare stations, sports, school, university, everything was on the state. And we had culture, with theatre and everything. Later, things became very difficult. They collapsed. I was working in a factory and I was laid off. It shut down. I felt fear and insecurity. I said, how long will I stay here, here with the children who were having a hard time and I could not do a thing about it. I took the decision on my own, I had no husband, we were separated, I gave some money to my parents, to someone who brought immigrants here, not legally, and I reached the **intercity bus service** in Athens. Don't ask how I got here…" (Olga, 58, Ukrainian, interview in Igoumenitsa 2011)

In their self-representations as immigrants they appear to decide, act, and develop subjectivities and identities that are embodied in limited networks of chiefly familial relations that simultaneously connect them to their country of origin and their country of residence. As domestic workers, they form supplementary networks of values and emotions in order to manage their difficult position, to strengthen their stamina and to give meaning and value to their identity. In their interviews on emotional and other embodied expressions they define themselves, their identity formation, but chiefly through their role as mothers and not as salaried workers, as workers in low-salaried jobs in particular. Through highlighting their motherly emotions that converge with their ability to engage in salaried labour, and their proven ability to secure through their labour the improved present and future of their children, they define their existence as subjects who have achieved something in life.

"I gather all the money I make, which is everything because I spend nothing on myself, and I send it to my children, this makes me happy… my children should have everything they need. Now I also have grandchildren, and I care for them. As for myself, I don't care very much." (Maria, 58, Ukrainian, interview in Arta, 2013)

They themselves thus see their own labour and remuneration merely as an *instrument for* achieving rather than as *source of* individual and social worth. Their work allows them to provide for their children. Moreover, all women represent themselves as the sole member of the family, who through their salary support children; most of them have, in fact, become the head and breadwinner of their transnational household.

> "I make 700 euros a month. I have no expenses of my own. For the past four years, I have a residence permit. The money that I make I send to my children. Last year one of my children was married, and I bought him a house back home. Now I also want to help my younger son. The husband? He exists but it's as if he didn't. I could say that all men over there are indifferent to their families, the only thing they do is drink vodka all day long, they believe that either way they will die of the side-effects of Chernobyl" (Maria, 55, Bulgarian, interview in Nafpaktos, 2009).

As demonstrated in studies on feminist analyses of globalization, which underscore how such processes place growing responsibility on women, it is shown that it is women's remittances that support both their families and the economies of their home countries (Sassen 2000, Rosenbaum 2017:10).

3.1. Weak and Informal Social Networks

In nearly all narrations, the function of a weak, informal social network that spreads over a small circle of domestic workers of every nationality seems to dominate. The notion of the network as a practice of survival proved decisive in interpreting migratory movements and their economic and social outcomes in the country of arrival, and indeed it constituted a new perspective on the job market. (Macdonald and Macdonald 1964:82-96). However, the immigrant domestic workers that I approached relied only on informal networks (family, friends, social), which functioned effectively for the organization of the journey, job finding, hospitality and support in difficult times. From the moment they settled and began work in rural environments, their networks gradually became limited to contact with the scarce compatriots of the city in which they lived3. Their encounters are in the square, the café, the street, or in church, but this form of socialization and communication that takes places in spaces (public) and times (midday), that is *beyond space and time,* spacetimes *irregular* for the female gender, exposes them to the gaze of the Others—men (Siotou 2016: 77-88), as vulnerable and available; it renders them constantly scrutinized, and largely surveilled. This informal, controlled and brief public socialization, on the one hand registers the spacetimes of gendered and class heterogeneity as being in limbo and on the other intensifies among domestic migrant workers the feeling of insecurity that they experience. However, it is noteworthy that their public socialization is developed also at a level that is part of the recreation of the gendered self as an independent social subject. In their own evaluation, but as study too has shown, under the conditions of the communist regime, gendered, familial and generally social relations have set aside their traditional forms and have become more equal.

> "With Anna we have managed to take our day off at the same time. Every afternoon, between two and four. We meet in the square, we buy a takeaway coffee, we have a cigarette and we chat. I would like to invite Anna to my house, we have grown close over the past four years that we live here, but where should I invite her? I have no home and neither does she… What pains me is that I don't have a home in which I can do as I please, to which I can invite whomever I please, but this does not happen in this foreign home in which I live. So we always meet outdoors. Rania comes to see me frequently, we sometimes meet here in the square, sometimes we walk to the lake and back, that is kind of how we spend those two hours. When we sit here in the heat of noon, several passersby stare with a cheeky look, they taunt us, as they consider Bulgarian women

[3]It should be stressed that in rural environments, the networking made possible by various collectives of a public character (e.g., labour unions or cultural organizations) is not possible, as the latter were never created.

to be "loose," and we find it entertaining… It's not that we are loose because we came here as single women. We are, how should I say, powerful. With the regime we had in Bulgaria, we were on an equal footing with men, though of course we took on a lot of responsibilities and equality would easily be set aside, but we learned to be strong, ready for anything. That's why I'm here. I need to take care of my home and my family." (Tonia, 59, Bulgarian, interview in Yiannena, 2012).

3.2. "I Always Work and Live in a Place That Is Not My Own, Even if I Have My Own Room"

The non-operation of the household space in which immigrant domestic workers live and work as though it were their own *household,* as they called it, leads to intense feelings of social alienation and cultural backwardness. The house is a *par excellence* real and symbolic space in which the female engages with and obtains a social value and recognition and is for the most part the most dynamic field of action in the process of forming several aspects of female identity; as such, the inability of domestic workers to develop a household space that is familiar, one that may shape their sense of familiarity, one that may create a gap in their gendered and social identity. Delving deeper into the narratives, it appears that some of the dimensions of the ethnic origin or even the home may be negotiated by immigrant domestic workers in their habits of interaction with elderly men whom they look after, and with their family members too. It appears that the cultivated sense of a "home," familiarity, and homeliness, is developed and works only for the employers (Boccagni 2018). Even where certain different 'modes of domesticity' are developed at the intersection between continuous expectations of home-making and discontinuous ways of feeling at home (e.g., through the practice of cooking a dish from one's home country, and sharing it with a member of the employing family, through knitting and gifting a handicraft), do not create a deeper sense of home for them.

"I have been to several homes, because I was good at my work and they made me feel at home, but within limits of course. I understood this

> and I was deliberately careful. Er… you do not go to a stranger's home for you to change what the owner wants, you go there to work. I was there all day, but I didn't exist. In none of these did I ever feel that it was my home, what we women call 'my home', and this makes me feel a gap inside, a sadness… Perhaps, even if I didn't want it, if I could ever have, to feel that house as my own, because in my mind and soul I had a home—that of my children—I didn't want to be attached to a home every day, because if the granddads I took care of passed away, and I went for work to another home, I would leave… I didn't want to feel that I left my home, so I left (Rania,58, Ukranian, interview in Agrinio, 2014).

3.3. In the Realm of Roles and Emotions

Delving deeper into the real or imagine spacetimes of the life of immigrant domestic workers, as they express themselves in their public appearance, in their daily life in the home and in their integration practices in workplace environments (Boccagni and Baltassar 2015), we found that their integration is ultimately a marginal one, temporary, and in a state of limbo.

The sense of "belonging" that they cultivate is not shaped on the basis of their identity as immigrant workers, but as strangers in a strange city. The rejection of the identity as immigrant women, is coming from the difficulty in accepting their new identity as domestic workers. Vasilikou (2009:117) notes that the difficulty in identifying is not so much an outcome of the desire to negate a title that stigmatizes them, that of the 'worker—domestic worker', but more a result of the dead-end that results from an overlap of identities, which leads them to develop feelings of confusion and psychological disruption. The state in which they find themselves is rather complex as it entails dimensions related to the reality of immigration, to issues of gender, justice and of course the absence of a social recognition of their trade as domestic workers." In addition, the narratives of the life cycles of most women I interviewed entail another experience and interpretation on denial; of identity of the immigrant and live-in domestic worker: a deep internalized feeling of shame and trauma because they felt unprotected, deprived of love and alone.

> "I had no one to rely on, to work alongside me and support the entire family. Even my father urged me to leave. It was painful for me to feel so alone, and to be the only person capable of supporting everyone else. If communism gave women an equal position, after 1990 their position became worse than it was before. No support from the state, or the family. I was unemployed with three children and there was no protection. No subsidies or anything else. My husband might as well never have been, we then split, and the father was there but when I said I was leaving, he didn't say "let's think about it," and no one told my sister anything either. It was convenient, I thought, for me to be the man, the breadwinner of the home." (Olga, 61, Ukranian, interview in Igoumenitsa, 2011)

If, however, the denial of the immigrant and work identity is attributed to the web of dead-ends which the concealing of identity shapes, and leads to the development of feelings of deprivation, alienation and shame, overcoming this also entails stressing their identity as mothers who love and care through their work for a better life for their children and their family in general. The matricentric identity becomes the vehicle for obtaining strength, self-respect and respect from others. Denial also comes with the construction of an identity based on feelings and ties that tend to substitute actions and feelings of love and care towards parents.

Previously, I discussed the form of emotional labour that they are forced to cover up and experience as exhausting. Often, however, they appear to treat incapacitated parents of the Others as their own, especially when they spent a long period of time beside them.

> "I was in this house for ten years. The grandma and grandpa I looked after were parents to me, I loved them and they loved me. After the first period I spent with them I became attached, I felt that I was not working with them, that I looked after them as I would after my incapacitated parents. That is how I saw it, I say that with candour. When grandma died first I mourned for six months, I dressed in black for six months, that is how I felt it. I also took care of the memorial services, I was present in all

of them and now, years after grandpa passed, I visit their grave, I feel like they are my own (Olga, 61, Ukrainian, interview in Igoumenitsa, 2011).

Conclusion

Prior to the ethnography, my research hypothesis could be summed up in the position that immigrant women domestic workers—those working jobs intertwined with precariousness, poor remuneration and poor social recognition—are of determining character for global and local inequality, a category.

The ethnography, however, bases its efficiency on its ability to undermine the hypotheses of the researcher. After the recording and analysis of the interviews of 25 domestic workers, the carrying out of an ethnography and the analysis of ethnographic data, what I apprehended at first was that employment in domestic work *per se* itself did not make for a category distinguished from the broader experience of immigrants; they have in common the experience of the struggle for survival and success in a specific context of economic and social reference.

Though domestic work is really *par excellence* the trade that emanates from and supports global relations of power, the reproduction of global asymmetries and the consequent creation of new family structures, focusing only on the means of employment may obscure other aspects of the lives of immigrants (as well as those of local domestic workers). Through the analysis of the material, I discovered for instance that immigrant domestic workers are acting subjects who develop arenas and practices of real and symbolic action, in order to manage or negotiate the terms of dependence of their subjugation. More analytically, daily labour at home with the elderly is not uni-dimensional, but embodied in daily acts, in emotional and sensual expressions, in good practices which of course have as an immediate recipient the employer and the satisfaction of their expectations vis-à-vis the sector of their personal care, but also the securing of their own sense of familiarity. Yet the daily adaptation of the internal domestic worker to the rules that the employing house/family imposes, is bound to lead to subjugation and ultimately to the terms of the domestic life of the employers and society at large. In this light there are very few margins to express, at least in domestic daily life, a degree of their heterogeneity. They choose to move away from it, to become merely alien, with an integration that is marginal and temporary. The biographies of narratives and the local research show in conclusion that they themselves (domestic workers) exhaust whatever limits there are to their abilities, there in the crevices, in the unseen mundane social practices, they find the informal social networks for the internal world of feelings in precious functionalities and meanings that attribute value and meaning to their identity and make their position of subjugation bearable. Through this context they understand and signal their personal existence as an existence for others. Thus their identity is preserved primarily through their role as mothers and not as salaried workers, as workers especially in work with a low-ranking social recognition. Through stressing the motherly role and emotions, which intersect with their ability to be salaried workers, their proven ability to secure through work a better present and future for their children, they define their existence as subjects who have achieved something in their lives.

References

Abu-Lughod, Lila, Lutz A. Catherine (eds.). (1990). *Language and the Politics of Emotion*. Cambridge: Cambridge University Press.

Angelidou, A. (2010). When women travel: Female Migration from Bulgaria, Economic Practices and Gender Identities. In Avdikos, V. and Papakostas C. (eds.). *Borders and Popular Cultures in the Balkans,* Athens: Pedio, pp 157-188 (In Greek).

Bauer, E. and Thompson, P. (2004). "She's always the person with a very global vision: The Gender Dynamics of Migration, Narrative Interpretation and the Case of Jamaican Transnational Families" *Gender & History,* 16 (2) : 334-375.

Boccagni, Paolo (2018). “At home in home care? Contents and boundaries of the ‘domestic’ among immigrant live-in workers in Italy,” *Housing Studies,* 33 pp. DOI: 10.1080/02673037.2017.1367366.

Boccagni, Paolo – Baltassar Loretta (2015). “Emotions on the move: Mapping the emergent field of emotion and migration,” *Elsevier*, Special Issue “*Emotion, Space and Society* 16 : 73-80.

Boeschoten, Van Riki (2015). Transnational Mobility and the Renegotiation of Gender Identities: Albanian and Bulgarian Migrants in Greece. In Vermeulen,H., Baldwin-Edwards, Martin, Boeschoten, Van Riki (eds.), *Migration in the Southern Balkans From Ottoman Territory to Globalized Nation States*, IMISCOE Research Series, DOI 10.1007/978-3-319-13719-3, 9 : 168 – 182.

Castles, Stephen and Miller, J. Mark (2003). *The age of Migration. International population movements in the modern world,* third edition, New York : Palgrave Macmillan.

Christou, Anastasia and Michail, Domna (2018). “Post-socialist narratives of being, belonging and becoming: eastern European women migrants and transformative politics in an era of European crises”. *New Formations*, Doi: 10.3898/NewF:95.05.2018 : 70 - 86.

Greenm L. N. (2004), *The roads of migration. Modern theoretical perspectives.* trans. D. Parsanoglou. Athens: Savvalas (in Greek).

Hantzaroula, Pothiti (2012). *Skulpting the subordination: Paid domestic workers in Greece in the first half of the twentieth century.* Athens: Papazisis (in Greek).

Hatziprokopiou, Panos, Markova M., Hans Eugenia (2015). “Labour Migration and other Forms of Mobility Between Bulgaria and Greece: The Evolution of a Cross-Border Migration System,” In Vermeulen H., Baldwin-Edwards Martin, Boeschoten Van Riki (eds.). *Migration in the Southern Balkans From Ottoman Territory to Globalized Nation State*s. IMISCOE Research Series, DOI 10.1007/978-3-319-13719-3_9 : 183-208.

Hochschild, Russell Arlie (1979). “Emotion Work, Feeling Rules, and Social Structure,” *American Journal of Sociology* 85 (3) :5 51-575.

Macdonald, J. S. and Mackdonald, L (1964). "Chain migration, Ethnic Neighborhood formation and social network," *The Milbank Memorial Fund Quarterly* 42: 82 – 96.

Maratou-Alipranti, Laura (ed.), (2007). *Female migration in Greece: Contemporary trends and processes of settlements*, Athens ΚΕΘΙ (in Greek).

Nikolova, Marina (2013). Bulgarians in Greece: Phases and trends. In. Triandafyllidou, A. & Maroukis, T. (eds.), *Migration in 21st Century Greece*, Athens: Kritiki: 257-308 (in Greek).

Nikolova, Marina (2015). *The dynamic of migration of Ukrainians in Greece: Trajectories, decisions and practices.* Athens: Hellenic Foundation for European & Foreign Policy (ELIAMEP) (in Greek).

Nitsiakos, V., Manos, I., Dalkavoukis, V., Angelopoulos, G., Angelidou, A .(eds.), (2019). *The multiple boundaries of a Changing World: The Proceedings of the Konitsa Summer School (2006-2016).* Athens: Gutenberg (in Greek).

Psimmenos, Iordanis (ed.), (2013). *Work and social inequalities. Personal services and servant labor.* Athens: Alexandria (In Greek).

Psimmenos, Iordanis (2017). "The social setting of female migrant domestic workers". In Psimmenos Iordanis (ed.), *Unveiling Domestic Work in Times of Crisis, Journal of Modern Greek Studies,* Vol. 35 (1) : 43- 66 (special section, John Hopkins University Press)

Ricoeur, Paul (2004). *Memory, History, Forgetting*, trans. Kathleen, Blamey and David Pellauer. Chicago: University of Chicago Press.

Rosenbaum, Susanna (2017). *Domestic economies: women, work, and the American Dream in Los Angeles.* Durham: Duke University Press.

Sassen, Saskia (2000). "Women's burden: Counter-geographies of globalization and the feminization of Survival". *Journal of International Affairs*, 53 (2).

Siotou, Alexandra (2016). The Park of 'unwanted lovers': readings of public space through the emotional daily life of women Bulgarian migrants. In Boeschoten, Van Riki, Vervenioti, T., Lambropoulou, D., Mouliou, M., Xantzaroula, P. (eds.), *Memory narrates the city. Oral history and the memory of urban space.* Athens: Plethron : 77-88. (In Greek).

Vasilikou, Katerina (2009). "Immigrant women-domestic workers and "transnational" family". *Social Cohesion and Development,* 4 (1): 109-125.

Ventoura, Lina *(2009).* National state and contemporary migrations: tendencies, policies, approaches. *Sigchrona Themata,* 1(7): 32 – 36 (In Greek).

Vermeulen, Hans (2004). Back home in a roundabout way. The Anthropology of international migration in Greece: Suggestions for a historical and comparative approach. In Greek Society of Ethnology (ed), *Perspectives of Anthropological thought and research in Greece*. Athens, Greek Society of Ethnology : 175 – 202 (in Greek).

Xypolytas, Nikos (2012), *Live – in domestic work: The contribution of family and solidarity in the reproduction of labor*. Athens: Papazisis (in Greek).

Xypolytas, Nikos, Vassilikou, K., and Fouskas, Th. (2017). "Migrant Domestic Workers: Family, Community, and Crisis" *Journal of Modern Greek Studies,* 35 : 88–109.

About the Editors

Michalis Christodoulou

Assistant Teaching Staff, Department of Philosophy,
University of Patras, Patras, Greece

Michalis Christodoulou has studied sociology (Department of Sociology, University of Crete) and philosophy (Department of Philosophy, University of Patras) and holds a PhD in the sociology of education (University of Patras). He has published several articles on the sociology of youth transitions and on the philosophy of qualitative research. He is the author of *Researching post-secondary social pathways. Decision making, identities and risk in adolescence, (2017)* (in Greek) and of *Critical Realism and Biographical Methods in qualitative research. Philosophical issues and research applications (2019)* (in Greek). He is member of the academic staff at the Department of Philosophy, University of Patras, Greece. https://michalischristod.blogspot.com/

Manos Spyridakis

Professor, Department of Social and Educational Policy,
University of the Peloponnese, Corinth, Greece

Manos Spyridakis is Associate Professor of Social Anthropology. He teaches Anthropology of Work and Economic Anthropology in the Department of Social and Educational Policy at the University of the Peloponnese. He studied History and Archaeology in the University of Crete; he got his Master's degree in Social Anthropology from the University of Durham, and his Ph.D. in Anthropology from the Sussex European Institute in the University of Sussex. His most recent publications include, *Liminal Worker* (2013), the edition of the volume, *Market versus Society. Anthropological Insights* (2018) and the Homo Precarius (2018 in Greek).

ABOUT THE CONTRIBUTORS

Giorgos Bithymitris

Giorgos Bithymitris received his PhD from Panteion University of Social and Political Sciences, Social Policy Department. He is a Researcher (Grade C) at the National Centre for Social Research (EKKE), with expertise in social stratification and social inequalities. His current research interest focuses upon working-class identities and nationalism in a crisis and post-crisis context. Drawing on cultural approaches of social class, he explores the emotional and cultural components of class identifications and their political implications. He has published a book on trade union movement, and several academic articles and book chapters on working-class identities, nationalist discourses, Greek trade unionism, industrial relations. Giorgos is member of the Board of the Hellenic Political Science Association (www.eepe.gr) and co-founder of the EEPE's research network "Methodology in Political Science" (www.methodosnet.gr).

Eleni Giannakopoulou

Eleni Giannakopoulou is a PhD candidate in Social Anthropology at the University of Peloponnese, Department of Social and Educational Policy.

She studied Philosophy, Pedagogy and Psychology at the National and Kapodistrian University of Athens. She holds an MA degree in Contemporary History from The University of Bristol and an MSc degree in Public Policy from the University of Queen Mary and Westfield College, University of London. Her research interests concern second generation immigrants from Albania in secondary education in Greece, immigration policy, inequalities, qualitative analysis. She has published various articles and participated in several collective volumes. She works as a high school teacher.

Christina Karakioulafi, PhD

Dr Christina Karakioulafi is Assistant Professor at the Department of Sociology, University of Crete (Greece), where she teaches Industrial Relations and Industrial Sociology. She holds a B.A. in Social Policy and Social Anthropology, an M.Sc/DEA in Human Resources Development and a PhD in Sociology. Since 2005 she is a member of the academic staff at the Hellenic Open University and Instructor at the Academy of Work of the General Confederation of Greek Workers. Her main research interests and contributions focus on employment and unemployment issues, trade unions, industrial relations trends and theory, work place violence and artistic work. From 2012 to 2015 she was research coordinator at the research project "the crisis as an agent of cocial change and social disorganization", financed by the Labour Institute of the General Confederation of Greek Workers. From 2016 to 2017 she participated at the European Program "TransSOL: European Paths to Transnational Solidarity at the time of crisis". She is co-editor of two books (with Manos Spyridakis): *Unemployment, Society and Social Reproduction*, Athens: Gutenberg-Dardanos (2017) and *Work and Society*, Athens: Dionikos (2010), and author of the book Industral Relations: Theoretical approaches and empirical issues, Athens: Papazisis (2012) (all in Greek).

Spyros Sakellaropoulos

Spyros Sakellaropoulos completed his undergraduate studies in the Sociology Department of the Panteion University (1989), with postgraduate studies at the Paris VIII University D.E.A. (Diplôme d'Etudes Approfondies), 1992, and a Ph.D. in Political Sociology, 1995. He is Professor in the Social Policy Department of the Panteion University, specializing in the subject *State and Political Theory*. His research interests are centred on the theory of the State, the study of the Modern Greek and Cypriot societies and the theory of development of the capitalist mode of production. He has written numerous books and articles on his research interests in Greek, English, French, Spanish and Italian.

Ioannis Kyriakakis

Ioannis Kyriakakis holds a PhD in anthropology. He has conducted fieldwork in England and Ghana. He is concerned with global inequality, religion-cosmology and the anthropology of capitalism. He teaches social theory at the Hellenic Open University and cultural economy at the Open University of Cyprus.

Nikolaos Papachristopoulos

Nikolaos Papachristopoulos is a psychoanalyst. He teaches Psychology and Psychoanalysis at the Philology Department in the University of Patras. Monographs (indicative): *Art and unconscious* (2013), *The psychoanalytical trace* (2010), *Psychoanalysis and social symptoms* (ed., 2006), *Psychoanalysis and writing. Theory of sublimation in Freud and Lacan* (2005), *The songs "rebetika". A semiotic approach* (2004). He has also translated books and articles concerning psychology and psychoanalysis.

Kalliopi Orfanaki

Kalliopi Orfanaki is Criminologist, PhD (University of Athens) and she is an expert on prison research. She has studied Social Anthropology, Sociology of Social Exclusion, Political Theory and Sociology. Kalliopi Orfanaki has a teaching experience in Secondary and Higher Education (Hellenic Open University, University of West Attica), in the education of vulnerable social groups (prisoners, refuges, drug addicts) and currently works as a Coordinator of Refugee Education in Refugee Hosting Structures in Athens, Greece. At the same time, she has been selected by the IEP as a member of the Committee of Experts for the Development of Programs of Studies in the Thematic Fields of the Social Sciences of General Lyceum and for the creation of educational material for the Reception Classes for the Refugees and for Prison Schools. She has participated in conferences, educational and research programs and her research interests focus on issues of criminology, social exclusion, education, human rights and qualitative research.

Konstantina Bada

Konstantina Bada completed her undergraduate studies in ancient literature at the University of Ioannina (1975). From 1977 to 1985 she worked as a scientific collaborator in the Folklore Museum of Faculty of Philosophy of Ioannina University and received her PHD in 1983 in the field of Folklore and Historical Anthropology. In 1985 she jointed with the Department of History and Archeology of Ioannina University, Greece, where she was member of its teaching and scientific staff. From 2004 until her retirement in 2017, she held the position of a professor in the subject of Social Folklore. Using her annual and semi-annual sabbatical, she expanded her scientific interests to the broader area of Social Anthropology - at the Cambridge University (1986-87, 1991), as well as in the field of Oral History and Women's Studies - at the Department of Sociology at the

University of Essex (1997-98). She was also a Visiting Scholar of the Center for Hellenic Studies at King's College (2006).Her academic and research interests focuses on the study of popular culture , material culture, oral history and memory studies, gender studies, anthropology of work, of migration, and in the last years on the ethnography of the decade 1940 - 1950 in Greece. She has published books and articles in Greek and International Journals. She also is editor of the on - line Journal "*O Kosmos tis Ergasias*", http://kosmos-ergasias.unit.uoi.gr/

INDEX

C

D

E

F

G

H

I

P